The Abolition of Serfdom in Russia, 1762–1907

SEMINAR STUDIES   IN HISTORY

The Abolition of Serfdom in Russia, 1762–1907

DAVID MOON

An imprint of **Pearson Education**

Harlow, England · London · New York · San Francisco · Toronto · Don Mills, Ontario · Sydney · Tokyo
Singapore · Hong Kong · Seoul · Taipei · Cape Town · Madrid · Mexico City · Amsterdam · Munich · Paris · Milan

PEARSON EDUCATION LIMITED

Head Office:
Edinburgh Gate
Harlow
Essex CM20 2JE
Tel: +44 (0)1279 623623
Fax +44 (0)1279 431059

London Office:
128 Long Acre
London WC2E 9AN
Tel: +44 (0)20 7447 2000
Fax: +44 (0)20 7240 5771
Website: www.history-minds.com

First published in Great Britain in 2001

The right of David Moon to be identified as author
of this work has been asserted by him in accordance
with the Copyright, Designs and Patents Act 1988.

ISBN 0-582-29486 X

British Library Cataloguing-in-Publication Data
A CIP catalogue record for this book can be obtained from the British Library

10 9 8 7 6 5 4 3 2 1

Typeset by 7 in 10/12 Sabon Roman
Printed in Malaysia, LSP

The Publishers' policy is to use paper manufactured from sustainable forests.

CONTENTS

LIST OF TABLES AND MAP

INTRODUCTION TO THE SERIES

Such is the pace of historical enquiry in the modern world that there is an ever-widening gap between the specialist article or monograph, incorporating the results of current research, and general surveys, which inevitably become out of date. *Seminar Studies in History* is designed to bridge this gap. The series was founded by Patrick Richardson in 1966 and his aim was to cover major themes in British, European and World history. Between 1980 and 1996 Roger Lockyer continued his work, before handing the editorship over to Clive Emsley and Gordon Martel. Clive Emsley is Professor of History at the Open University, while Gordon Martel is Professor of International History at the University of Northern British Columbia, Canada, and Senior Research Fellow at De Montfort University.

All the books are written by experts in their field who are not only familiar with the latest research but have often contributed to it. They are frequently revised, in order to take account of new information and interpretations. They provide a selection of documents to illustrate major themes and provoke discussion, and also a guide to further reading. The aim of *Seminar Studies in History* is to clarify complex issues without over-simplifying them, and to stimulate readers into deepening their knowledge and understanding of major themes and topics.

NOTE ON TRANSLITERATION

Russian words have been transliterated according to the British Standard system. In the text, but not the references and bibliography, soft signs (') have been omitted. English versions of Christian names have been used where close equivalents exist, e.g., Alexander rather than Aleksandr. Likewise, St Petersburg and Moscow have been preferred to Sankt Peterburg and Moskva.

LIST OF ABBREVIATIONS

AHR   *American Historical Review*
JGO   *Jahrbücher für Geschichte Osteuropas*
JMH   *Journal of Modern History*
PSZ   *Polnoe sobranie zakonov Rossiiskoi imperii*
RGIA   *Rossiiskii gosudarstvennyi istoricheskii arkhiv*
SEER   *Slavonic and East European Review*
SR   *Slavic Review*
SSH   *Soviet Studies in History*

AUTHOR'S ACKNOWLEDGEMENTS

The research for this book was supported financially by the Universities of Newcastle upon Tyne and Strathclyde. I owe debts of gratitude to the staffs of the libraries of these two universities, in particular the inter-library loans desks. I should also like to acknowledge the help of the staffs of the libraries of the Universities of Glasgow and Birmingham, the British Library (both St Pancras and Boston Spa), the Slavonic Library of the University of Helsinki, and the Russian National Library and Russian State Historical Archive in St Petersburg. A number of colleagues have been generous with advice, comments and suggestions. As ever, I am grateful to David Saunders. In addition, David Christian, Terry Cox, Conan Fischer and Maureen Perrie kindly read and commented on draft chapters. Sole responsibility for any errors or shortcomings lies, of course, with the author. Unless otherwise indicated, the documents in Part Four of this book were translated from the original Russian by the author.

PUBLISHER'S ACKNOWLEDGEMENTS

We are grateful to the following for permission to reproduce copyright material:

HarperCollins Publishers for permission to reproduce extracts from *The Call to Honour, 1940–1942* by Charles de Gaulle translated by Jonathan Griffin, and *Paris in the Third Reich: A History of the German Occupation, 1940–1944* by David Pryce-Jones.

Table 2.1 from 'Consequences of the price revolution in eighteenth-century Russia' in *Economic History Review*, 45, reprinted by permission of Blackwell Publishers (Mironov, B. N. 1992); Table 8.1 from *The Abolition of Serfdom in Russia*, edited and translated by S. Wobst, reprinted by permission of Academic International Press (Zaionchkovsky, P. A. 1978).

In some instances we have been unable to trace the copyright owners of material and we would appreciate any information which would enable us to do so.

CHRONOLOGY

All dates in this book are in the Julian calendar, which was used in Russia from 1700 to 1918. In the nineteenth century, it was 12 days behind the Gregorian calendar, which was used in most of the rest of Europe. It is not possible to include trends in social, economic and intellectual aspects of the history of the abolition of serfdom in a chronology.

1762

12 February	Peter III announced his intention to withdraw the Russian Empire from the Seven Years' War.
18 February	Abolition of compulsory noble state service.
21 March	Secularization of the estates and peasants of the Russian Orthodox Church.
28 June	Catherine the Great succeeded to the throne after Peter III was deposed and murdered in a coup.
1765	Foundation of the 'Free Economic Society for the Encouragement of Agriculture and Good Husbandry'.
1766	Catherine's Instruction to the Legislative Commission hinted at need to reform serfdom.
1772–95	Annexation of Belorussia, Kurland, Lithuania and right-bank Ukraine by the Russian Empire in the Partitions of Poland.
1773–74	Revolt led by Pugachev, who claimed to be Peter III.
1775	Provincial reform, which included some provisions to protect serfs from cruel and exploitative nobles.
1785	'Charter to the Nobility' codified nobles' rights and privileges.
1789	Outbreak of the French Revolution.
1790	Radishchev published *A Journey from St Petersburg to Moscow*, which attacked serfdom.
1796	Paul succeeded to the throne on the death of Catherine.
1797	
5 April	Proclamation banning labour services on Sundays and recommending that work on the other six days of the week be divided equally between noble and peasant land.
1801	Alexander I succeeded to the throne after Paul was deposed and murdered in a coup.

1803

20 February   Decree on 'Free Agriculturalists' permitted nobles to free their serfs and sell them land.

1804   Regulation by law of relations between nobles and serfs in Baltic provinces of Estonia and Livonia.

1807   Start of abolition of serfdom in Prussia.

1814–15   Russian army occupied Paris at the end of the Napoleonic Wars.

1816–19   Landless abolition of serfdom in Baltic provinces of Estonia, Kurland and Livonia.

1825

14 December   Nicholas I succeeded to the throne after the death of Alexander I.

Failed 'Decembrist' revolt in St Petersburg by army officers who aimed to abolish the autocracy and serfdom.

1829   Start of Perovskii's reforms of the appanage peasantry.

1830   Outbreak of a Polish nationalist revolt in the Russian Empire's western provinces in November.

1837   Start of Kiselev's reforms of the state peasantry.

1842

2 April   Decree on 'Obligated Peasants' permitted nobles to regulate their relations with their serfs.

1847

January   Publication of the first of Ivan Turgenev's 'Sportsman's Sketches', which indirectly attacked serfdom, and Gogol's *Selected Passages from Correspondence with Friends*, which defended serfdom.

26 May   Ratification of the 'inventory regulations', which governed relations between nobles and serfs in right-bank Ukraine.

8 November   'Auctions Decree' permitted serfs to buy their land and freedom under certain circumstances. Effectively repealed in 1849.

1848–49   Revolutions in many European states, but not in the Russian Empire. Agrarian reform in the Austrian Empire.

1849   Decree permitted peasants in Livonia to buy land from nobles.

1853–56   Crimean War. Russian Empire defeated by Turkish Empire, Great Britain and France.

1855

18 February   Alexander II succeeded to the throne on the death of Nicholas I.

1856

29 March	Dmitrii Milyutin presented a memorandum to a committee on military reform, arguing that serfdom needed to be abolished in order to reform the system of recruitment.
30 March	Alexander II told Marshals of the Nobility in Moscow that it was better for serfdom to be abolished from above than below.
April	Alexander II issued a secret directive to Minister of Internal Affairs Lanskoi to draw up proposals to abolish serfdom.
October	Grand Duchess Elena Pavlovna presented her plan to free the serfs on her estate of Karlovka to Alexander II.
	Decree (published in April 1858) permitted peasants in Estonia to buy land from nobles at prices set by the latter.

1857

1 January	Alexander II set up the 'Secret Committee on the Peasant Question' under the chairmanship of Orlov.
August	Secret Committee proposed gradual reform.
20 November	Alexander II's Rescript to Governor-General Nazimov of Lithuania laying down principles for the abolition of serfdom.
Late 1857–summer 1858	Provincial nobles elected committees to draw up plans for reform on the basis of the principles in the rescript to Nazimov. They submitted their proposals to St Petersburg in 1859.

1858

January	The 'Secret Committee' renamed the 'Main Committee on the Peasant Question'.
April	The Main Committee produced its 'April Programme', based on the rescript to Nazimov. This was the government's first programme. It did not ensure the freed serfs would have land.
Spring	Wave of disturbances among peasants in Estonia after the publication of the 1856 decree (see above).
Summer	Alexander II toured the provinces.
August–September	Rostovtsev sent four letters to Alexander II arguing for freed serfs to acquire land.
4 December	The Main Committee adopted a new programme for reform, with a guarantee that the freed serfs would acquire land.

1859

February	Alexander II approved the creation of the Editing Commissions, under the chairmanship of Rostovtsev, to draft the Statutes abolishing serfdom. Members included several 'enlightened bureaucrats', e.g. Nicholas Milyutin.
5 March	Rostovtsev presented his programme for reform, based on that of the Main Committee of 4 December 1858, to the Editing Commissions.

Late summer	First convocation of deputies from nobles' provincial committees in St Petersburg.
1860	
6 February	Death of Rostovtsev. Replaced as chairman of the Editing Commissions by Panin.
February	Second convocation of deputies from nobles' provincial committees in St Petersburg.
October	The Editing Commissions sent the draft statutes to the Main Committee, under the chairmanship of Grand Duke Constantine Nikolaevich, which approved them with minor amendments in January 1861.
1861	
January	The draft statutes approved by the State Council with minor amendments.
19 February	Alexander II signed into law the Proclamation and Statutes abolishing serfdom.
5 March	Publication of the Proclamation and Statutes.
21 April	Dismissal of Minister of Internal Affairs Lanskoi and his acting deputy Nicholas Milyutin.
April	Massacres of peasants protesting against the terms of the reform in Kandeevka, Penza province, and Bezdna, Kazan province.
15 July	Publication of the first part of Ogarev's very critical article on the Statutes in *The Bell*.
Early summer	Peace mediators began to arrive in the villages to oversee the implementation of the reform.
Winter 1861–62	Campaign of 'noble liberalism'.
1863	
19 February	Formal start of 'Temporary Obligation'.
	Polish nationalist revolt. The Russian government revised the terms of the abolition of serfdom in the formerly Polish western provinces in favour of the peasants.
	Reform of the appanage peasants throughout the Russian Empire. They were permitted to redeem their land from 1865.
1866	Reform of the state peasants. They were transferred to the equivalent of 'temporary obligation'.
1874	
1 January	Military service reform. All males liable to serve in the ranks for a maximum of seven years.
1881	
1 March	Assassination of Alexander II, succeeded by Alexander III.

28 December	Transfer to redemption made compulsory for all peasants still temporarily obligated to nobles with effect from 1 January 1883. Reduction of the redemption payments paid by peasants and the compensation received by nobles.
1883–87	Abolition of the Poll Tax in the European provinces of the Russian Empire.
1886	State peasants permitted to redeem their land.
1889	The post of land captain created to supervise the peasants.
1894	Nicholas II succeeded to the throne on the death of Alexander III.
1905	
January	Outbreak of Revolution.
3 November	Announcement of the end of redemption payments, with effect from 1 January 1907.
1906	
5 October	Peasants granted freedom of movement.
9 November	Stolypin's decree permitted peasant households to leave village communes.
1907	
1 January	The end of the Redemption Operation.

Map xviii

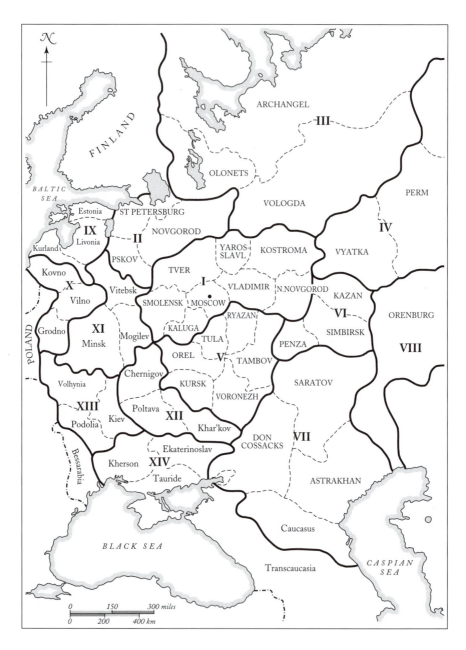

Map Regions and provinces of the European part of the Russian Empire, *c.* 1850

Map   xix

KEY TO MAP: REGIONS AND PROVINCES OF THE EUROPEAN PART
OF THE RUSSIAN EMPIRE, *c.* 1850

Regions

A. Russia ('Great Russia')

I	Central Non-Black Earth
II	Northwest
III	Northern
IV	Northern Urals
V	Central Black Earth
VI	Mid-Volga
VII	Lower Volga and Don
VIII	Southern Urals

B. Western Provinces

IX	Baltic	
X	Lithuania	
XI	Belorussia	
XII	Left-bank Ukraine	
	('Little Russia')	
XIII	Right-bank Ukraine	
	('Southwestern provinces')	
XIV	Southern Ukraine	
	('New Russia')	

Note: Samara province was formed from the eastern parts of Saratov and Simbirsk and the western part of Orenburg provinces in 1851. Ufa province was created from northern Orenburg province in 1865.

PART ONE   BACKGROUND

CHAPTER ONE

INTRODUCTION

On 19 February 1861 Tsar Alexander II signed into law the Statutes abolishing serfdom in the Russian Empire. The reform directly affected around 22 million peasant men, women and children, and around 100,000 noble estate owners to whom they belonged as serfs. The magnitude of the reform is demonstrated by the fact that, on the eve of the reform, serfs of noble estate owners made up around 35 per cent of the Empire's total population. The abolition of serfdom was not, however, a single 'event' that took place in early 1861 and led to the immediate 'emancipation' of the serfs. Rather, it was a process spread out over several decades (Kolchin, 1996: 52–5; Mironov, 1996: 335–46). It is argued in this book that the process of abolishing serfdom in the Russian Empire lasted almost a century and a half, from 1762 to 1907.

In 1762 Tsar Peter III enacted two reforms that, with the benefit of hindsight, can be seen as precursors to the end of serfdom 99 years later. The first was the abolition of compulsory noble state service, sometimes called 'the emancipation of the nobility' [*Doc. 1*]. This measure ended the original rationale behind serfdom. For at least two centuries prior to 1762 nobles had been obliged, at least in principle, to serve the state. Most nobles served either as officers in the armed forces or officials in the civil bureaucracy. In return, state servitors had originally been paid in land. Between the late sixteenth and mid-seventeenth centuries, the Russian state had ensured its servitors had a labour force to cultivate their land – and thus provide them with an income – by binding peasants to it, thereby creating the institution of serfdom. Peter III's act in 1762 ended this hierarchy of service in which nobles served the state and serfs served the nobles. After 1762 noble state service was voluntary, and nobles were free to live where they chose. The peasants on their estates, however, remained bound to the land, and were still serfs.

Peter III's other act in 1762 that indirectly concerned serfdom was the secularization of the estates and peasants of the Russian Orthodox Church [*Doc. 2*]. Peasants who lived on nobles' estates – the serfs – were only a part of the total peasant population. Another part were peasants who lived on church estates. They served monasteries and churches in much the same way as serfs served nobles. In 1762 Peter III converted the church's land and peasants into state lands and peasants. Thus – and this was Peter III's motive – the immense landed wealth of the Russian Orthodox Church now belonged to the state. However, if the state could take land and peasants from the church, then in theory it could also take the nobles' estates and serfs away from them, thus abolishing serfdom.

Throughout the rest of the eighteenth and the first half of the nineteenth centuries, the 'peasant question' – in particular the future of serfdom – was the subject of considerable discussion inside the government and among wider society. Over the same period the government enacted further reforms that touched on serfdom directly or indirectly.

The culmination of this process of discussion and reform was the Statutes of 1861, which set in motion a complex, three-stage process to undo the ties that bound the serfs and noble estate owners to each other. The details will be explained later. Suffice to note here that during the first two stages, relations between the freed serfs and estate owners were regulated by law. In the third stage, the former serfs bought part of the land from the estate owners in a process known as 'redemption'. The government paid compensation to the estate owners, and the former serfs repaid the government in 'redemption payments' spread over 49 years. The 'redemption operation' came to an end when Tsar Nicholas II's decision to write off the freed serfs' outstanding redemption payments came into effect on 1 January 1907 [*Doc. 28*]. The previous year, the former serfs – or more likely their children and grandchildren – had regained the legal right of freedom of movement, which their forebears had lost in the late sixteenth century with the onset of serfdom.

HISTORIANS AND THE ABOLITION OF SERFDOM

The majority of the works cited in this book were published in the former Soviet Union, Western Europe and North America in the second half of the twentieth century (Gleason, 1994). Historians working in the Soviet Union from the early 1920s until the end of the 1980s were constrained by an official interpretation of history that was imposed by the ruling Communist Party. It was based, crudely, on the writings of Karl Marx and Vladimir Ilich Lenin. As a result, most Soviet historians emphasized social and economic rather than political and intellectual history, stressed the role of 'class struggle', and presented the history of tsarist Russia as leading inevitably towards revolution and the triumph of Lenin and the Bolsheviks in the revolution of 1917.

Nevertheless, a number of Soviet historians produced important work on the subject of this book. The most prominent was Peter Zaionchkovsky. His major book, *The Abolition of Serfdom in Russia,* has been translated into English (Zaionchkovsky, 1978). In contrast to many Soviet historians, Zaionchkovsky paid due attention to political history and the role of the state bureaucracy in the abolition of serfdom (Saunders, 2000a). In addition, Zaionchkovsky supervised a number of postgraduate students, Russian and Western, who went on to produce significant work on the abolition of serfdom. Zaionchkovsky's students included such prominent scholars as Terence Emmons, Daniel Field, W. Bruce Lincoln and Larisa Zakharova (Zakharova, 1998: 16–17).

Both Soviet and Western historians drew on the considerable scholarship of historians working in the Russian Empire in the decades prior to 1917. Historians such as Vasilii Semevskii and his colleagues and students produced pioneering studies of the peasantry and the 'peasant question'. In 1911 a six-volume work entitled 'The Great Reform', which contained essays by many major scholars, was published in Moscow to mark the fiftieth anniversary of the Statutes (Dzhivelegov, 1911).

THE STRUCTURE OF THE BOOK

In order to understand the abolition of serfdom, it is necessary to consider the origins of the institution, the ways it linked the nobility and the state, and how it operated in the villages. Although the main focus of this book is on the Russian part of the multinational empire, some attention is paid to the non-Russian western borderlands (the Baltic provinces, Lithuania, Belorussia and Ukraine). All these are discussed in Chapter 2. The range of motives for reforming and abolishing serfdom are analysed in Chapters 3 and 4. Rural reforms enacted between 1762 and 1855 are discussed in Chapter 5. One of the major concerns of the tsars was their empire's international status and the armed forces that supported it. The connection between Russia's defeat in the Crimean War of 1853–56, the need for military reform, and the decision to abolish serfdom is explored in Chapter 6. Once the decision had been taken, it took several years to prepare the reform. This is the subject of Chapter 7. Chapter 8 seeks to explain the terms of the Statutes of 19 February 1861. Responses to the reform and its implementation in 1861–63 are the subject of Chapter 9. The reform process over the years 1863–1907 is examined in Chapter 10, and the wider impact of the reform on the economy, society and politics of the Russian Empire is discussed in Chapter 11. Concise conclusions and an assessment of the reform process and its aftermath are presented in Part Three.

Throughout the book, more attention is paid to peasants than nobles, but the treatment of the nobility is still out of proportion to their small numbers. While the book discusses social and economic aspects of the process of abolition, centre stage is taken by the relationship between the imperial Russian state and its nobles and peasants.

PART TWO   ANALYSIS

CHAPTER TWO

SERFDOM IN THE RUSSIAN EMPIRE

Throughout the period of serfdom – from the late sixteenth century until 1861 – the Russian Empire was an overwhelmingly rural society. 80–90 per cent of its population were peasants, most of whom supported themselves largely, but not solely, by farming the land. Very roughly, half the peasantry were the serfs of the nobility. Nobles, however, made up less than 1 per cent of the empire's population. Under serfdom, peasants were bound to the landed estates of nobles and, in practice, also to the nobles themselves. They were banned from leaving the estates without the owners' permission. In addition, serfs were required to serve or pay obligations for or to their estate owners, usually in labour (*barshchina*) and/or dues (*obrok*) in cash and kind. In return, serfs received the use of allotments of land. Noble estate owners had considerable administrative and judicial authority over their serfs, and could buy and sell them with or without the land they lived on (Blum, 1961). From an economic point of view, the main feature of serfdom was that it enabled nobles to extract more income from their estates – in the form of their serfs' obligations – than they would have been able to do if a free peasantry had had the rights to rent land or sell their labour at the best rates they could get in an open market. In an economic sense, therefore, serfdom enabled nobles to get as big a share as they could of the product of peasant labour (Smith, 1968: 3).

THE RUSSIAN STATE, THE NOBILITY AND SERFDOM

The origins of serfdom in Russia lay in the process of binding peasants to the landed estates of the nobility by the state, which began in the fifteenth century, but developed most rapidly between 1580 and 1649. Terms in the law code of 1649 laid down that serfs (and other peasants) were bound to the land they lived on in perpetuity, and were permanently liable to be caught and returned if they fled. The main reason why the state bound a large part of its peasant population to nobles' land was to support its military forces. This requires some explanation. The state needed armed forces that were powerful enough to maintain its power inside Russia, and to defend and expand its borders. In the south and east, in the fertile steppe regions, the Russian state came up against the Tatars and other nomadic peoples. In the west, Russia bordered the states of east-central Europe. The Russian state lacked the financial resources to pay adequate salaries to its military servitors. Nor did it have a sufficiently large or effective administration to raise the necessary money through taxation or other means. One resource it did have in large quantities was land. From the sixteenth century the state paid its servitors, both military and civil, with grants of land. Since landed estates were of little value unless they had labour to farm them, and since the estate owners were away serving the tsar, the state gradually bound peasants to the land, and permitted the owners of the land to exploit them. From 1556, in principle, all secular landowners were obliged to serve the state. This included wealthy aristocrats, or boyars, who inherited their estates. These two groups, state servitors and boyars, were the ancestors of much of the Russian nobility of the eighteenth and nineteenth centuries.

In the sixteenth and seventeenth centuries most estate owners served in the armed forces. The backbone of these forces was units of cavalrymen, which fought alongside the musketeers (*strel'tsy*), artillery, and irregular forces, including cossacks and non-Russians from the steppe frontier. The commanding officers were usually high-ranking nobles and boyars. Thus, much of the burden of military service was born by the Russian nobility, while a large part of the peasantry was bound to their estates to support them (Hellie, 1971). The Russian armed forces, and the ways they were manned and supported, underwent considerable changes in the seventeenth and early eighteenth centuries, culminating in the reforms of Tsar Peter the Great (1682–1725). The cavalry and musketeers were gradually replaced by 'new formation' regiments on the contemporary European model. These reforms were necessary if Russia was to hold its own on its western frontier against the superior forces of its neighbours, in particular Poland and Sweden. The officer corps of the 'new formation' regiments originally included many foreign mercenaries, but they were gradually replaced by Russian nobles. The rank-and-file soldiers of the 'new formation' units were conscripted from the mass of the population, chiefly peasants, including nobles' serfs. Levies of recruits were held in the late seventeenth century, and became more or less annual from 1705. For most of the eighteenth century recruits served for life, but the term was cut to 25 years in 1793. Serfs who were recruited into the army, together with their families, were freed from serfdom. This was little compensation, however, for the onerous burden of military service. Peter the Great's system of recruitment lasted until the Military Service Reform of 1874, 13 years after the abolition of serfdom. Peter the Great made another reform which is significant for the history of serfdom. From 1714, in theory if not always in practice, noble state service was paid with monetary salaries rather than grants of land with a serf labour force (Keep, 1985).

The cost of Russia's armed forces could not be met solely through serfdom and conscription, but also depended on tax revenues extracted from the mass of the population, mainly the peasants. The reformed army of the seventeenth and eighteenth centuries was much more expensive than its predecessors, forcing the state to increase taxes. Between 1645 and 1679, the old land tax was replaced by a tax on households, and in 1718–24 Peter the Great introduced a poll tax on all male members of the lower orders. In order to assess and collect the poll tax, Peter ordered a census to be taken, and introduced internal passports to control the movement of tax-payers. Peter's poll tax, like his system of conscription, outlasted serfdom, surviving until the 1880s. In an attempt to ensure the collection of taxes, from medieval times the Russian state had enforced the principle of 'joint responsibility' (*krugovaya poruka*) of communities of tax-payers. If one man defaulted, his neighbours were responsible for his taxes (Anisimov, 1993: 160–2, 197–202, 233–5). Another major source of state revenue was the monopoly on vodka. Rather than administer this itself, the state sold the rights to distil and sell vodka in franchises to merchants and nobles, who were thus able to share in the profits of the trade in hard liquor (Christian, 1990).

The military and tax reforms of the seventeenth and early eighteenth centuries had major implications for serfdom and relations between the state and nobility:

> the original connection [between the armed forces and] serfdom was ended. The bulk of the manpower was now provided not by [noble] cavalrymen, but by men conscripted mainly from the peasantry, around half of whom were the nobles' serfs. The material support for the reformed army came not only from serfs working on the land of the nobles, but also from taxes paid mostly by the peasantry, including the serfs. There was now a potential conflict … between [the] state and nobility [over who would] … get the greater share of the product of peasant labour. (Moon, 1996a: 490)

In the mid- and late eighteenth century it was the nobles who were winning the struggle to get the larger share of the product of peasant labour. Nobles' incomes from their serfs' obligations grew much more quickly than the state's revenues from the poll tax (Table 2.1). The state came to rely on the dues paid by the state peasantry (see below), the vodka monopoly, and indirect taxes (Mironov, 1992).

Table 2.1 Serfs' state and seigniorial obligations in the eighteenth century

This table shows how, on average, estate owners increased the obligations, in both dues and labour, they extracted from the serfs on their estates faster than the rate of inflation, measured in grain prices (col. 11), while the state increased the direct taxes it extracted from the peasants, including nobles' serfs, much slower than the rate of inflation. As a result, over the eighteenth century, the average male serf's seigniorial obligations increased in real terms by 1.69 times (col. 7) and labour services by 2.5 times (col. 10). Over the same period, the average serf's direct taxes fell in real terms by two-thirds (col. 4). Thus, a growing part of the product of serf labour was extracted by estate owners rather than the state.

1	2	3	4	5	6	7	8	9	10	11
	STATE OBLIGATIONS			SEIGNIORIAL OBLIGATIONS						
	Direct Taxes			1. Dues (obrok)			2. Labour (barshchina)			
								Value of harvest		
Years	Roubles	Index A	Index B	Roubles	Index A	Index B	Area desyatiny	Index A	Index B	Index of grain prices
1700–9	0.27	100	100	0.40	100	100	0.60	100	100	100
1710–19		259		0.50	125	69				180
1720–29	0.70	259	96	0.70	175	67				263
1730–39	0.70	259	115	0.90	225	100				226
1740–49	0.70	259	94	1.20	300	108				277
1750–59	0.70	259	103	1.60	400	159				251
1760–69	0.70	259	72	3.00	750	207	0.75	452	125	362
1770–79	0.70	259	58	4.50	1,125	253	1.20	1,130	200	444
1780–89	0.70	259	37	6.00	1,500	219				686
1790–99	0.96	356	32	7.50	1,875	169	1.50	2778	250	1,110

All obligations are averages per male serf (soul).

1 Direct taxes: household tax to 1723, poll tax from 1724.

Columns 3, 6, 9   **Index A:** all figures in nominal levels, not taking account of price rises.

Columns 4, 7, 10   **Index B:** all figures have been deflated to take account of inflation (in grain prices), see column 11.

Columns 8–10   Labour services (*barshchina*) are calculated in the area cultivated (in *desyatiny*) and the value of the harvest from that land.

Source: Mironov (1992), p. 458.

The conflict over who would extract more income from the enserfed peasantry was long and drawn out because of the mutually dependent relationship between the state and nobility. The state relied on nobles to serve as officers in the armed forces and civil servants in the bureaucracy. Nobles, in turn, depended on the state to maintain their elite status in society, including the institution of serfdom. Moreover, most nobles did not earn enough from their estates to support their lifestyles, and thus relied on the salaries they received for state service. For this reason many nobles continued to serve after the abolition of compulsory state service in 1762 (Kahan, 1966). In the long run, since at least the sixteenth century, however, the nobility depended on the state more than the other way round (Crummey, 1983; Jones, 1973; Meehan-Waters, 1982). It was the state's eventual assertion of its dominance that lay behind the abolition of serfdom in 1861.

Throughout the servile period by no means all peasants were nobles' serfs. But, all peasants were bound to the land they lived on and were obliged to pay taxes and supply recruits to the state. A relatively small proportion of the peasantry lived on the estates of, and owed obligations to, members of the imperial family. After 1797 they were known as 'appanage peasants'. Until 1762 larger numbers of peasants lived on the extensive landholdings of the Russian Orthodox Church, to which they owed obligations. The other main category of peasants was the state peasantry, who lived on lands belonging to the state, to which they paid dues. In contrast to the other categories of peasants, there was no intermediary between the state peasants and the state. The numbers of state peasants were substantially increased in 1762 when the church's land and peasants were taken over by the state [*Doc. 2*] (Moon, 1999: 97–106). The existence and growth of the state peasantry suggested an alternative to serfdom as a way of organizing the social structure of rural Russia: a landed peasantry directly subordinate to the state without an intermediate layer of noble (or church) estate owners.

SERFDOM IN THE WESTERN BORDERLANDS OF THE RUSSIAN EMPIRE

The development of serfdom in Russia over the late sixteenth and early seventeenth centuries coincided with the emergence of similar systems of unfree labour in east-central Europe to the west of the Russian frontier and east of the River Elbe that flowed through the middle of the German lands. In these territories, in contrast to Russia, it was noble estate owners, rather than the state, that played the principal role in the enserfment of the local peasantry (Blum, 1957). From the mid-seventeenth century, however, the growing military might of the Russian state enabled it to expand its borders westwards, at the expense of Poland and Sweden, into east-central Europe. Over the eighteenth century, the Russian Empire incorporated the Baltic provinces of Estonia, Livonia and Kurland, together with Lithuania, Belorussia and the part of Ukraine on the right bank of the River Dnieper. In most of these areas the Baltic German and Polish nobilities had enserfed the local peasantries long before Russian annexation. By the eighteenth century, however, the Swedish and Polish governments had put some restrictions on noble estate owners' authority by regulating the sizes of serfs' seigniorial obligations and land allotments. After annexation the Russian government initially did away with these restrictions. Later, it extended the poll tax to these regions, and granted local nobles the same rights and privileges as Russian nobles. These rights included extensive authority over the serfs on their estates. In the late eighteenth century the Russian variant of serfdom also spread to the part of Ukraine on the left bank of the River Dnieper that had come under Russian rule in the mid-seventeenth century (Blum, 1961: 349, 416–19, 460–2, 542; Kakhk, 1988: 19–20, 41–8; Kohut, 1988: 237–48).

NOBLE ESTATES AND PEASANT VILLAGES

Serfdom gave the nobility control over the labour of roughly half the peasant population of the Russian Empire. While noble estate owners enjoyed immense theoretical authority over the serfs on their estates, they had less power in practice. Many nobles lived away from their estates on account of either their state service obligations or personal choice. Since many nobles owned several estates, moreover, it was impossible for them to live on, or even visit, all of them. Therefore, many nobles hired stewards and set up estate administrations to manage and organize the exploitation of their estates and serfs. To varying degrees these administrative structures incorporated or relied on the elders of the serf communities and village communal organizations (the *mir* or *obshchina*), which included the heads of individual serf households under a village elder appointed or approved by the estate owner (Aleksandrov, 1976).

Recent case studies of individual estates have shown that many elders and village elites – who were themselves serfs – were prepared to cooperate in the enforcement of the estate owners' authority in return for a share of that authority and the privileges that went with it. There was also a hierarchy of power inside serf households. This was especially true of the large households containing more than one married couple – often parents and married sons – that were widespread in central Russia in the eighteenth and first half of the nineteenth centuries. The result of this hierarchy of power inside the enserfed peasantry was that male heads of households, village elders, and members of elite factions of serfs benefited at the expense of their fellow villagers, especially the women, the younger generation, and those with less clout in the village commune (Hoch, 1986; Melton, 1993).

Table 2.2   Forms of obligations in the 1850s

Region	% serfs on labour services (barshchina)	% serfs on dues (obrok)
A. Russian non-black earth		
Central Non-Black Earth	32.5	67.5
Northwestern	60.4	39.6
Northern	16.5	83.5
B. Russian black earth		
Central Black Earth	73.1	26.9
Mid-Volga	77.2	22.8
Lower and Trans Volga	69.8	30.2
C. Western Borderlands		
Belorussia and Lithuania	92.3	7.7
Right-bank Ukraine	97.4	2.6
Left-bank Ukraine	99.3	0.7

Note: Serfs on mixed obligations (labour and dues) are counted under the form that was the greater.
Source: Koval'chenko (1967), p. 58.

Nobles' estate administrations did not organize serfs' economic activities. Nobles' estates in the Russian Empire were not like slave plantations in other parts of the world, where the plantation owners made the important decisions about what crops to grow and how they were to be cultivated. Instead, on most Russian nobles' estates, the basic economic decisions about production were taken by serfs in their village communes and households. The main purpose of Russian nobles' estate administrations was to extract obligations in labour and/or dues from the serfs. Labour services were more common in the fertile black earth regions to the south and east of Moscow, where agriculture was the main economic activity of the peasants. Dues prevailed in the less fertile central and northern regions, where handicrafts, trade and wage labour played a large part in the rural economy. The geographical distribution of the two main forms of obligations was not as clear-cut as this might suggest. Some nobles with estates near large cities in central and northern Russia used serf labour to produce foodstuffs for urban markets. In the non-Russian western borderlands, including less fertile regions, almost all estate owners demanded labour obligations. Figures on the proportions of serfs required to perform labour obligations or pay dues can be misleading, however, since some estate owners required both. (Table 2.2.) In the last few decades of serfdom the majority of estate owners expected their serfs to work for them for three days a week, or demanded a similar proportion of serfs' income as dues.

Most estate owners set total figures for the amount of money, agricultural produce, and/or days' labour they required from entire villages. Many held village communes jointly responsible for these obligations (Moon, 1999: Chapters 3 and 6).

There were few legal limitations on the levels of obligations estate owners could demand from their serfs, apart from a general provision dating back to the seventeenth century that they were not to work them to death. Over the eighteenth century, however, the state began to take very tentative steps to protect serfs from excessive exploitation and cruel treatment by their owners, and to insist that estate owners offered their serfs assistance in times of bad harvest and famine. In 1724 Peter the Great expressed the view that his peasant subjects, including the nobles' serfs, should be cared for and protected against excessive exploitation. He wrote that the peasants were 'the arteries of the state which is nourished by them as the body is fed by the arteries'. Peter was well aware that the peasants were his main sources of tax revenue and supplied most of the recruits for his armed services. Similar views were held by Peter's successors and several statesmen of the eighteenth century (Bartlett, 1996: 67–8). Some nobles, especially the owners of large numbers of serfs, shared this attitude. Their primary motive, however, was to secure their incomes from their estates, not concern for the welfare of their serfs (Melton, 1990).

In return for the obligations estate owners extracted from their serfs, most nobles granted them use of allotments of land to support themselves. Estate owners who demanded dues handed over most of the land on their estates. Those who required labour services kept some of the land for their own production – the demesne – and handed over the rest. Estate owners usually gave the land not to individual households of serfs, but to village communes, which then distributed it in strips in the village open fields to households. In central Russia from the late seventeenth and early eighteenth centuries, village communes not only held the land in communal tenure, but periodically redistributed strips of land between households to take account of changes in their size (Aleksandrov, 1990). In contrast, in the empire's western borderlands, households held their allotments in individual tenure, and passed them on to their sons and heirs.

Households' allotments were made up of a number of different types of land. The most important was their arable land on which they grew the grain that was the staple of their diet. In central Russia and the western borderlands most serfs grew grain under a three-field system, in which one-third of the land was left fallow each year to recover its fertility. Serfs also had household plots. These included the land their houses were built on and their garden plots, where they grew vegetables and kept domestic livestock. In addition, serf households had access to pastures, which were usually held in common, where they grazed their cows and horses in the summer. In the winter serfs fed their livestock hay which they had mown in the village meadows the previous summer. Finally, households had access to woodland, where they could gather fuel and timber, and to streams, ponds or other sources of water. Households cultivated their land by themselves, but village communes regulated crop rotations, pasturing livestock, and haymaking (Moon, 1999: Chapters 4 and 6). On most estates the land set aside by some estate owners for their own cultivation using serf labour – the demesne – was intermingled with the communal land in the villages' open fields. Moreover, serfs grew the same crops and used the same implements, draught animals and techniques on their own plots and the demesne (Confino, 1963).

Thus, most noble estates were peasant villages far more than they were the 'nests of gentry' portrayed in some nineteenth-century Russian literature. Nobles' country houses and elegant gardens (which existed on only a small minority of estates) were largely cut off from their serfs. The only serfs to enter this 'noble world' were some household serfs (*dvorovye lyudi*), who comprised a small minority – 6.8 per cent in 1858 – of the total numbers of serfs. A few wealthy nobles, such as the Sheremetevs, even had some household serfs trained to play in orchestras and operas for their entertainment. A few serfs were trained as architects and painters to help beautify their owners' houses. These were a tiny minority. More household serfs worked as domestic servants. The majority worked as clerks, smiths, wheelwrights, millers and in other skilled occupations on their owners' estates (Roosevelt, 1995).

Wealthy estate owners such as the Sheremetevs were a tiny minority of the Russian nobility, but they owned a large part of Russia's serfs. In the late 1850s Count Sergei Sheremetev was the largest single serfowner in the Russian Empire, with a total of nearly 150,000 male serfs (Lieven, 1992: 44). At the same time, the 3.4 per cent of the nobility who owned more than 500 male serfs possessed over 40 per cent of all serfs. On the other hand, the three-quarters of nobles who owned fewer than 100 male serfs possessed only about 20 per cent of the total. Smaller landowners had been losing out to magnates over the preceding century and a half. (See Table 2.3.)

Table 2.3 Noble serfownership in Russia, 1719–1858

Number of serfs owned	1719–27		1857–58	
	% nobles	*% serfs*	*% nobles*	*% serfs*
501+	0.80	26.20	3.40	41.50
101–500	7.90	32.50	20.90	38.00
<100	91.30	41.30	75.70	20.50
Totals	100.00	100.00	100.00	100.00

Source: Shepukova (1964), p. 393

CONCLUSION

Serfdom emerged in Russia in the late sixteenth and early seventeenth centuries in the interests of the state and its noble servitors. In the seventeenth and eighteenth centuries the tsars acquired territories in east-central Europe (the Baltic provinces, Lithuania, Belorussia and Ukraine) where similar systems of serfdom had emerged. By the eighteenth century there were four main features of serfdom in the Russian Empire: the serfs' subordinate legal status, including the prohibition on moving; the rights of access to allotments of land that noble estate owners granted to serfs (in the Russian provinces via village communes); the obligations serfs owed in return to estate owners, usually in the forms of labour services and/or dues in cash or kind; and the estate owners' administrative and judicial authority over their serfs. These were the features of the institution that would have to be dealt with once the state had decided to reform, or indeed abolish, serfdom.

CHAPTER THREE

A CRISIS OF SERFDOM?

Some historians have argued that the main cause of reform and, eventually, abolition of serfdom in Russia was that it was in a state of crisis in the decades before 1861. The strongest proponents of this thesis were historians writing in the Soviet Union under the influence of the official Soviet interpretation of history (see Chapter 1). There were two main components of the 'crisis thesis': that the servile economy had reached a state of crisis, and that serfs, who were suffering from growing exploitation, were protesting in increasing numbers and with growing strength against their servile status. It was further argued that the developing economic crisis and rising tide of 'the peasant movement' influenced radical intellectuals in campaigning for the abolition of serfdom.

AN ECONOMIC CRISIS?

Soviet historians, for example P. I. Lyashchenko and I. D. Kovalchenko, identified, and endeavoured to find evidence for, a 'crisis of the feudal-serf system' in the late eighteenth and first half of the nineteenth centuries. They argued that 'feudal' exploitation of serfs by noble estate owners and the state not only increased over this period, but did so out of proportion with serfs' incomes and economic potential. Many Soviet historians also maintained that grain yields, agricultural output per capita, and the average sizes of serfs' land allotments and livestock holdings were all declining. As a result, serfs' living standards were falling. They were so bad, many asserted, that serfs were literally 'dying out'. Indeed, over the first half of the nineteenth century, the numbers of serfs fell as a proportion of the total population and, from the 1830s, in absolute terms (Table 3.1a). It was also argued that although nobles were trying to squeeze more out of their serfs, serfdom was becoming unprofitable for them. Soviet historians saw these 'negative' factors as evidence for the 'decay of feudalism'. The perceived 'crisis' also had 'positive' elements indicating the 'genesis of capitalism'. There was increasing regional specialization between the largely agricultural black earth regions to the south and east and the less fertile forested region around Moscow and to the north, where serfs spent more time engaged in craft production. This led to growing production of agricultural and craft produce for the market, and increasing trade both between and inside regions. However, these developments were hindered by the increasing burden of 'feudal' exploitation and the continued existence of serfdom (Koval'chenko, 1970; Lyashchenko, 1949: 358–69).

Table 3.1a   The decline in the serf population, 1811–57

1	2	3	4
Year	Total Male Population	Male Serf Population	Serfs as % Total Population
1811	20,863	10,455	50.11
1815	21,538	9,987	46.37
1833	25,957	10,963	42.24
1850	28,555	10,859	38.03
1857	29,608	10,795	36.46

Columns 2 and 3: all figures in thousands.

Column 2: figures include army and navy, but exclude Poland, Finland and Transcaucasus.

Source: Hoch and Augustine (1979), p. 406.

There were two major problems with the 'crisis' thesis. First, critics – including Soviet scholars B. G. Litvak and V. A. Fedorov – pointed out that it depended to some extent on sources that they regard as unreliable and, crucially, which overstated the very factors that were central to the 'crisis' argument. Kovalchenko used data from provincial governors' annual reports, which appear to have understated grain yields. The crisis argument also relied on information on the sizes of serfs' land allotments and their obligations to estate owners from the 'Descriptions of Seigniorial Estates'. These were compiled by the estate owners themselves in 1858–59, on the eve of the abolition of serfdom. Litvak, Fedorov and other historians approached data from the 'Descriptions' more critically, and made greater use of the 'Regulatory Charters', which were also drawn up by estate owners, but under official supervision and subject to peasant approval, immediately after the end of serfdom in 1861. The 'Charters' contained higher figures for serfs' allotments and lower figures for their obligations than the 'Descriptions'. The discrepancy strongly suggests that, in anticipation of abolition, some estate owners deliberately falsified the figures in the 'Descriptions' with the aim of maximizing the amount of compensation they might receive and minimizing the area of land they might have to hand over to the freed serfs (Fedorov, 1974; Koval'chenko, 1967; Litvak, 1972).

A second serious problem with the 'crisis' thesis is that it was based to a large extent on *a priori* assumptions derived from Marx's theory of historical development. As Marxists, Soviet historians believed that societies passed through a series of 'modes of production', for example 'feudalism' and 'capitalism', and that the transition from one mode to the next was marked by a 'crisis' in the old 'mode'. For Soviet historians, the 'crisis of the feudal-serf system' was not just a cause of the abolition of serfdom, but the precursor to the development of capitalism (Baron, 1972). Since Soviet scholars were obliged to adhere to an official 'Marxist' interpretation of history, many set out with the intention of finding evidence to support a preconceived view. The end of the Soviet Union in 1991 was accompanied by the demise of the official interpretation of history. Few Russian historians now believe there was a 'crisis of the feudal-serf system' in the last decades before 1861. A major specialist, Boris Mironov, has recently stated categorically that there was no 'crisis' (Mironov, 1999, vol.1: 400).

Table 3.1b   Transfers from the serf population, 1833–57

Type of Transfer	Number
Law of 1803	*58,225*
Law of 1842	*27,173*
Law of 1847	*964*
Other transfers to state peasantry (on state initiative)	*232,213*
Purchased by Appanage Department	*25,000*
Sub-total	343,575
Recruits to regular army and navy	433,750
Sons of recruits (*kantonisty*)	122,500
Exiles to Siberia	60,000
Estimated natural growth after transfer	22,800
Total	**982,625**

All figures are for males only.

On laws of 1803, 1842 and 1847, see Chapter 5.

Other transfers to state peasantry included serfs confiscated from Polish rebels after the revolt of 1830–31, serfs on estates purchased by the Ministry of State Domains, and peasants who were found to have been illegally registered as serfs.

Recruits no longer counted as serfs (see Chapter 6).

Sons of recruits became boy trainee soldiers (*kantonisty*).

Source: Hoch and Augustine (1979), p. 410.

Historians in the West have put forward different, and more positive, views of the Russian economy in the late eighteenth and first half of the nineteenth centuries (Blum, 1961: 342). Steven Hoch has shown that some serfs in the fertile Central Black Earth region were relatively well fed in years with good harvests (Hoch, 1986: 15–64). The idea that serfs were 'dying out' because their living standards were so bad has been refuted. The decline in the relative and absolute size of the serf population was due largely to serfs transferring to other categories of peasants, for example the state peasantry, and out of the peasantry altogether, in particular as recruits to the armed forces (Hoch and Augustine, 1979) (Tables 3.1a and 3.1b). Moreover, two American economic historians have denied that serf estates were unprofitable for their owners in the last decades before 1861 (Domar and Machina, 1984).

What is not in dispute is that, over the late eighteenth and first half of the nineteenth centuries, the Russian economy was increasingly lagging behind the economies of some western European countries, which were experiencing agricultural and industrial 'revolutions'. Serfdom, however, may not have been the decisive factor retarding the development of the Russian economy. Olga Crisp pointed to the endemic transport problems in a country as large as Russia, and to the weakness of domestic demand. She concluded: 'Serfdom was a symptom not the cause of the slowness of Russia's economic growth until the 1850s' (Crisp, 1976: 95). Nevertheless, Russian serfdom was becoming an anachronism as similar systems of unfree labour were being abolished throughout east-central Europe, and had largely disappeared in western Europe by the end of the middle ages (Blum, 1978).

Russia's growing, relative economic 'backwardness' preyed on the minds of Russia's rulers and senior officials as well as intellectuals. They were influenced at least as much by contemporary economic theories, mostly from western Europe, however, as by their impressions of Russia's actual economic performance (Kingston-Mann, 1991). From the mid-eighteenth century liberal economic theorists – for example the Scot Adam Smith – objected to systems of forced labour for three reasons. They argued that forced labour impeded the development of a free market in labour; that it led to the impoverishment of a large part of the population and thus in-hibited the growth of domestic demand; and that free labour was more productive, and more profitable, than forced labour. Catherine the Great (1762–96), who was well versed in the latest European ideas, promoted the dissemination of 'liberal' economic thought in Russia. Under her patronage, the 'Free Economic Society for the Encouragement of Agriculture and Good Husbandry' was founded in 1765. The society held an essay competition on the subject of peasant property rights in 1766. Almost all entries came from western Europeans. The winning entry was by Beardé de l'Abbaye, a doctor of laws from Aachen in western Germany. He proposed that serfs should be allowed to acquire property, including land. In addition, once they had received the necessary education, they should be granted personal freedom. The state, nobles and peasants, he wrote, would all benefit economically. The fact that Catherine permitted the publication of the essay suggests that she agreed with its contents. Indeed, at the same time, she hinted that serf-dom was in need of reform for economic reasons in her 'Instruction' to the Legislative Commission. However, her arguments fell mostly on deaf ears (Bartlett, 1998; Madariaga, 1981: 134–6, 156–9).

The only part of the Russian Empire where noble estate owners favoured reform for economic reasons was the Baltic provinces. In the early nineteenth century, moreover, they advocated the abolition of serfdom (see Chapter 5). The Baltic nobles were mostly German and had far greater knowledge of general European intellectual thought than their Russian counterparts (Kakhk, 1988: 168–79). In so far as most Russian estate owners understood concepts such as profitability, or collected the necessary figures to be able to judge whether their estates made a profit, most seem to have believed that they gained financially from the existing ways of running their estates. In any case, most Russian nobles preferred to mortgage their serfs than contemplate major changes in order to get their hands on ready cash. In 1820, 20 per cent of all serfs in Russia were mortgaged to state credit institutions by their owners. By 1859 this had increased to 66 per cent (Emmons, 1968a: 20–9).

Some enlightened members of the Russian bureaucracy, however, were persuaded by the theoretical economic arguments for abolishing serfdom. In 1841 a senior official, Andrei Zablotskii-Desyatovskii, put forward economic objections to serfdom in a confidential memorandum to the Minister of State Domains, Paul Kiselev [*Doc. 9*]. Zablotskii-Desyatovskii's convictions were shared by a number of officials of his generation. Nicholas Milyutin, an official in the Ministry of Internal Affairs, wrote in a confidential memorandum in February 1847: 'Serfdom serves as the main – even the only – hindrance to any development in Russia at the present time. … Only with the emancipation of the serfs will the betterment of our rural economy become possible.' A future Minister of Finance, Michael Reutern, also believed that the Russian economy would benefit from the abolition of serfdom. All three officials were involved in the preparation of the legislation to abolish serfdom in the late 1850s (Kipp, 1975; Lincoln, 1982: 48–9, 78, 174, 195–7). Liberal and radical intellectuals also put forward economic arguments for abolishing serfdom. In 1790, the nobleman Alexander Radishchev (see Chapter 4) criticized serfdom partly on economic grounds. In the 1840s and 1850s, Nicholas Turgenev and Boris Chicherin among others made similar points in works that were published abroad to avoid censorship. The slavophile noble Alexander Koshelev appealed to the economic self-interest of noble estate owners. In his 1847 essay 'Voluntarism is better than Compulsion', he argued that freely hired labour was more productive than labour obligations under serfdom [*Doc. 12*]. He restated this argument in an 1858 memorandum to Tsar Alexander II (see Chapter 4). Koshelev and other intellectuals had close contacts with reform-minded officials (Davidson, 1973).

However, although economic arguments were advanced in favour of reforming serfdom in Russia, and some government officials shared such views, it is difficult to make a case that economic motives were the decisive factor in the Russian government's decision to reform and later abolish

serfdom. In 1858–61, when Russian officials drew up the Statutes abolishing serfdom, they did not legislate for an immediate reduction in the
exploitation of the former serfs in order to increase domestic demand to
stimulate economic growth. Nor did the reformers create a free and mobile
labour force, but left the former serfs bound to the land (see Chapters 7 and
8). One of the reasons for the continued ban on peasant movement was to
ensure that the former serfs would continue to pay their taxes and dues
(Skerpan, 1964: 186–213). Thus, crisis or no crisis, economic factors did
not play the central role in the demise of serfdom in Russia.

'THE PEASANT MOVEMENT'

Another of the reasons why the reformers were reluctant to create a freely
mobile peasantry in 1861 was their concern for social stability. They were
worried that a mobile peasant population could pose a serious threat to the
social order. In the decades prior to 1861, Russia's rulers, officials and
nobles were particularly anxious to avert the threat, as they perceived, of a
large-scale serf revolt. There is some evidence, furthermore, that the scale of
serf protests was increasing over the first half of the nineteenth century, or
at least that some officials believed it was. This concern for social stability
has been seen by many historians, Western as well as Soviet, as one of the
main reasons for the abolition of serfdom.

   In the seventeenth and eighteenth centuries Russia had been shaken by
four massive revolts. The most serious were led by Stepan Razin in
1670–71 and Emelyan Pugachev in 1773–74. In the final stages of both
revolts, serfs in the mid-Volga region – about 400 miles east of Moscow –
rose up and slaughtered many estate owners and officials (Avrich, 1972).
Pugachev, who claimed to be the late Tsar Peter III, went so far as to issue
proclamations in Peter's name abolishing serfdom [*Doc. 3*]. However,
peasants in general and serfs in particular were only one group among a
number who took part in the wider revolts. Cossacks, townspeople and
non-Russians were as prominent as peasants, and all had their own agendas
and aims. The revolts began and were strongest on the peripheries of the
empire, where serfdom was weakly established or absent altogether. In each
case, once the rebels approached the central regions of Russia they were
defeated. None of the rebel armies stood a realistic chance of victory once it
came up against the full might of the Russian state and its armed forces.
The growing strength of the state meant that the prospects of a successful
social revolt against serfdom became ever more remote (Hart, 1988;
Khodarkovsky, 1994).

   More localized and lower-level unrest among serfs continued both
between the four revolts and after 1774. Serfs fled their owners' estates in
attempts to find greater freedom elsewhere. Many moved to the border-

lands of the empire where serfdom was absent. There were numerous, mostly non-violent, confrontations between serfs and estate and state authorities in which serfs tried to gain some improvement in their lives. Some serfs sent petitions to the authorities, including the tsar, or filed law suits. Like oppressed people in other societies, many Russian serfs resorted to 'weapons of the weak': shirking work on estate owners' land, not paying dues in full or on time, lying, feigning illness, getting drunk, etc. At most, serfs who used such tactics attained redress of particular grievances. Many, however, received only retribution from the authorities (Bohac, 1991: 236–60; Ignatovich, 1911a; Moon, 1999: 237–81).

Many Soviet historians devoted enormous energies to attempts to quantify what they called 'the peasant movement'. At their crudest, these efforts amounted to counting the numbers of 'disturbances' with little or no regard to what had happened or why it had taken place. Not surprisingly, the deeper historians delved in the archives, the more 'disturbances' they found. Back in the 1880s, Semevskii had uncovered 556 'disturbances' between 1826 and 1854. By the early 1960s, Soviet researchers had raised this figure to 1,365, and found many more for the years 1855–61 (Table 3.2). Many Soviet historians connected the apparent rising tide of peasant unrest with the increasing exploitation by nobles and declining living standards that were part of the alleged 'crisis of the feudal-serf system'. They aimed to demonstrate, moreover, that the scale of 'the peasant movement' provoked by this 'crisis' was one of the main reasons for the decision to abolish serfdom (Lyashchenko, 1949: 370–4; Nechkina, 1970). This interpretation bore the hallmarks of the official Soviet interpretation of history, which followed Marx's assertion that 'class struggle' was the motor behind historical development. Soviet historians wished to show that 'class struggle' between serfs and nobles was a major cause of the demise of 'feudalism' and its replacement with 'capitalism'.

Table 3.2 Numbers of peasant 'disturbances', 1826–61

Years	Historians		
	Semevskii [1888]	*Ignatovich [1925]*	*Druzhinin series [1961–36]*
1826–29	41	88	172
1830–34	46	60	158
1835–39	59	78	184
1840–44	101	138	191
1845–49	172	207	357
1850–54	137	141	303
1855–61	–	474	926
Totals	*[556]*	*1,186*	*2,291*

Sources: Semevskii (1888), vol. 2, p. 595; Ignatovich (1925), pp. 331–2; Predtechenskii (1961), p. 817; Okun' (1962), pp. 732–3; Okun' and Sivkov (1963), p. 736.

Not all historians working in the Soviet Union were content with this view. Zaionchkovsky subjected the work of some historians of 'the peasant movement' to withering criticism. He pointed out that it was not adequate simply to add up the numbers of completely different phenomena (he drew a parallel with adding 'one camel plus one chicken'). He also claimed that some historians exaggerated the scale of peasant unrest. There are also problems with the sources. Historians of 'the peasant movement' relied heavily on the work of the tsarist police. There were two police forces: the rural police, who were subordinate to provincial governors and the Ministry of Internal Affairs, and the Third Section (the secret police). The figures produced by the two organizations are not comparable since they used different criteria. In addition, the rural police tended to report fewer disorders, since larger numbers would have suggested to their superiors that they were not carrying out their duty to maintain law and order. The agents of the Third Section, however, usually reported higher numbers, since they were anxious to justify their role (Zaionchkovsky, 1978: 26–7).

The numbers of incidents of peasant unrest the police reported also depended, to some extent, on their instructions from the central government. Not surprisingly, more disorders were reported at times when the government asked the police to pay particular attention to peasant unrest. The more worried the central authorities, the more orders they sent out on the need to maintain surveillance over the peasantry to provincial officials, who in turn responded with more detailed reports on more disturbances. Thus, the original fears in St Petersburg to some extent confirmed themselves. For example, higher numbers of disturbances were reported in 1826 (after the Decembrist revolt – see below), 1848 (following the outbreak of revolutions in many European states), and in the late 1850s (after the decision to abolish serfdom had been taken). Peasant discontent probably was higher than average in these years, but so was government concern for law and order in the provinces (Nifontov, 1961: 186–8; Tokarev, 1960).

This is not to say that peasant disturbances played no role in the government's decision to abolish serfdom. Russian rulers and state officials did consider enacting reforms of serfdom with the aim of removing causes of discontent among serfs. The idea of reforming serfdom from above rather than waiting until the oppressed serfs rose in violent revolt to overthrow the institution from below became a recurring theme among Russia's rulers. Early in her reign Catherine the Great wrote 'if we do not agree to reduce cruelty and moderate a situation intolerable for human beings, then they themselves will take things in hand' (Madariaga, 1981: 123–7). Several decades later, in his annual report to the tsar in 1839, the chief of the Third Section argued for reform from above rather than wait for revolt from below [*Doc. 8*], a sentiment which was echoed by Nicholas I in 1842 [*Doc. 10*]. The most famous occasion when this argument was used was in March 1856 by Alexander II [*Doc. 14*]. Although Alexander's speech is sometimes seen as starting the process that led to the abolition of serfdom five years later, there is no direct evidence that fear of peasant unrest was the decisive factor in the decision. Successive rulers were certainly concerned by the regular reports they received about disturbances among enserfed peasants. But, Nicholas I and Alexander II may have been playing on the nobility's fear of a revolt to scare them into the realization that one day they would have to give up their serfs for other reasons (Rieber, 1966: 33–6). Nevertheless, however worried the authorities were, the case for a central role for peasant protest in the demise of serfdom remains not proven.

On the other hand, there is evidence that fear of serf revolts was a reason why Russia's rulers were reluctant to enact major reforms of serfdom. Popular unrest, both actual and feared, acted as a brake on reform for two reasons. First, it persuaded most rulers that their interests were best served by maintaining their close relationship with the nobility. This meant continued state support for serfdom. Back in 1649 the legal consolidation of serfdom had cemented the alliance between the state and nobles in face of riots in Moscow. The four great revolts of the seventeenth and eighteenth centuries served to strengthen this alliance, and to convince the state of the value of the nobility as a police force in the provinces. The defeat of Pugachev in 1774 was followed by a *rapprochement* between Catherine the Great, who had considered reforms of serfdom in the 1760s, and the serf-owning nobility, who favoured the *status quo*. Catherine's Charter to the Nobility of 1785, which codified the nobility's privileged status, is often seen as evidence for a renewed and strengthened alliance between the state and nobility (Hellie, 1971: 108, 138–42, 246–9, 260–1, 329, 381; Jones, 1973: 196–209). Although Pugachev's was the last great rising in servile Russia, and serfs were only a minority of the rebels, the 'spectre of Pugachev' continued to haunt noble manor houses and the corridors of power in St Petersburg long into the nineteenth century. The 1848 revolutions in much of continental Europe prompted renewed fears in the mind of Nicholas I. Over the preceding decade he had alarmed many nobles by enacting a few limited reforms of serfdom as well as major reforms of the appanage and state peasants (see Chapter 5). In March 1848, however, shortly after news of the revolution in Paris reached St Petersburg, Nicholas I addressed the marshals of the nobility of St Petersburg province. He urged them to forget recent disagreements and to act together against the threat from below (Saunders, 2000b: 145–9).

Another reason why the threat of revolt was a reason for caution was that rulers feared that a major reform of serfdom might provoke rather than avert rebellion. They were worried that some serfs might interpret any action as a signal that the tsar was on their side, and then rise up against the nobility. Rulers also feared that serfs might revolt if, as was likely, they were disappointed by a reform that did not match their hopes. Nicholas I, ever cautious, expressed such a view in 1842 [*Doc. 10*].

CONCLUSION

With the partial exception of the Baltic provinces, serfdom in the Russian Empire was not abolished by noble estate owners who decided that it would be economically advantageous to free their serfs and hire free labourers to cultivate their land instead. Nor was serfdom overthrown from below by a violent serf revolt. Nevertheless, both economic factors and social stability influenced intellectuals, nobles, state officials and the tsars themselves when they considered the future of serfdom. In gauging the significance of the two main components of the 'crisis thesis' – economic crisis and peasant unrest – it is important to distinguish between what subsequent historians have argued on the basis of their research and theoretical perspectives, on the one hand, and the attitudes and perceptions of contemporaries, on the other. Thus, these two factors seem to have been more important in the writings of Soviet historians than they were in the minds of contemporaries. In order to assess the relative importance of economic factors and peasant unrest as causes of reform and the eventual abolition of serfdom, it is necessary to consider other factors that affected the thinking of both the men who took the crucial decisions and those who, directly or indirectly, influenced them.

CHAPTER FOUR

FURTHER CAUSES OF REFORM AND ABOLITION

In addition to their perceptions of the influence of serfdom on the economy and the threat of serf protests, Russia's rulers and senior state officials took account of other factors when considering whether to reform or abolish serfdom in the decades prior to the 1850s. A similar range of factors was also discussed by members of the growing radical intelligentsia – which included some nobles – who sought to influence the government.

HUMANITARIAN CONSIDERATIONS

Another argument for reforming, and ending, serfdom was that allowing the ownership and subjugation of some human beings by others was immoral, offended natural justice, and corrupted all members of a society – including serfowners as well as their serfs – that tolerated such an institution. Some thinkers of the eighteenth-century European Enlightenment argued that human beings were essentially good, but were constrained by oppressive institutions, such as serfdom, which should therefore be reformed (Hampson, 1968). Enlightened, humanitarian arguments against personal bondage were a secular version of older, radical religious objections (Hilton, 1973: 207–13). Catherine the Great, who was a keen student of the Enlightenment, seems to have abhorred serfdom on humanitarian, as well as economic, grounds. Some historians have argued, however, that she did little to ameliorate the serfs' lot and actually intensified the institution (Lappo-Danilevskii, 1911/1972). This has led to the claim that Catherine's main concern was that Russian serfdom had an adverse effect on her, and her empire's, reputation among her enlightened friends in the salons of western Europe. Isabel de Madariaga, however, has strongly defended Catherine (Madariaga, 1974).

During Catherine's reign a few educated Russians were less equivocal in their humanitarian objections to serfdom. Most notably, the nobleman Radishchev made a thinly veiled attack on the inhumanity of serfdom in his book *A Journey from St Petersburg to Moscow*, published in 1790.

Radishchev had been educated at the German University of Leipzig between 1766 and 1771 at the expense of the Russian government, which had paid for his studies because it needed educated men to serve in the bureaucracy. Radishchev, however, used the critical talents he developed under the guidance of his enlightened tutors to question the social and political order of his motherland. Under the guise of a traveller's account, in some sections of *A Journey* he depicted the fate, at the hands of their noble owners, of serfs his narrator met on his way from St Petersburg to Moscow. Radishchev also raised the spectre of a social revolt if nothing was done to end the abuses inherent in serfdom [*Doc. 4*]. Catherine the Great was horrified. Shocked by the outbreak of revolution against absolute monarchy in France in 1789, and despairing of achieving wide-ranging reforms at home, she banished Radishchev to Siberia (Radishchev, 1790/1966).

In spite of state repression and censorship, criticism of serfdom on humanitarian grounds by Russian intellectuals increased over the first half of the nineteenth century. Some confined their attacks to unpublished papers circulated among a few friends or discussions in small circles of radicals that met in each others' houses and salons. Members of both main intellectual movements – slavophiles and westernizers – were opposed to serfdom. At the time, however, the only people who paid much attention to such radicals, besides themselves, were secret policemen. Another way around the censorship was to publish abroad. Nicholas Turgenev published his book *Russia and the Russians*, in which he criticized the existing order in Russia, including serfdom, in Paris in 1847. In the same year, appalled by the repression of intellectuals in Nicholas I's Russia, Alexander Herzen went into self-imposed exile, from where he conducted propaganda campaigns against serfdom and the autocracy. From 1853 he published a series of periodicals – *The Polar Star*, *Voices from Russia*, and *The Bell* – in London. They were smuggled into Russia, where they were read not just by sympathizers, but also state officials, secret policemen, members of the imperial family, and even Alexander II (Saunders, 1992: 148–72, 211–12, 223, 227). Humanitarian arguments for reforming serfdom were also held, confidentially, by state officials. Zablotskii-Desyatovskii expressed moral objections to serfdom in his 1841 memorandum to Kiselev (Lincoln, 1982: 48–9).

Some humanitarian attacks on serfdom did make it into print in Russia. The best known is the collection of short stories by Ivan Turgenev, 'A Sportsman's Sketches', which were published in the literary journal *The Contemporary* between 1847 and 1851 (Turgenev, 1847–51/1967). Aware that the censors would not permit direct attacks, Turgenev followed Radishchev's example and used a literary device. His stories were ostensibly about a nobleman out hunting, the game he shot, the countryside he passed through, and the people he met along his way. Many of the people he met, however, were serfs. Turgenev made a point of describing their lives and stories in realistic and sympathetic terms. By portraying serfs as full human beings, it can be argued that he was implying that the institution of serfdom that oppressed them was inhumane. It has often been asserted that Turgenev's short stories had a powerful influence on the future Alexander II, and even that they were an important factor in his eventual decision to abolish serfdom (Hanne, 1994: 43–74). This final claim is an exaggeration. David Saunders probably went too far in the other direction, however, with his mischievous suggestion that Alexander II may have enjoyed Ivan Turgenev's stories simply because he liked hunting (Saunders, 1992: 205). Alexander II was less happy when, in early 1858, the slavophile noble Koshelev sent him a memorandum – laying out a plan for ending serfdom – in which he argued that abolition: 'is more necessary for the welfare of our class itself even than for the serfs. The abolition of the right to dispose of people like objects or like cattle is as much our liberation as theirs: for at present we are under the yoke of a law that destroys still more in us than in the serfs any human quality' (Seton-Watson, 1967: 334).

Not all Russian intellectuals opposed serfdom. One of the most prominent writers of the first half of the nineteenth century, Nicholas Gogol, defended the institution in a collection of letters published in 1847 as *Selected Passages from Correspondence with Friends*. In contrast to many of his educated contemporaries, Gogol did not accept the enlightened, liberal notion that people were inherently good but were constrained and oppressed by institutions, such as serfdom, that inhibited human freedom. Rather, he adhered to the Christian belief in 'original sin', which taught that, after Adam and Eve's fall from grace, people were innately sinful and needed to be protected from their own base instincts. In a letter to a 'Russian landowner', Gogol advised him to tell his serfs: 'that you are compelling them to labo[u]r and work not because you need money for your pleasures ... [but] because it has been commanded by God that man must earn his bread in the sweat of his brow, and then read them a lesson in the Holy Writ [Genesis 3:17–19] so that they may see it' (Gogol, 1847/1969: 138). Gogol was subjected to a vitriolic attack by the liberal literary critic Vissarion Belinskii in an unpublished, and thus uncensored, letter which circulated widely among the intelligentsia (Dmytryshyn, 1967: 184–92).

Although Gogol's defence of serfdom was to some extent consistent with the Christian doctrine of original sin, some *opponents* of serfdom, including some already mentioned, were also motivated by Christian beliefs. Hostility to forced labour on humanitarian grounds can be found in some of the oldest texts of the Judæo-Christian tradition. One of the best-known stories in the Old Testament is God's deliverance of the Israelites from slavery in Egypt (Exodus 1–14). Some Russians, including serfs, made a direct comparison between the lot of the enslaved Israelites under Pharaoh and Russian peasants under serfdom (Moon, 1992: 130). Some Orthodox clergymen were unhappy with serfdom. Gregory Freeze has revised the older view of the Russian Orthodox Church as a submissive 'handmaiden of the state' that helped maintain the servile social order. The church, he emphasized, concentrated on spiritual rather than worldly matters. Priests who did address the issue of serfdom tended to stress the duty of nobles, as Christians, to show regard for the material and moral welfare of their serfs, as well as the serfs' obligation to obey their owners. By the mid-nineteenth century some Orthodox churchmen began to express moral repugnance of an institution that was undermining their attempts to reinforce the religious faith of their mostly peasant parishioners (Freeze, 1989).

In spite of the vehemence of their arguments, humanitarian churchmen and radical intellectuals did not make a direct contribution to reforming or abolishing serfdom in Russia. There is no doubt, however, that most Russian rulers from Catherine the Great to Alexander II, as well as more enlightened state officials, were well aware of, and to an extent shared, humanitarian objections derived from Christianity and the Enlightenment. Nevertheless, such concerns were not a major reason for the government to tackle the vexed question of serfdom. It is difficult to believe that Russia's rulers or senior officials would have risked alienating the nobility – the section of society that provided most of their officers and bureaucrats – and taken the chance of undermining their systems of taxation and recruitment, unless they had come to the conclusion for other reasons that the maintenance of serfdom was no longer in the best interests of the state.

STATE INTERESTS

From the mid-eighteenth century some of Russia's more far-sighted rulers and officials became aware, for a variety of reasons already discussed, of the incompatibility between the persistence of servile relations in the countryside and the long-term interests of the Russian state. Reforms of the social structure of rural Russia depended ultimately on the state's per-ception of the best way to mobilize and exploit Russia's resources in pursuit of its aims, chiefly the consolidation of state power inside Russia and the defence and expansion of its frontiers. The military reforms of the seven-teenth and early eighteenth centuries had contributed to Russia's imperial expansion into east-central Europe and rise to the status of a major European power. These developments had coincided with the consolidation and intensification of serfdom. The height of imperial Russia's international standing came in 1814, when Russian troops occupied Paris at the end of the Napoleonic Wars. Together with its allies, the Russian Empire's huge army of peasant-conscripts and noble-officers had defeated the mass army of Napoleon's French Empire. The Russian army continued to be victorious, against the Turkish and Persian Empires to the east, in the three decades after 1814. In the eighteenth and first half of the nineteenth centuries, therefore, the Russian state continued to support serfdom, at least in part, because it seemed to provide the basis for, or seemed to be compatible with, the persistence of Russian military might (Fuller, 1992).

Since the peasantry, including the serfs of the nobility, supplied the overwhelming majority of soldiers and paid the bulk of the tax revenues, however, the state took steps to ensure that they met, and were in a position to meet, these obligations (see Chapter 5). From the mid-eighteenth century, moreover, some of Russia's rulers began to give serious consideration to the question of abolishing serfdom. It seems most likely that they thought about such a measure not in terms of 'emancipating' the serfs, but of converting them to state peasants. This would bring the nobles' peasants under the direct control of the state, which would then be able to exploit the product of their labour without the intermediary of noble estate owners who took a share in the form of seigniorial obligations. The secularization of the church's estates and peasants by Peter III in 1762 [*Doc. 2*] – when peasants on the estates of the Russian Orthodox Church were converted to state peasants – can be seen as a step in the direction of the state bringing all Russia's peasants under its direct jurisdiction (Leonard, 1993: 73–89).

RELATIONS BETWEEN THE STATE AND NOBILITY

Rural reforms, especially changes that touched serfdom, reflected the evolving relationship between the Russian state and the estate-owning and serfowning nobility. The enserfment of the peasantry had reinforced the mutually dependent relationship between them that was based on noble service for the state and state support for serfdom. Although Peter the Great had ended the principle of granting land inhabited by peasants in return for state service in 1714, he had strictly enforced compulsory noble state service and upheld serfdom. Over the seventeenth and eighteenth centuries, service in the officer corps of Russia's growing armed forces and the civil bureaucracy became more professionalized. The state increasingly needed educated, competent and experienced men who were able to perform their duties effectively. An important step in this direction was Peter the Great's 'Table of Ranks' of 1722, under which qualifications and service were given precedence over birth as criteria for promotion in the officer corps and civil bureaucracy (Pintner, 1980; Raeff, 1966). In the long run, if the state could hire sufficient professional army officers and bureaucrats, or if officers and bureaucrats of noble origin came to identify with their professions and the state ahead of their social origins, then Russia's rulers would be able to dispense with compulsory noble state service and abolish the nobles' privileges, including serfdom.

Indeed, in February 1762, Peter III proclaimed the 'emancipation of the nobility' from obligatory state service, thereby ending the original rationale behind serfdom. Noble state service became voluntary and, with the exception of officers in the armed forces at the start of campaigns, nobles could retire from service whenever they wished, or choose not to enter service in the first place [*Doc. 1*]. It could be argued that Peter III's reform was a reversion to the less rigid patterns of noble service of the sixteenth and seventeenth centuries. However, the fact that the abolition of compulsory noble state service was spelled out in a proclamation was very significant as it defined formally in law the new relationship between state and nobility. The reform has been interpreted as a concession wrested from the state by the nobility, who resented the burdens of state service and wanted to enjoy the privileged life of landed nobles, residing on their estates and living off the labour of their serfs (Blum, 1961: 345–51). This view was challenged by, among others, Marc Raeff (1970: 1291–4) and Robert Jones (1973: 32–6). They argued that, on the contrary, the state wanted to emancipate itself from the expense of having to employ large numbers of poorly-qualified noblemen who were not able or willing to serve effectively. This view is supported by the timing of the act. Peter III proclaimed his measure towards the end of the Seven Years' War (1756– 62/63). Fighting Frederick the Great's Prussia had put a severe strain on the Russian treasury. Demobilizing superfluous noble officers in anticipation of peace was one way of cutting state expenditure. In addition, echoing the reforms of Frederick the Great (Rosenberg, 1958: 75–6) – who was Peter III's role model – the proclamation of 1762 stressed the professionalization of the civil service. It emphasized education, encouraged appointments based on competence, and increased the opportunities for capable officials from non-noble backgrounds to advance. Another reason why Peter III ended compulsory state service was that nobles were needed in the provinces to manage their estates and participate in local government. The most recent authority on Peter III concluded that he 'dissolved the obligatory bond between the nobility and the state and replaced it with a voluntary union with mutual benefits' (Leonard, 1993: 72). The enduring importance of the nobility to the state is indicated by the 99 years that separated the proclamations ending compulsory noble state service in 1762 and serfdom in 1861.

In the meantime, several tsars were concerned that if they attempted to reform serfdom, especially if such a reform seemed to presage abolition, they might alienate the nobility. They had good reason to be concerned. Between 1725 and 1801 factions of nobles and army officers had staged a number of coups or 'palace revolutions' in support of their favoured candidates for the throne. Two tsars, Peter III in 1762 and Paul in 1801, were deposed and murdered. (In neither case, however, was the tsar's policy on serfdom the main source of discontent.) It is not surprising, therefore, that both Alexander I (1801–25) and Nicholas I (1825–55) were conscious of the need not to provoke the hostility of important sections of the nobility. Tsars were not just worried about provoking 'palace revolutions'. The future of the autocracy itself was at stake. Over the previous centuries Russian nobles had acquiesced in the consolidation and maintenance of the tsars' autocratic powers in return for state support for their privileged position in society, in particular their authority over the serfs on their estates. Following this logic, if nobles were deprived of their serfs, then they might demand a constitution giving them the right to participate in the government of Russia (Riasanovsky, 1968: 274–5).

On the other hand, both Alexander I and Nicholas I became aware that by not introducing major reforms of serfdom they were alienating a minority of nobles who were members of the emerging radical intelligentsia. These nobles were opposed to serfdom in spite, or perhaps partly because, of the fact that they owned serfs themselves. After the end of compulsory noble state service in 1762 some nobles turned their attention to enlightened, liberal, and even revolutionary political and social ideas from western Europe. A few, for example Radishchev, began to take an interest in the peasantry beyond exploiting them. The most radical nobles went so far as to reverse their traditional loyalties, seeing their new role as serving the 'common people', that is the peasantry, rather than the state. Indeed, some also opposed the autocratic state that supported serfdom (Raeff, 1966: 148–71).

THE DECEMBRIST REVOLT

Although the main weapon used by noble critics of serfdom was the pen, some turned to the sword. In the decade after the end of the Napoleonic Wars in 1815, a number of mostly aristocratic army officers, together with a few civilians, formed conspiratorial secret societies. Men such as Paul Pestel and Nikita Muraviev drew up detailed plans for reforms, including the abolition of both serfdom and the autocracy [*Doc. 7*]. The movement culminated in the Decembrist revolt by some units of the army in St Petersburg on the day the army was due to swear allegiance to the new tsar, Nicholas I, in December 1825.

One of the chief causes of the Decembrist movement and revolt was that, early in his reign, Alexander I had aroused the hopes of members of the educated, noble elite that he would carry out major changes, including reforms of serfdom and the autocracy. Many of the rebels of 1825 had been educated in an intellectual and cultural environment orientated towards western Europe, where the last remnants of serfdom had long since died out and, more recently, absolute rulers had been overthrown in the wake of the French Revolution of 1789. Some of the conspirators had seen western Europe at first hand during the European campaigns of 1813–14 and the occupation of Paris. The Russian campaigns against Napoleon had also contributed to a growth in patriotic sentiment among noble army officers. Their feelings for Russia were increased by their daily contact with ordinary soldiers, most of whom came from peasant backgrounds. Noble-officers came to respect the endurance and bravery shown by their peasant-soldiers, and some began to think of the 'common people' as patriotic Russians not so different from themselves. On their return to Russia after 1815, the officers awaited the reforms Alexander I had seemed to promise. By the early 1820s, however, it was clear that they were waiting in vain. Disappointment and frustration turned them and their associates to rebellion (Moon, 1996b). Alexander I's sudden death in December 1825 gave the conspirators a chance. However, lack of planning and support doomed their revolt to failure. In any case, a young officer named Yakov Rostovtsev – who had been approached by the rebels but declined to join them – had felt it his duty to inform the new tsar of the plans. Nicholas I put down the revolt, spilling the blood of some of his subjects on the first day of his reign. He had five of the rebels executed and over a hundred exiled to Siberia. For the rest of his reign, however, Nicholas never forgot the Decembrists' critique of the social and political order in Russia, nor how far a minority of nobles were prepared to go to achieve radical aims, including ending serfdom. Nicholas also feared, however, the possible reactions by the majority of nobles if he took decisive action to tackle the 'peasant question' (Lincoln, 1978).

CONCLUSION

Thus, in the late eighteenth and first half of the nineteenth centuries there was growing opposition to serfdom among many sections of the population in Russia. A range of motives, moreover, spurred Russia's rulers and state officials seriously to contemplate the reform and even abolition of serfdom. But, there were also reasons for caution. Until the midpoint of the nineteenth century there was no decisive factor that impelled Russia's tsars to act. In the meantime, however, several rulers did enact reforms of serfdom and other aspects of life in rural Russia.

CHAPTER FIVE

RURAL REFORMS, 1762–1855

Peter III's two measures in 1762 marked an important turning point in state policy towards nobles and peasants that would culminate in the abolition of serfdom itself in 1861. His abolition of compulsory noble state service ended the original rationale behind serfdom. And, the secularization of the church peasants established a precedent for transferring peasants from the jurisdiction of intermediaries to the state. Peter III's measures were followed by other rural reforms over the following decades.

CATHERINE THE GREAT, THE NOBILITY AND SERFDOM

The policies with respect to the nobility and serfdom of Catherine the Great, who succeeded Peter III in 1762, reflected the balance of power between state and nobility in the latter part of the eighteenth century. Many of Catherine's policies can be seen as supporting the interests of the nobility at the expense of tne serfs. Her measures were also, however, in the interests of the state. She confirmed Peter III's 'emancipation of the nobility', but only in 1785, in her 'Charter to the Nobility'. This document codified the nobility's rights and privileges, including the rights to own and exploit land and serfs, exemptions from the poll tax, recruitment obligation and corporal punishment, and the right to participate in provincial noble associations. The charter increased noble involvement in the new system of provincial administration set up in 1775. While provincial governors and the holders of some positions were appointed by the central government, other officials were elected by and from the local nobility. Although this looks like a concession to the nobility, there was no realistic alternative. There were not enough professional bureaucrats to administer the provinces, and the state would not countenance peasant self-government. It was in the state's interests, of course, to have a system of provincial administration that would ensure the population met its obligations and maintained internal security (Jones, 1973).

Earlier in Catherine's reign she had apparently hoped to enact a major reform of serfdom. These hopes came to little. The activities of the Free Economic Society founded in 1765 did not lead to a widespread interest in 'improving' agriculture by reforming serfdom. The sections of the first draft of Catherine's 'Instruction' of 1767, in which she criticized serfdom, were toned down for the published version. One of her more enterprising provincial governors, Yakov Sievers of Novgorod, failed to get approval for a scheme that would have permitted serfs who engaged in trade to buy their freedom. In each case, Catherine's senior advisers – most of whom came from wealthy noble families – were able to convince the empress that it was not in the interests of political expediency to force the issue (Dukes, 1967: 249; Jones, 1984: 106; Madariaga, 1981: 159). Throughout her reign, moreover, Catherine rewarded her favourites, statesmen and victorious generals with estates inhabited by peasants, who thus became their serfs. Most of these gifts did not come from the state's domains and peasants, however, but from estates that had been confiscated from nobles who had fallen into disfavour in previous reigns, or whose owners had died without heirs, or from the lands annexed from Poland between 1772 and 1795 (Madariaga, 1974). Nevertheless, this policy does show that Catherine was prepared to use serfdom for political purposes.

If the nobility was still sufficiently strong in the late eighteenth century to resist pressure for major changes to serfdom, the state did have the power to take tentative steps in the direction of reform. Some of the measures enacted in the late eighteenth and early nineteenth centuries were attempts to shore up the existing order in rural Russia. Others were preparing the way for the transition to a new social and economic order without serfdom.

PROTECTION

Catherine the Great tried to curtail the worst abuses of serfdom by noble estate owners. The introduction of serfdom had meant that the state had largely withdrawn from interfering in relations between estate owners and serfs, thus leaving the state little opportunity to protect a large part of the rural population. After the introduction of regular levies of recruits and the poll tax in the early eighteenth century, the state became especially concerned to make sure that serfs had the wherewithal to fulfil these obligations. The state was also concerned that enserfed peasants did not pose a threat to social stability. As a result, the state extended some protection to serfs. Peter the Great and his successors insisted that nobles did not ruin their serfs by making excessive demands on them for dues and services, or by subjecting them to cruel treatment or harsh punishments. For most of the eighteenth century, however, little was done in practice to protect serfs. In addition, laws issued in the 1760s increased nobles' arbitrary powers over their serfs.

Nobles were permitted to exile recalcitrant serfs to Siberia or for penal servitude without trial. In 1767 the existing ban on serfs submitting collective complaints about their owners directly to the ruler was repeated.

From the 1770s, however, Catherine and subsequent rulers enacted measures aimed at reducing serfowners' powers. A significant step was taken in 1775 when the provincial government reform included provisions enabling governors to prosecute estate owners who ruined their serfs with burdensome obligations or cruel treatment. The procedure was tightened up by Alexander I in 1817 and Nicholas I in the late 1820s. In extreme cases the authorities could step in, remove the estate owners, put them on trial, and hand their estates over to be managed by trustees. In 1845 the levels of corporal punishment estate owners could subject their serfs to were restricted in the penal code. Nicholas I was especially concerned to reduce possible causes of disorders since his accession in 1825 had been marked not only by the Decembrist revolt, but also by wide-scale peasant disturbances. There was, of course, a big difference between issuing laws and enforcing them. Supervision of noble–serf relations was entrusted to the rural police and marshals of the nobility. Since they were elected by the local nobility, serfowners were effectively policing themselves. Nevertheless, the measures had acquired some bite by Nicholas I's reign, during which a few thousand nobles were put on trial for 'abuses of seigniorial authority'. A few hundred were convicted. On the other hand, the large number of decrees, orders and circulars sent to governors and marshals, impressing on them the need to maintain surveillance over 'abuses', are evidence both for the central government's concern and that the local authorities were less than assiduous in following them (Ignatovich, 1925: 58–68; Mironov, 1994).

Another 'abuse of seigniorial authority', in the opinion of Catherine and later rulers, was the practice of selling serfs separately from the land on which they lived. This was of particular concern to the state authorities since, if serfs were deprived of land, they would not have the means to support themselves and pay their taxes. Tsar Paul banned the sale of serfs without land in left-bank Ukraine in 1798. Although the law was not extended to Russia, several later laws touched on the issue. Decrees banned advertisements offering serfs for sale without land, and made splitting up families for sale illegal. Like so many laws affecting serfdom, however, they were not properly enforced. In 1827 an important principle was established when estate owners were prohibited from selling or mortgaging parts of their estates that would leave less than 4.5 *desyatiny* of land (about 12 acres) per male serf. This established in law the idea that peasants were entitled to a certain minimum amount of land (Ignatovich, 1925: 35–6, 41–2; Semevskii, 1888, vol.1: 547–55).

The state also tried to protect serfs against the periodic threat of hunger. From the early eighteenth century, estate owners were required by law to assist their serfs if the harvest failed. This requirement was regularly repeated, suggesting that many estate owners ignored it. Some were unable to help their serfs in the event of bad harvests. Others were unwilling to offer aid. Repeated bad harvests and famines in the early nineteenth century, especially in 1822 and 1833–34, compelled the government to introduce new measures. Estate owners were obliged to keep stocks of grain in reserve. In very bad years, moreover, the state was prepared to step in with assistance. Famine relief measures were hindered by mutual suspicion on the part of the state authorities and estate owners that the other were trying to shirk their responsibilities (Kahan, 1989: 115–22).

In 1797 the state took what has been seen as a tentative step in the direction of regulating serfs' seigniorial obligations. On the day of his coronation, Paul issued a proclamation banning estate owners from obliging their serfs to perform labour services on Sundays. This was not new, but the proclamation went on to suggest that the serfs' labour on the other six days of the week should be divided equally between the estate owners' demesne and their own land allotments [*Doc. 5*]. The proclamation was not a legal prohibition on estate owners demanding labour services for more than three days a week, but it became widely interpreted as such. Two Soviet historians suggested that it was a clever way of limiting labour obligations without seeming to interfere between estate owners and their serfs. They argued that the force of the proclamation lay in the fact that it was read out in churches throughout the empire. Everyone, in particular estate owners and serfs, now knew the tsar's views on labour services. Estate owners who tried to make their peasants work for more than three days a week may have been courting trouble. In spite of his proclamation, Paul was not 'pro-serf'. During his short reign he converted tens of thousands of state and appanage peasants into serfs by handing them out to his favourites. Paul's motives in touching on labour services seem to have been the interests of the state. He was especially concerned for social stability since his accession in 1796 had been marked by a rash of disturbances by discontented serfs. It is likely that he was also concerned to prevent excessive noble exploitation of their serfs, since it would leave them unable to pay their taxes and less likely to supply fit recruits for the army.

In the decades after 1797 Paul's proclamation evolved into a legal limitation on labour services to three days a week. In 1832 it was reformulated by Michael Speranskii in the *Digest of Laws of the Russian Empire*. In addition to the ban on Sunday work, the law now stated that serfs were obliged to work for their estate owners for three days a week. The other three days, presumably, were to be left for the serfs' own work. Enforcement was entrusted to the rural police and provincial administration. There is little evidence to suggest that they took much notice. In 1853, however, following a serious serf revolt in the North Caucasus caused by excessive labour services, the Minister of Internal Affairs ordered governors and marshals of the nobility to enforce a limit of three days a week for labour services (Okun' and Paina, 1964).

Jerome Blum attached great weight to Paul's proclamation, and argued that Paul's reign 'proved to be the turning point in the history of the lord–peasant relations. Up to Paul's reign the status of the peasantry had steadily deteriorated as a result of imperial legislation. From Paul's time the current ran the other way' (Blum, 1961: 539). Although Paul's proclamation was undoubtedly important, it is argued in this book that the tide had already begun to turn against serfdom in 1762 with the abolition of compulsory noble state service and the secularization of the church peasantry. Even after 1797, however, it was a long time before the tide ebbed very far. A significant proportion of all laws concerning serfs in the first half of the nineteenth century upheld estate owners' authority over them (Krutikov, 1978: 127–9).

For 60 years after 1797 successive tsars were extremely reluctant to make more than very minor reforms of serfdom in the Russian provinces of the empire. They were prepared, however, to introduce significant reforms in the non-Russian western borderlands, and of the appanage and state peasants throughout the empire. The common factor is that very few of the peasants involved were the serfs of Russian nobles.

LIMITED REFORMS OF SERFDOM IN RUSSIA, 1801–48

When Alexander I ascended the throne in 1801 it seems that he intended to introduce far-reaching reforms, including even the abolition of serfdom. Yet the measures he enacted were only half-hearted. In 1801 he broke the nobles' monopoly on landownership, allowing merchants, townspeople and state peasants to own land that was not populated by serfs. Two years later he issued the law on 'free agriculturalists' [*Doc. 6*]. Estate owners who wished to do so were permitted to conclude agreements with whole villages of peasants, granting them full ownership of the land and personal freedom in return for payment in a lump sum or instalments spread over a period of time. The agreements were legally binding on both parties. The 'free agriculturalists' became part of the state peasantry. The law was very important in theory because it established two principles: that freed serfs should have land, and that they should pay for it. It had little impact in practice, however, since its implementation depended on the voluntary initiative of estate owners. By 1855 only 114,000 male serfs had been converted to 'free agriculturalists'. Alexander I considered further reforms, and had several of his advisers draw up plans to abolish serfdom throughout the empire. None of the plans was implemented (Hartley, 1994: 44–9, 173–9; Semevskii, 1888, vol.1: 252–81).

Historians have explained Alexander's reluctance to act with reference to his contradictory character and the dominance of foreign policy concerns – especially the Napoleonic Wars – in his reign. Russian historian S. V. Mironenko has recently made a strong case that Alexander I did indeed want to abolish serfdom, but was not able to carry out his wishes because most nobles and senior officials were opposed. In spite of the modernization of the administration and growing professionalization of the bureaucracy, the upper echelons of officialdom were still filled with wealthy nobles. Alexander was not prepared to compel them to give up their serfs (Mironenko, 1989: 61–146).

Nicholas I, who came to the throne in 1825, followed his brother's pattern of considering major reforms, but enacting only minor measures. He convened ten secret committees of his leading advisers to discuss the 'peasant question'. They spent a great deal of time deliberating on possible reforms, including regulating and even abolishing serfdom, but the few laws on serfdom in Russia that emerged were limited and largely ineffective.

In 1842 the law on 'obligated peasants' [*Doc. 11*] was issued. It allowed estate owners, if they wished, to conclude contracts with their peasants in which the two parties agreed on the size of the peasants' land allotments and the level of obligations in labour and dues they owed in return. Thus, relations between estate owners and 'obligated peasants' would be regulated and not subject to the arbitrary will of the nobles. The estate owners were freed from the obligation to provide for 'obligated peasants' in times of dearth, but retained judicial and police powers over them and, significantly, full ownership of the land. The law was, therefore, a step back from that of 1803 on 'free agriculturalists'. This was deliberate. By making the terms of the 1842 law more favourable to estate owners than those of the 1803 law, the government hoped that more would make use of it. It proved to be forlorn. By 1858 only 27,000 male serfs had been converted to 'obligated peasants'. Nicholas I and Kiselev had hoped to enact a more significant measure, but seem to have backed off in order to avoid offending the nobility. The introduction of this measure in the State Council was the occasion of Nicholas's speech in which he tried to mollify the nobility [*Doc. 10*]. Nevertheless, the decree on 'obligated peasants' was intended by Kiselev to be a 'middle way' between serfdom and freedom – regulated estate owner–peasant relations – that would prepare the way for more far reaching reform (Vernadsky, 1972, vol.2: 548).

A further decree of November 1847 gave serfs the right to buy the estates they lived on if they were sold at public auction in order to repay their owners' debts [*Doc. 13*]. The serfs who took advantage of the decree would receive both the land and their freedom, and be converted to a special sub-category of state peasants who were the full legal owners of their land. Just under a thousand male serfs managed to do so. Many who wished to were unable to raise the money in the 30 days allowed. Nevertheless, the new law aroused considerable alarm among the nobility. Some feared that their serfs might deliberately withhold their obligations with the intention of ruining them, so that their estates would have to be sold and the serfs would then be given the opportunity to buy their land and freedom. As a result of noble opposition, and the government's heightened concern for social order in the wake of the 1848 revolutions in Europe, the law was changed in 1849 to require the former owners' approval before serfs were given the chance to buy estates. In the wake of the 1848 revolutions, Nicholas decided to batten down the hatches and seek a *rapprochement* with the Russian nobility. The last seven years of his reign – 1848–55 – saw no further reforms concerning serfdom in Russia (Moon, 1992: 62–71, 80–7, 106–8; Semevskii, 1888, vol.2: 529–70).

REFORMS OF SERFDOM IN THE WESTERN BORDERLANDS

Alexander I and Nicholas I were both prepared to enact more significant reforms of serfdom in the western borderlands of their empire that had been annexed from Sweden and Poland in the eighteenth century. Significantly, neither the estate owners nor the peasants in these regions were Russian.

Serfdom was abolished in the three Baltic provinces (Estonia, Livonia and Kurland) in 1816–19. The reforms were carried out partly on the encouragement of Alexander I, and partly on the initiative of the local Baltic German nobility, many of whom were familiar with contemporary arguments in favour of reform (see Chapter 3). Indeed, the first systematic critic of serfdom in the Russian Empire, before Radishchev, was Johann Georg Eisen. He was a German-born Lutheran pastor who settled in Russia's Baltic provinces and wrote extensively about the rural social order (Bartlett and Donnert, 1998).

Rural reforms were enacted in the Baltic provinces over the first half of the nineteenth century in three stages. First, in 1804, the state regulated relations between estate owners and serfs in Estonia and Livonia. It gave force of law to the existing registers (*wackenbücher*) recording serfs' land allotments and seigniorial obligations that had been introduced by the Swedish government before the provinces were annexed by the Russian Empire. In addition, the serfs were guaranteed hereditary use-rights of their allotments, and their obligations were set in conformance with the size and productivity of their land. The reform of 1804 was not very successful, and provoked objections from both nobles and serfs. This led to the second stage. Following petitions from some Baltic estate owners and pressure from Alexander I, serfdom was abolished in all three Baltic provinces in 1816–19. The Estonian historian Juhan Kahk has convincingly presented the Baltic 'emancipation' as the liberation not of the peasants from their estate owners, but of the estate owners from the regulation of their relations with their serfs. The freed serfs lost security of tenure. Henceforth, the sizes of their allotments and obligations were set by 'voluntary agreements' with the estate owners. This put the peasants at a considerable disadvantage. The end of serfdom was followed by a decline in the material conditions of the Baltic peasantry, and waves of serious peasant disturbances. These prompted the third stage in the reform process. Laws of 1849 in Livonia and 1856 in Estonia allowed peasants to buy part of their allotments at prices set by the estate owners. The laws did not, however, abolish the peasants' labour obligations. The implementation of the reform in Estonia provoked another wave of serious peasant unrest in 1858. The situation in the Baltic provinces after 1816–19 influenced officials who were interested in reforms elsewhere in the Russian Empire. They were concerned about the threat posed to the social order by the emergence of a class of landless and rootless peasants. By the 1840s, Nicholas I and Kiselev were convinced that abolishing serfdom without ensuring that the freed peasants had guaranteed access to land, on the model of the Baltic 'emancipations', was not the answer to the 'peasant question' (Blum, 1978: 228–30; Kakhk, 1988).

In 1847–48 a reform of serfdom was implemented in another of the Russian Empire's western borderlands: the three provinces of right-bank Ukraine (Kiev, Volhynia and Podolia). Here there were ethnic and religious divisions between the estate owners and their serfs. The former were mainly Polish and Roman Catholic, while the latter were mostly Ukrainian and Orthodox. The reform, known as the 'inventory reform', was similar to the 1804 measure enacted in the Baltic provinces. Estate inventories, which recorded serfs' land allotments and the obligations they owed in return, had been introduced by the Polish government before Poland was partitioned. The inventory reform was also similar to plans to regulate serfdom that had been discussed in the secret committee of 1839–42 that had drawn up the decree on 'obligated peasants' (see above). If Nicholas was reluctant to introduce a major reform of serfdom in the Russian provinces of his empire lest he provoke the discontent of the nobility, he could have no such qualms in right-bank Ukraine since most of the local Polish nobles were already hostile. Some had participated in the Polish nationalist rising against Russian rule in 1830–31. Nicholas I and his governor-general in the region, Dmitrii Bibikov, introduced the inventory reform with the specific intention of weakening the Polish nobles by limiting their powers over their serfs and, they hoped, winning the support and loyalty of the Ukrainian peasantry. The reform guaranteed the serfs permanent use of their allotments, and regulated their seigniorial obligations very precisely in estate inventories. The reform was not a success. The new estate inventories were based on standard regulations for the whole region that did not take account of local variations and were far too rigid. There was no attempt, moreover, to ensure that serfs had sufficient land. Relations between Polish estate owners and Ukrainian peasants were usually tense. The inventory reform only made them worse. The reform provoked massive discontent on both sides. The regulations were revised in December 1848 in response to some of the problems that had arisen. Plans to extend the inventory reform to other western borderlands (Belorussia and Lithuania) were eventually shelved in the face of obstruction from the local nobility (Moon, 2001; Vasilenko, 1911).

In spite of their limitations, the reforms in the Baltic provinces and right-bank Ukraine were significant measures directed at serfdom. They can be contrasted with the much more limited measures implemented by Alexander I and Nicholas I in the Russian provinces of the empire.

REFORMS OF THE APPANAGE AND STATE PEASANTS

Also in contrast to the limited reforms of serfdom in the Russian provinces of the empire were more significant measures addressed at the appanage and state peasantry. These were peasants who lived on the lands of, and owed obligations to, members of the imperial family and the state, rather than noble estate owners.

The Appanage Department had been set up by Paul in 1797 to manage the estates and peasants of the imperial family. The appanage peasantry was a small part of the total peasantry in Russia, 5–6 per cent in the early nineteenth century. Paul proposed that the peasants' dues should be based on the value of their land allotments, rather than a flat-rate payment for every male, so that they would reflect the peasants' ability to pay. The proposal was implemented only in 1829, as part of a wider reform of the appanage peasantry carried out by Leo Perovskii. The aim of the reforms was to improve the condition of the appanage peasants in order to max-imize the Appanage Department's income, but without overburdening the peasants. Attempts were made to increase the peasants' productivity by encouraging them to 'improve' their farming methods, use better imple-ments, raise better quality livestock, and grow new and more productive crops, for example potatoes. Perovskii also ordered appanage peasants to cultivate part of their village land communally to stock reserve granaries in case of bad harvests. The reforms tackled the problem of land shortages on appanage estates, but to the advantage solely of the Appanage Department. The department exchanged some overcrowded estates in central Russia for state-owned land and peasants in the more outlying, and less densely pop-ulated, mid-Volga region. In the view of some historians, Perovskii's reforms of the appanage peasantry were not very successful. The state lacked sufficient officials of the necessary calibre to make them work.

Above all, however, the reforms, especially those concerning agriculture, aroused peasant suspicion and provoked disturbances (Blum, 1961: 496–9; Pintner, 1967: 73–5, 117–19).

Of greater significance were the reforms of the far larger category of state peasants, who comprised around half the peasantry in the first half of the nineteenth century. The reforms were planned and implemented in the late–1830s and 1840s by Nicholas I's 'chief of staff of peasant affairs', Kiselev. He was appointed first to a special section of the tsar's personal chancery then, in 1838, to head the new Ministry of State Domains that was set up to manage the state's lands and peasants in place of a department of the Ministry of Finance. Kiselev ordered a general survey into the condition of the state peasantry to provide the necessary data to prepare the reforms. It revealed a picture of maladministration, corruption, embezzlement and abuses that were harmful both to the welfare of the state peasants, and the revenues the state collected from them. One of the reasons for this state of affairs was that the Ministry of Finance had treated the state's domains and peasants solely as sources of income without concern for their condition or management. The maladministration of the state peasantry had also led to many disturbances that posed a serious threat to law and order.

Kiselev created an entirely new administrative structure at a series of levels from the ministry in St Petersburg to agencies in the provinces and officials at two lower levels. Peasant self-government through village communes was retained at the lowest level. Kiselev tackled the endemic corruption, embezzlement and other abuses. He attempted to appoint educated and competent officials at all levels, and paid them higher salaries to dissuade them from supplementing their incomes illegally. He also attempted to improve the 'moral' standards of the state peasantry. Steps were taken to discourage drunkenness, and primary schools for state peasant children were founded in a few areas. An important aim of the reforms, like those of the appanage peasants, was to make sure that the peasants had the wherewithal to support themselves and meet their obligations to the state. Attempts were made to encourage the peasants to 'improve' their farming. A few agricultural colleges and model farms were set up. New breeds of livestock and crops, including potatoes, were introduced, and famine relief measures were improved. Land shortages were addressed. Large acreages of uncultivated land, mainly forest, were granted to state peasant communes. Some state peasants were resettled on vacant lands away from their villages. And, efforts were made to recover land that had been seized illegally by nobles. Attempts to set norms for state peasant households' land allotments were not successful. However, the reforms did bring state peasants' obligations to the state more in line with their ability to pay. Starting in 1842, obligations were no longer assessed per head, but in conformance with the value of peasants' land or their incomes from non-agricultural activities. A lottery system was introduced to select peasants for military service in order to make the distribution of this burdensome obligation fairer, and to stop villages sending the dregs of rural society to the army.

The consequences of Kiselev's reforms have been the subject of debate. The Soviet historian, N. M. Druzhinin, stressed their negative results. He argued that the reforms failed, left the state peasantry worse off, and led to an increase in unrest as peasants resisted what they saw as officials meddling in their lives, committing further abuses, and increasing exploitation (Druzhinin, 1946–58). Western historians have been less critical. Some have argued that Kiselev's reforms were a qualified success, that the condition of the state peasantry improved, abuses and exploitation were reduced, and the state's income from its peasants increased (Adams, 1985; Crisp, 1976: 79–92; Pintner, 1967: 153–81).

Kiselev's reforms of the state peasantry, like Perovskii's of the appanage peasantry, were paternalistic. They endeavoured to improve the material and 'moral' welfare of the peasantry by direction from above, on the basis of the reformers' perceptions of the peasants' needs and interests. There was no room for initiative from the peasants themselves. Nor, of course, were the interests of the peasants the primary motivation behind the reforms. It was state interests that were paramount.

CONCLUSION

Nicholas I was prepared to enact wide-ranging reforms of the state and appanage peasantry throughout his realm. Together with Kiselev, the tsar hoped that the reforms of the state peasantry would serve as models for noble estate owners to follow on their estates. This hope was largely in vain. Overall, however, Kiselev's reforms need to be seen, as the Minister of State Domains intended them, as the start of a general reform of the entire peasantry. Nicholas I and Alexander I were also willing to carry out significant reforms of serfdom in the non-Russian western borderlands of their empire. While local factors and political reasons were important motives for the reforms in the Baltic provinces and right-bank Ukraine, to some extent the tsars were using the western borderlands as test-beds for the sort of reforms they were considering for the rest of the empire. However, the prospects for significant reform of serfdom in the Russian part of the empire broke down over two issues: landownership and compulsion. Nicholas I was not prepared to sanction a large-scale transfer of land from the nobility to the peasantry. On the other hand, he recognized that a landless abolition of serfdom on the Baltic model would be a disaster. Moreover, Nicholas was not willing to make any reform of serfdom compulsory for Russian nobles. But, the nobility clearly demonstrated their extreme reluctance to take advantage of the voluntary measures that were introduced. The resulting deadlock between the state and Russian nobility was not broken until the reign of Nicholas's son and successor, Alexander II. Field maintained that the legacy of Nicholas I's actions on 'the peasant question' was frustration and failure (Field, 1976a: 50). Blum, on the other hand, gave a positive evaluation to Nicholas's work. He argued that Nicholas's constant preoccupation with the vexed 'peasant question' helped prepare Russia for the eventual abolition of serfdom. Nicholas's secret committees and reforms in the western provinces and of the appanage and state peasantry, moreover, gave considerable experience to a new generation of reform-minded bureaucrats (Blum, 1961: 551). Subsequent developments suggest that Blum's evaluation is the more accurate. Before reform-minded bureaucrats could take part in the preparation of major reform of serfdom, however, Russia's rulers and senior state officials needed to be convinced that such a step would be in the best interests of the state.

CHAPTER SIX

MILITARY REFORM AND THE CRIMEAN WAR

As Nicholas I and several of his senior advisers recognized, the arguments in favour of major reform, or indeed abolition, of serfdom were strong. While it is unlikely that the decision to act was taken by his son Alexander II as a result of one factor alone, the issue that seems finally to have convinced him and some of his officials that abolition was in the state's best interests was the Russian Empire's defeat in the Crimean War of 1853–56 by Great Britain, France and the Turkish Empire. The war exposed Russian weaknesses compared with other European powers. In particular, defeat drew attention to the state of the Russian army.

THE NEED FOR MILITARY REFORM

Russia's armed forces were the pride and joy of the tsars. They loved the military parades they held in the imperial capital of St Petersburg. Several tsars took a keen, and in some cases obsessive, interest in their soldiers' dress uniforms and drill. The tsars were also aware, of course, of the practical significance of their armed forces. The army had played a large part in the creation and defence of Russia's vast empire. During the last century and a half of the existence of serfdom, the Russian Empire enjoyed the status of a major European and world power. The defeat of Napoleon in 1814 marked the zenith of Russian military might. There was a close connection between the armed forces and serfdom. Supporting Russia's military forces had been the original reason behind the development of serfdom. Serfdom had survived the transition over the seventeenth and early eighteenth centuries to a more modern army – with noble officers and peasant conscripts – that was capable of taking on the more advanced and larger armies of European states such as Poland and Sweden (see Chapter 2). In most years from 1705, large numbers of men were conscripted for long and onerous terms of military service. Most conscripts came from the peasantry, and those from the enserfed peasantry, together with their wives and any children born subsequently, were freed from serfdom. Moreover, soldiers of serf origins who completed their terms of service did not return to their previous status (Wirtschafter, 1990 and 1995). The Russian Empire maintained an enormous army in times of war and peace, which put considerable strains on the state treasury. It was the peasants, however, who shouldered the biggest burden by providing much of the tax revenues as well as recruits (Pintner, 1984). In the half-century prior to the Crimean War, Alexander I and Nicholas I both recognized that the way their armed forces were manned and supported needed reform. But, the existing social structure, with serfdom at its heart, put limits on the reforms that could be made.

MILITARY SETTLEMENTS

Alexander I thought he had found a solution in the 'military settlements' that were set up by his adviser A. A. Arakcheev after the end of the Napoleonic Wars. Settlements were founded around Novgorod in northwestern Russia, in Ukraine, and in the south of the empire. They were inhabited by regiments of soldiers and by farmers drawn from the state peasantry. The farmers were freed from the obligations to pay the poll tax and provide conscripts for the army, but had to support settled soldiers, along with their families, who were billeted in their households. In return, the soldiers helped them farm the land. While they were away on campaign, the soldiers' families continued to live with, and be supported by, the farmers. The settlements were intended to be self-sufficient, thus greatly reducing the cost to the treasury of supporting the army. In addition, the settlements provided recruits. All male children in the settlements were trained for military service. In time, it was hoped that the need for levies of recruits from the rest of the peasantry would be reduced or even eliminated. By the mid-1820s around one-third of the army lived in military settlements.

In spite of the investment in establishing the settlements and the basic soundness of the idea, they did not work as Alexander I and Arakcheev had hoped. The settlers were alienated by an excess of petty regulations and all households were subjected to regular inspections. Infringements of the regulations were severely punished. The problems were exacerbated by poor quality and ill-trained officers, unrealistic plans, and the infertility of the land around Novgorod. There were disturbances on some settlements, for example those at Chuguev in Ukraine in 1819. The most serious unrest came in 1831, during the cholera epidemic, when the settlements near Novgorod erupted in revolt. The rebels were harshly punished, but the revolt persuaded Nicholas I to introduce major reforms. The farmers were redesignated 'farming soldiers', and freed from military discipline. But, they had to produce food to feed military units, and became liable to conscription and high dues. The reformed settlements lasted until 1858 (Keep, 1985: 275–307).

INDEFINITE LEAVE AND THE CREATION OF RESERVES

Nicholas I tried to tackle the problem of the expense of maintaining an enormous army in peacetime with a rather more modest measure. Following the example of other countries, for example Prussia, he aimed to reduce the size and cost of the active forces in peacetime by creating a reserve of men with military training who could be called up in the event of war. In 1834, the term of active service was reduced from 25 years to 20 years, after which soldiers were released on 'indefinite leave'. They were free to choose where they lived and the occupations they pursued. But, they had to report for annual military training and were liable to be called up to resume active service until the end of their full term of 25 years. In addition, soldiers with good conduct records were released from active service after 15 years and spent five years in reserve units. The reform was not very successful. By the 1850s, the number of trained men in reserve was only 210,000, most of whom were middle aged. Even this relatively modest measure, moreover, aroused opposition. Some army officers, civilian officials and nobles were very concerned that sending men with military training back to the villages could pose a threat to internal security. Since many of the men were former serfs, it was feared that they might lead revolts against their former masters. In 1839, the chief of the Third Section reported his concerns to the tsar [*Doc. 8*]. Although some of the released soldiers did cause trouble and were put on trial, the fears were not fully justified. Given the increasing concern in the government and among the nobility about peasant unrest, however, Nicholas I did not continue reform in this direction (Curtiss, 1965: 111–12, 253–72; Kagan, 1999: 209–36).

THE CRIMEAN WAR, 1853–56

When war broke out in 1853, initially with the Turkish Empire, neither the military settlements nor the modest reserves built up since 1834 proved adequate sources of additional manpower for the armed forces. Overall, the Russian Empire was ill-equipped to fight a major war in the mid-1850s. Its problems increased when the Turkish Empire was joined by Great Britain and France in 1854. Russia's victory over Napoleonic France 40 years earlier had created an exaggerated illusion of Russian military might, both inside Russia and abroad, which had led to complacency in St Petersburg. Over the first half of the nineteenth century, the technological and societal changes associated with the industrial revolution had had a considerable impact on the armed forces of northwest European states. The extent to which the Russian forces had fallen behind became apparent, however, only when they came up against the armies of Great Britain and France in the Crimea. The Russian army's smooth-bored muskets and cannon were hopelessly outclassed by the rifles and better artillery of the allies. No amount of heroism by Russian soldiers – and there was a great deal – could compensate for the inferiority of their equipment. Even though they were fighting on Russian territory, moreover, the Russians found it difficult to supply their army in the Crimea because there were no railways south of Moscow. All supplies had to be sent on slow-moving ox-carts. In contrast, the allies were able to supply their forces more easily by ship across the Black Sea from Constantinople (Curtiss, 1979; Fuller, 1992: 217–78).

Furthermore, although the Russian army was very large – numbering around a million men – it was not large enough. Many troops were needed to defend the empire's long borders in case other countries, for example the Austrian Empire and Prussia, joined the alliance against Russia. As a result, only a quarter of the enormous Russian army was sent to the Crimea. The size of the army could not be increased quickly on the outbreak of war, moreover, because Russia still lacked a sufficiently large reserve of trained men. In order to reinforce the armed forces, the government raised several extra levies of recruits, who were to serve for the full 20 to 25 years. In addition, calls were made for volunteers to serve in the regular army and in two temporary militia. There was little time to train the men who were conscripted or volunteered. The appeals for volunteers served to create further problems. Thousands of serfs responded, even though the calls were not directed at them. They tried to join the army or militia for short terms of service, apparently in the belief, or hope, that they would thus avoid being called up for far longer terms of service as regular recruits, and/or attain freedom from serfdom. In 1855, the 'volunteer phenomenon' in some provinces, in particular Kiev, posed a serious threat to internal security. Troops had to be diverted from the war effort to pacify the would-be volunteers (Moon, 1992: 113–64).

Meanwhile, at the front in the Crimea, the Russian forces were being badly defeated. The naval base of Sevastopol fell to the allies in August 1855 after a siege lasting nearly a year. To compound Russia's misery, Nicholas I had died in February 1855. His successor, Alexander II, initially vowed to continue the fight. He had little choice but to sue for peace, however, after the Austrian Empire threatened to join the allies at the end of 1855. Under the terms of the Peace of Paris of March 1856, the Russian Empire lost only a narrow strip of territory on the Danube delta, but had to dismantle its forts on the coast of the Black Sea, and give up its Black Sea naval fleet. The psychological blow was much greater. Defeat cast serious doubt over the Russian Empire's continued status as a major power.

FROM DEFEAT TO REFORM

While the loss of the war can be attributed partly to diplomatic failings (in particular the failure to get a guarantee of Austrian neutrality) that were not connected with serfdom, the defeat laid bare Russia's weaknesses compared with more economically advanced states of northwestern Europe. Many contemporaries believed that at the heart of Russia's relative backwardness was the persistence of serfdom. Alexander II's proclamation to his subjects announcing the Peace of Paris, issued on 19 March 1856, contained tentative hints about the possibility of social change. The tsar praised all social estates for their bravery in the war, singled out the peasants who had left their fields to take up arms, and promised that all loyal subjects would share in the fruits of peace. Pointedly, there was no explicit mention of the nobility (*PSZ*, 2nd series, 31: 131–2 [no.30273, 19 March 1856]).

At around this time, as at the start of most reigns since 1762, rumours began to spread among the population that the new tsar intended to abolish serfdom. On 30 March 1856, Alexander II made his famous speech to the marshals of the nobility of Moscow province. The ostensible purpose of the speech was to put a stop to the rumours, and reassure the nobility that he did not intend to undertake such a measure. Instead, however, Alexander II gave a stronger indication of his desire for a major reform of serfdom [*Doc. 14*].That the tsar did intend to take action is indicated by the fact that in April 1856 he issued a secret directive to his new Minister of Internal Affairs, Sergei Lanskoi, to draw up proposals for abolishing serfdom (Lincoln, 1982: 173–5). With the benefit of hindsight, many historians have argued that Alexander's Moscow speech marked the start of the developments that led to the Statutes of 1861, and that it was the shock of the Crimean defeat that prompted the tsar to take the decisive step from tentative reform towards abolition of serfdom (Gerschenkron, 1965: 708–10; Zaionchkovsky, 1978: 40).

The American historian Alfred Rieber made a strong case that the link between the defeat and the decision to abolish serfdom was more than just psychological shock. The Austrian ultimatum was not the only issue that had persuaded Alexander II to sue for peace. In early 1856, his Minister of War, Vasilii Dolgorukov, advised him that Russia did not have the military, monetary and industrial resources to defeat the more developed states of northwestern Europe, and that to continue the war would invite disaster. Back in July 1855, the tsar had formed a special committee to consider the question of military reform in the light of the army's poor performance. On 29 March 1856 – the day before Alexander's speech in Moscow – one of his advisers on military affairs, Dmitrii Milyutin, presented a detailed memorandum to the special committee entitled 'Thoughts on the deficiencies of the existing Russian military system and on means to overcome them'.

Milyutin identified the need to keep an enormous and expensive standing army in peacetime as the key problem. He pointed out that other European states had smaller armies that could be reinforced quickly in wartime by calling up trained reserves who existed in adequate numbers. Milyutin proposed changing the existing Russian system of conscription, in which a relatively small number of men were drafted for very long terms of service, and instead conscripting far larger numbers for a much reduced term of two or three years. The conscripts would be sent home at the end of this shorter term, but would be liable to be called up in the event of war. Milyutin recognized that there were problems in changing the system of conscription. The immense size of the empire and its multinational population were obstacles to reform, but they could not be altered. Another barrier, and one that could be eliminated, was serfdom. Since serfs (together with their families) were freed when they were enlisted in the army, a reform along these lines would fairly rapidly free large numbers of serfs. Moreover, given the concern for social stability, releasing thousands of freed serfs with military training back to the villages every year would be very risky. Milyutin drew the conclusion that in order to implement the reform of conscription that he believed necessary, serfdom would have to be abolished. Milyutin certainly made a strong argument. As Rieber admitted, however, the case for the link between reforms of the army and serfdom is not conclusive. There is no direct evidence that Alexander II decided to abolish serfdom because of the need to reform the system of recruitment. Circumstantial evidence, however, in particular the timing, does suggest that there was a connection. The end of the Crimean War was followed by the start of military reforms, and by steps that led eventually to the abolition of serfdom (Rieber, 1966: 17–29, 96).

In the years immediately after 1856 the Russian army was re-equipped (with rifles), retrained and re-organized. Alexander II began at once to address the expense of maintaining a massive army in peacetime and the system of conscription. On the occasion of his coronation in August 1856, he suspended recruitment under the old system for three years. In 1859, he reduced the full term of military service from 25 to 15 years (Brooks, 1984). In November 1861, a few months after the Statutes abolishing serfdom were issued, Alexander appointed Dmitrii Milyutin as Minister of War. The new minister quickly presented the tsar with a plan for military reform, including radical changes to the system of conscription along the lines he had suggested in March 1856 (Zakharova, 1999: 244–6). It was not until 1874, however, that Milyutin finally won the battle over conservative opponents and his reform of military service was enacted (Miller, 1968).

CONCLUSION

This was not the first time in Russian history, of course, that major reforms of military service directly, and serfdom indirectly, were enacted in the aftermath of a major war. Around a century earlier in 1762, at the end of Russian involvement in the Seven Years' War, Peter III had abolished compulsory noble state service. After the Crimean War, however, Alexander II turned attention from the nobles, who still provided most of the officers, not just to the peasants who supplied most recruits for the rank and file, but to serfdom itself. If Rieber was right – and certainly not all historians have accepted his argument (Emmons, 1968b: 44–5; Field, 1976a: 54–5, 386; Lincoln, 1982: xii) – then the main reason why serfdom was abolished was the same as the reason why it had been introduced: in the interests of supporting Russia's armed forces (Hellie, 1971: 261–2). Once again, as in the seventeenth century, the Russian armed forces were found to be inadequate when they came up against more advanced, western European armies. This time, however, it was not possible to reform the Russian armed forces without fundamentally altering the social structure. In the 1850s, the Russian army could have upgraded its weapons without altering serfdom; the Russian state could have built more railways to supply its armies on all its frontiers without abolishing serfdom; Russian diplomats could have made sure they did not again blunder into war without ensuring other powers would remain neutral regardless of whether serfdom continued to exist. But, as Dmitrii Milyutin pointed out in early 1856, the Russian armed forces could not modernize their recruitment system without eradicating the institution of serfdom. If the Russian Empire was to maintain its status as a major power, then the army needed to follow its counterparts in western Europe by creating a large reserve of trained men who could be called up in wartime to reinforce a smaller, cheaper, better armed and better trained regular army. This was not possible when around half the pool of recruits were the serfs of the nobility. Moreover, simply maintaining an enormous standing army in peacetime as well as wartime was draining financial resources that could have been used, among other things, for new weapons. Before the Crimean War, for a variety of reasons, the tsar and a number of state officials already felt that serfdom was a liability that no longer served the interests of the state. It seems to have been the military factor, however, that prompted Alexander II to take the decision in the spring of 1856 that led eventually to the Statutes of 1861 that abolished serfdom.

It is very important to note, however, that the decision Alexander II seems to have taken in the spring of 1856 was certainly not the end of the matter. It was not made public, may well have been tentative, and was likely to provoke considerable opposition both inside and outwith the government.

CHAPTER SEVEN

PREPARING TO ABOLISH SERFDOM, 1856–61

Almost five years separated Tsar Alexander II's apparent decision in the spring of 1856 to abolish serfdom and his ratification in February 1861 of the Statutes that converted the decision into law. The time was taken up overcoming opposition and planning the reform.

Historians have debated the role of the tsar in both the decision to end serfdom and the preparation of the reform. Many have seen him as an irresolute figure who tried to compensate for this with stubbornness (Saunders, 1992: 214–18; Zaionchkovsky, 1978: 42–3). Other historians, however, have stressed the personal role of Alexander II in taking the initiative and, by intervening at key points, in bringing the reform to fruition (Pereira, 1980). Alexander benefited from the support of two members of the imperial family – his aunt, the Grand Duchess Elena Pavlovna (Lincoln, 1970), and brother, the Grand Duke Constantine Nikolaevich (Zakharova, 1994), both of whom were committed to reform.

A crucial role in turning the tsar's decision into law came to be played by the rather improbable figure of General Yakov Rostovtsev. He was a military man and confidant of Alexander II with a reputation as a conservative. He had first come to wider attention, as a young man, in 1825 when he informed on the Decembrists (see Chapter 4). In the 1850s, Alexander II appointed him to serve on the special committees set up to prepare the reform. Rostovtsev's role was important, not least because he acted as a bridge between Alexander II and a group of reformist 'enlightened bureaucrats' who did not enjoy such a close relationship with the tsar (Field, 1976a: 165–70). The enlightened bureaucrats were a group of educated, competent and professional officials who had emerged inside the imperial bureaucracy by the 1850s. They put the interests of the state first, ahead of their particular interests as nobles. It may be significant that, together with Rostovtsev, several enlightened bureaucrats came from relatively poor noble backgrounds and owned few, if any, serfs.

Among the most influential enlightened bureaucrats were Dmitrii Milyutin, who had argued that military reform was impeded by serfdom (see Chapter 6), and his brother Nicholas, who worked in the Ministry of Internal Affairs. Earlier in their careers, several of these men had been protégés of Perovskii and Kiselev, the ministers responsible for the reforms of the appanage and state peasants (see Chapter 5). The planning and discussion of reforms in the previous reign had given this younger generation of bureaucrats valuable experience. They learned the importance of investigating the extent of Russia's problems and gathering data to assist in the preparation of reforms to address them. This interest in the collection of information about Russian conditions brought them into contact with the Imperial Russian Geographical Society, and such men as the geographer and explorer Peter Semenov. The enlightened bureaucrats and their aims had an influential supporter in the Grand Duchess Elena Pavlovna. Once Alexander II had decided to abolish serfdom, therefore, there was a body of competent and committed officials who had the ability and motivation to turn the decision into legislation. The enlightened bureaucrats were not just civil servants who carried out the tsar's orders, however, but men who sought to promote their own ideas. They had recognized before the Crimean War the need to end serfdom and to allot land to the freed serfs. Some time was to elapse, however, before Nicholas Milyutin and his associates came to occupy centre stage (Lincoln, 1982 and 1990: 72–5).

Outwith the governing circles, abolition of serfdom was supported by radical intellectuals, many of whom were from noble families (see Chapters 3 and 4). In the mid-1850s a number committed their ideas to paper. Constantine Kavelin, for example, wrote a memorandum proposing that serfs be freed and allocated allotments of arable land. The slavophiles Koshelev and Yurii Samarin also wrote about the need to end serfdom. Herzen published articles by intellectuals inside Russia in his *émigré* journals. In 1856, in an article published anonymously in *Voices from Russia*, the westernizer Chicherin saw the abolition of serfdom as a precursor to a range of reforms he believed Russia needed. Many of these works were read by senior officials (Saunders, 1992: 210–12; Zakharova, 1984: 25–38).

There was also, of course, considerable opposition to ending serfdom. Most provincial noble estate owners were alarmed by the rumours of impending abolition that were soon to be confirmed. Many feared for their livelihoods and position without the institution that did so much to support them and define their elite status. Nobles in the provinces responded only slowly, reluctantly, and after much prodding to the tsar's appeal in March 1856 to the Moscow nobles asking them to take the initiative [*Doc. 14*].

It would be simplistic and inaccurate, however, to portray the struggle for reform as one between the tsar, his aunt and brother, Rostovtsev, the enlightened bureaucrats and radical intellectuals, on the one hand, and the land-owning and serfowning nobility on the other. The reformers were by no means united. Alexander II considered himself the first nobleman in the empire, and was far happier in the company of aristocrats and senior military officers than enlightened bureaucrats. The last he sometimes suspected were 'reds' opposed to the entire social and political order. His secret police and censorship, moreover, kept careful watch over radical intellectuals, and sought to prevent them disseminating their views. The opponents of reform, on the surface, might have seemed the stronger in the mid-1850s. They had the added advantage that they were defending the *status quo*, and knew that it would take great efforts by the reformers to prepare and enact such a complex measure as abolishing serfdom. The suspicions and opposition of the majority of provincial nobles were shared by many officials, including some at the highest levels of government. A large proportion of these officials, of course, were themselves nobles who owned estates and serfs. Some senior officials tried stubbornly, if passively, to obstruct the preparation of reform. However, in the same way that a minority of bureaucrats favoured abolition, a few provincial nobles supported reform. Most notable was Alexis Unkovskii of Tver province (see below) (Emmons, 1968a; Field, 1976a).

Overcoming opposition was only part of the task facing the reformers. A number of key issues needed to be resolved. Was the reform to be immediate or gradual? Were the freed serfs to be guaranteed access to land? Were they, moreover, to be given the opportunity to acquire full property rights over land that belonged to the nobility? Would the freed serfs owe obligations, as rent for land, to their former owners? Were nobles to be compensated for the loss of their serfs and the obligations they extracted from them? In the event of a landed settlement, were nobles to be compensated for the loss of part of their land? If nobles were to be recompensed, who was to pay: the state, the freed serfs, or both? The questions of local administration and justice at village level also arose, since these were the responsibility of noble estate owners. The preparation of the reform sheds light on the prevailing relationship between the autocratic state and the Russian nobility that had been at the heart of the matter since the origins of serfdom. The identities of the nobles involved in the reform process – as state servitors, radical intellectuals or noble estate owners – were also demonstrated.

TENTATIVE FIRST STEPS

The only serious response to Alexander's appeal in March 1856 for nobles to put forward ideas for reform came from his aunt, Elena Pavlovna. She was already planning to free the serfs on her estate of Karlovka, Poltava province, in left-bank Ukraine. She turned for advice to Kavelin and Nicholas Milyutin. They proposed complete freedom for the serfs and state support for them to buy ('redeem') land from their former owners at prices set by provincial committees of noble estate owners. The Grand Duchess presented her plan to the tsar in October 1856 (Lincoln, 1969). The contrast between Elena Pavlovna's radical plan and the silence from most nobles gave an indication of the problems that were to follow. The main features of the Karlovka plan were at the heart of the enlightened bureaucrats' ultimate aims for the empire-wide abolition of serfdom (Zakharova, 1987: 25–6, 50, 102).

Most officials, even those who favoured reform, were more cautious. In late 1856, Nicholas Milyutin's boss, Minister of Internal Affairs Lanskoi, responded to the tsar's request in April for him to formulate proposals for reform (see Chapter 6). Drawing on the experiences of the landless abolition of serfdom in the Baltic provinces in 1816–19 and the inventory reform in the western provinces in the 1840s (see Chapter 5), Lanskoi argued that different measures would be needed in different provinces. He added that it would not be practical to free the serfs from the nobles and settle the land question at the same time (Zakharova, 1987: 25).

Alexander II's next step, in January 1857, was to convene the 'Secret Committee on the Peasant Question' under the chairmanship of Alexis Orlov. Its members were mostly conservative figures from the State Council, for example Dolgorukov, the new chief of the Third Section, Paul Gagarin, a major estate owner, Dmitrii Bludov, chairman of the legal department of the State Council, and Rostovtsev. They were joined in April by Michael Muraviev, the new Minister of State Domains. There were also a few more reform-minded men such as Lanskoi and M. A. Korf. Several members of the committee had served on Nicholas I's secret committees, and so had experience of the peasant question, and the difficulty of answering it.

At its first meeting the tsar told the Secret Committee that serfdom had 'almost outlived its time'. This does not seem to have been the view of most of its members. They opted for procrastination, probably in the hope that the tsar would give up his dangerous idea. Only when prompted by Alexander, who admonished them for trying to bury the question in the files, did the committee discuss the matter more seriously. At this point, Rostovtsev began to study the peasant question, including the papers of Nicholas I's secret committees and earlier reforms. This was the start of the gradual change in Rostovtsev's views. In August 1857, echoing Lanskoi's response a few months earlier, the Secret Committee reported to the tsar that it was not possible at that time to emancipate the serfs throughout Russia. It proposed instead a gradual measure based on the decrees of 1803 on free farmers – which allowed nobles to sell land and freedom to their serfs – and 1842 on obligated peasants – which permitted nobles to draw up contracts to regulate relations with the peasants on their estates (see Chapter 5). Alexander's reaction was to appoint his brother Constantine Nikolaevich to the committee to encourage them to take a more dynamic approach (Field, 1976a: 64–77; Zaionchkovsky, 1978: 44–52).

Opponents of reform were also trying more subtle means to dissuade Alexander, including raising the spectre of revolt 'from below'. As chief of the Third Section, Dolgorukov was responsible for reporting to the tsar on peasant unrest. In his annual report for 1856, submitted in early 1857, he had reported that there had been disturbances on 65 noble estates. This was a lot more than the 26 disturbances reported by the Third Section the previous year. In his report for 1857, moreover, Dolgorukov noted that the majority of nobles feared that peasants lacked the education to comprehend civil rights, and that if they were given full freedom they would behave like 'wild animals', leading inevitably to disorders, robberies and murders. Such fears were especially marked, he noted, in the Volga region where people still recalled the 'terrible time' of the Pugachev revolt (see Chapter 3). Although Dolgorukov also noted that the fears were exaggerated, he had brought to the tsar's attention the idea that abolishing serfdom might provoke a revolt (Morokhovets, 1931, vol.1: 102, 112–13). On the other hand, a different view was taken by the Ministry of Internal Affairs, which also reported on peasant unrest. In early 1857 Minister Lanskoi reported that there had been only 25 disturbances among serfs in 1856, less than half the number reported by Dolgorukov. The minister noted that there were rumours of impending 'freedom for the serfs' but that 'they had not had any important consequences' (Okun', 1962: 593–606). Even allowing for the fact that the ministry's figures on peasant disturbances were usually lower than the Third Section's (see Chapter 3), the differences between the figures and the attitudes to peasant unrest were significant. Since Dolgorukov was opposed to the reform while Lanskoi was in favour, it is not hard to detect a political explanation. Yakov Soloviev, a senior official in the Ministry of Internal Affairs, recalled in the 1870s that Dolgorukov was one of the 'fanatical opponents' of the peasant reform, and added that they frightened the tsar with 'peasant uprisings' (as well as 'serious opposition from the nobility') (Solov'ev, 1881: 756).

There is no doubt that the tsar and the government were concerned about unrest among the serfs, many of whom by then knew of Alexander II's intention to abolish serfdom. From December 1857 the tsar received weekly reports on the mood among the peasantry from the Ministry of Internal Affairs (Zakharova, 1987: 32). What was less certain at the time was how the government would react in view of its concern for social stability. Would it pull back, or push ahead with a more radical measure of reform?

THE GOVERNMENT'S FIRST PROGRAMME

Although most provincial nobles were as reluctant as the majority of the Secret Committee to put forward plans for major reform, manoeuvres had been taking place behind the scenes to engineer a response from the nobles of the Lithuanian provinces of Vilno, Grodno and Kovno in the northwest. In the 1840s inventories – which strictly regulated serfdom – had been drawn up for nobles' estates in the empire's western provinces. This measure proved very unpopular with the local, mostly Polish, nobility. Only in right-bank Ukraine was the reform implemented (see Chapter 5). Elsewhere in the western provinces, nobles had been able to resist the inventories. This gave the government a lever. Lanskoi and Governor-General Nazimov of Lithuania put pressure on the local nobles to come up with a proposal for reform under threat of enforcing the inventories. The nobles looked to the abolition of serfdom in 1816–19 in the Baltic provinces, which adjoined Lithuania to the north (see Chapter 5), and proposed the abolition of serfdom without granting land to the freed serfs. They saw this as preferable to serfdom regulated by inventories. The government kept its side of the tacit deal, and closed the inventory committees in early 1858 ('Zakrytie inventarnykh kometetov').

Armed with this response, Lanskoi outflanked the Secret Committee. He proposed that nobles in all provinces of the empire be called on to form committees to draw up plans for reform. Moreover, he advocated that the government lay down 'binding principles' to guide them. Alexander approved Lanskoi's proposal. The first nobles authorized to elect provincial committees were those of Lithuania. The authorization, and the principles that were to guide the committees, were contained in a rescript from the tsar to Governor-General Nazimov of 20 November 1857 [*Doc. 15*]. The rescript to Nazimov was published and circulated to all provincial governors and provincial marshals of nobility throughout the empire. The implication was clear: provincial nobles throughout the empire were to seek permission to elect committees to draw up proposals for reform based on the government's principles. The rescript described the projected reform as 'an amelioration of the way of life of the enserfed peasants', but was a little more specific on what this would involve. Estate owners were to retain property rights of all the land, but the freed serfs were to keep their household plots, and in time be permitted to buy ('redeem') them. In addition, they were to be granted 'use rights', but not full property rights, of sufficient arable land in return for cash dues or labour services. Estate owners were to retain some administrative and judicial authority over the peasants. The new arrangements were devised to ensure that the peasants could and would support themselves and meet their obligations to the state (Emmons, 1968a: 52–62; Field, 1976a: 77–88).

With the publication of the rescript to Nazimov the government's decision to abolish serfdom was out in the open. There was now no going back on the decision, and there was no reason for the committee of senior advisers to remain 'secret'. It was renamed the 'Main Committee on the Peasant Question' at the start of 1858. It then produced the 'April Programme', which added more detail to the principles in the rescript. Together these were the government's first programme for reform (Emmons, 1968a: 62–8; Field, 1976a: 119, 143–8). From the point of view of most provincial nobles and more conservative officials, the rescript and the April Programme seemed very radical. For the enlightened bureaucrats, and radical intellectuals, they fell short of the sort of reform they hoped for. In particular, the government's first programme did not rule out the possibility that, in the long run, the nobles would retain most of their land (Zakharova, 1987: 33). The next two to three years saw a struggle over the terms the reform was to take between conservatives and reformers, among the nobles who sat on the provincial committees and bureaucrats in St Petersburg, and between the provincial nobility and the bureaucracy.

THE PROVINCIAL COMMITTEES OF NOBLE ESTATE OWNERS

Between late 1857 and the summer of 1858 nobles in provinces throughout the empire sought, and were granted, permission to elect committees to draw up plans for reform on the basis of the government's programme. Each committee comprised around 20 members elected by the nobility and two appointed by the provincial governor. It is worth pausing to note that, in an autocratic state, the ruler was actively seeking the participation of some members of the population in the legislative process (Wortman, 2000: 61). There was no question, however, of involving the serfs in the preparation of legislation to free them.

By choosing to elect the committees, Field has argued that the nobles were expressing their assent to the end of serfdom. He attributed the nobles' assent to a number of factors. They feared a backlash from the serfs if they resisted the government's now public intention to abolish serfdom. There was an equal if not greater fear among nobles that, unless they responded to the invitation to take part in the preparation of the reform, then the bureaucracy would impose a settlement on them that was incompatible with their interests. Moreover, the government put pressure on provincial nobles to submit petitions to elect committees, and encouraged them in the idea that they could adapt the principles in the rescript to conditions in their provinces. The main reason, according to Field, why nobles assented was the tradition of deference to state authority. This itself was a legacy of serfdom, which, like the elite status of the nobility, ultimately depended on state support (Field, 1976a: 102–41). The argument has been taken further by Rieber. He attributed the nobility's 'inability to take collective and decisive action' in defence of its interests to its 'underdeveloped social identity'. By the mid-nineteenth century some nobles, caught up in the professionalization and bureaucratization of state service, had come to identify with the state. Others sought the advancement of

Russian society as a whole and identified with the radical intelligentsia. Only part identified primarily with their status as the elite of society and sought to defend its privileges, including the right to own and exploit serfs (Rieber, 1998; Saunders, 2000a: 175–7).

Alexander II did his best to win over the provincial nobility. In the summer of 1858 he toured the provinces, meeting his subjects and making speeches. He insisted on the convenient fiction that the initiative for reform had come from the nobles, rather than been imposed by the government. In Kostroma province, for example, he thanked the nobles for their readiness to assist in the work of 'ameliorating the peasants' lives', and asked them to follow the terms of his rescripts and 'justify his trust in them'. When he encountered opposition to aspects of the reform, however, he spoke sharply, insisting that nobles toe the line. In Moscow, the tsar upbraided the nobles for their tardiness in responding to his speech of 30 March 1856. While in Tver, the tsar announced that the provincial committees would be invited to send deputies to St Petersburg. Richard Wortman concluded that Alexander's speeches 'made clear his resolve to proceed with emancipation. ... By presenting emancipation as an expression of the emotional and personal bond between monarch and nobility, Alexander disarmed the enemies of emancipation. ... Disobedience would have violated their bond with the throne' (Wortman, 1990: 756–63).

By 1858 most provincial nobles seem to have been convinced that the tsar and his government were serious about reform. Rather than adopt the risky strategy of resistance, most chose to try to attain the best settlement possible: one that would compensate them for their losses and ensure their livelihoods. Inside the provincial committees there were disagreements which, to some extent, reflected their composition. The members appointed by the governors represented the government and generally advocated its programme, sometimes in the face of opposition from members elected by the nobility. Many provincial committees were not able to agree among themselves and submitted majority and minority reports. In almost all cases, with the important exception of Tver province, the majority reports were more conservative than those of the minorities.

There were also divergences in views between committees in different provinces. To a large degree they reflected the regional diversity of the empire. Committees in fertile provinces of the Central Black Earth, Volga and Ukrainian regions were anxious that nobles retain as much land as possible, since this was their most important source of wealth. They also sought to retain peasants' labour services for as long as possible. In the less fertile regions around Moscow and to the north, in contrast, committees were more concerned about the payments the freed serfs would make to redeem their household plots, and the obligations they would pay for the continued use of allotments of arable land. In these regions it was the serfs' obligations (often dues), rather than the land, that was most important to the noble economy. Some committees made it clear that they wanted the serfs to pay for their freedom as well as the land. These aims were reflected in the distorted data on serfs' land allotments and obligations, understating the former and overstating the latter, that were collected by the committees and included in the 'Descriptions of Seigniorial Estates' they drew up (see Chapter 3). Regarding the administration of the freed serfs, the majority of committees favoured retaining noble authority.

Several provincial committees put forward ideas that diverged from the government's first programme. Many ideas, such as the retention of all or most of the land by the nobles, were more conservative. The government rejected them, and instructed the committees to adhere to its principles. In contrast, under the leadership of Unkovskii, the majority of the Tver committee proposed a more radical settlement than the government's first programme. The nobles of Tver province, in the less fertile northwest, advocated that freed serfs be compelled to redeem not only their household plots, but also allotments of arable land. This would lead to the complete separation of noble estate owners and peasant landowners. Thus, the Tver committee also proposed the replacement of noble authority by peasant self-government. The majority of members of the provincial committee in Kharkov in Ukraine, together with minorities on other provincial committees, also proposed compulsory redemption. Some historians have argued that they were seeking to secure their economic interests, ensuring they would be paid for the land ceded to the freed serfs. Emmons, however, argued that Unkovskii and others were influenced by European thought and were genuinely 'liberal'. By the time the provincial committees submitted their proposals to St Petersburg in 1859, however, the government was planning a more radical measure than that outlined in its first programme (Emmons, 1968a: 73–205; Field, 1976a: 173–232).

THE GOVERNMENT'S SECOND PROGRAMME

On 4 December 1858 the Main Committee adopted a new programme for abolishing serfdom (Fedorov, 1994: 165–6). The government's second programme differed from the first in two very important ways. The government now committed itself to enabling the freed serfs, gradually, to become owners of allotments of arable land as well as their household plots. Moreover, the freed serfs were not to be subject to noble authority, but were to administer their own affairs through village communities. The new programme had been preceded by an order of 26 October on the procedure for reviewing the provincial committees' reports. They were to be assessed according to three criteria: would the freed serfs feel an immediate 'amelioration' in their way of life?; would noble estate owners be reassured that their interests were protected?; and would public order be guaranteed? These criteria, and the innovations in the government's second programme, were the work of Rostovtsev. They drew on four letters he had written to Alexander II to persuade him to change course (Field, 1976a: 159–72).

The government adopted a more radical programme in late 1858 for five main reasons (Saunders, 1992: 226–30). First, reform-minded intellectuals were actively campaigning for a landed settlement for the freed serfs. Following a relaxation in censorship in early 1858, Kavelin's memorandum advocating such a reform (see p. 57) was published in the influential journal *The Contemporary*. In the ensuing storm the government restored the ban on discussing the peasant question in print. This did not affect Herzen in London. In his journal, *The Bell*, he published anonymous articles (among whose authors was probably Koshelev or Samarin) arguing strongly for serfs to be freed with land. Regardless of the censorship, influential figures, including Rostovtsev and the tsar himself, are known to have read *The Bell*, and to have taken its contents seriously (Zakharova, 1984: 107–9). Second, disagreements within and between the provincial committees may have played a role in the government's change of programme. The tsar and his chief advisers realized that they could not rely on the provincial nobility to come up with workable proposals, and that it was up to the government to prepare the reform. The government may have been influenced by the proposals for redemption of arable land by 'liberal' nobles, such as Unkovskii and the Tver majority (Emmons, 1968a: 223). Third, the influence of the enlightened bureaucrats increased as that of the provincial nobility declined. In contrast to the nobles on the provincial committees, Nicholas Milyutin and his colleagues had clear ideas about the sort of reform they wanted: the abolition of serfdom with land for the freed serfs.

Fourth, a strong case has been made by Kakhk and Zakharova that some peasants played a significant role in the government's change of programme. In the spring of 1858 a serious wave of peasant disturbances broke out in Estonia following the government's latest attempt to address the problems created by the landless abolition of serfdom in the Baltic provinces in 1816–19 (see Chapter 5). General N. V. Isakov, who was sent by Alexander II to investigate, 'concluded that a landless emancipation [in the rest of the Russian Empire] would be a dangerous mistake and that the peasants must be granted land in order to avoid universal dissatisfaction'. The persistent unrest in the region since 1816–19 had already convinced some senior officials that the Baltic model was not one to follow. Isakov's report, which the tsar made sure was passed to the Main Committee, further discredited the case for a landless abolition of serfdom (Kakhk, 1988: 304–9, 314–20; Zakharova, 1987: 34–5 and 1984: 103–7, 120–1). Thus, although peasant unrest may not have been a decisive cause of the government's decision to abolish serfdom, the Estonian disturbances may well have had a major influence on the type of reform planned for the rest of the empire.

The most important factor in the government's shift to the new programme was the change over the summer of 1858 in the attitude of Rostovtsev, who was emerging as a key figure. Pilloried by radical public opinion since 1825 for informing on the Decembrists, it was probably this same trait – loyalty to the throne – that led him to take the task of planning the reform seriously and conscientiously, and to take account of all the factors just discussed. Crucially, because of his loyalty and conservative views, Rostovtsev enjoyed the confidence of the tsar. He was thus able to convince Alexander II, in his four letters of August and September 1858, of the necessity of adopting a more radical reform. It is very unlikely that men with long-held radical views, such as Nicholas Milyutin or Kavelin, could have done the same (Saunders, 1992: 229–30; Zakharova, 1984: 121–4).

The adoption of the government's second programme in December 1858 was the turning point in the preparation of the reform. Rostovtsev's conversion to the radical programme surprised the enlightened bureaucrats. They had previously seen him as an 'enemy alien', and changed their view of him only partly (Field, 1976a: 170). With the support of their new patron, however, the enlightened bureaucrats now moved to centre stage.

THE EDITING COMMISSIONS

In February 1859 Alexander II approved a plan to create Editing Commissions to review the proposals submitted by the provincial committees, and to draw up draft statutes for the abolition of serfdom. Four commissions were set up to deal with different aspects of the reform. In practice, however, they are better considered as one body. The chairman of the commissions was Rostovtsev. On the advice of his assistant, the geographer Semenov, Rostovtsev appointed several enlightened bureaucrats and intellectuals who shared their views. Many were associated with the Grand Duchess Elena Pavlovna and the Geographical Society. They included Nicholas Milyutin, Soloviev, Reutern, Zablotskii-Desyatovskii, Samarin and Vladimir Cherkasskii. Such men made up the majority of the Editing Commissions' 38 members. Semenov had also nominated Unkovskii and Koshelev, but Rostovtsev rejected them because he felt they might be 'disruptive'. On the tsar's suggestion, he added three great estate owners, including Peter Shuvalov. Shuvalov found himself in a minority of conservatives, and lacked the political skills to mobilize them. Thus, the crucial task of preparing the legislation to abolish serfdom had been handed to a converted Rostovtsev and a majority of committed reformers serving on an *ad hoc* body outwith the regular institutions of government which was responsible to a tsar who had complete faith in Rostovtsev and his new programme (Emmons, 1968a: 214–23; Field, 1976a: 233–6; Lincoln, 1982: 194–7).

The Editing Commissions reviewed and collated the proposals of the provincial committees. But Rostovtsev and the enlightened bureaucrats were well aware that these proposals were not a basis for the reform they believed was necessary. The Commissions also took account of other matters, including earlier reforms directed at the peasant question in the Russian Empire (see Chapter 5), and the experiences of other European countries, especially Prussia, Austria and France, in ending serfdom. In addition, Rostovtsev instructed members of the Commissions to read the press, including Herzen's *The Bell*. The most important guide for the Editing Commissions' work, however, was Rostovtsev's own programme of 5 March 1859 [*Doc. 16*], which expanded on the government's programme of 4 December 1858. Rostovtsev stressed the need for a settlement fair to both nobles and peasants, that the latter should experience an improvement in their lives, and that, in time, freed serfs should be allowed to buy, or 'redeem', with government assistance, as much land as they needed to support themselves. Over the next few months the Editing Commissions discussed and adapted Rostovtsev's programme. The experience and expertise of the enlightened bureaucrats, in particular Nicholas Milyutin, proved invaluable (Field, 1976a: 236–53; *Opis'*, vol. 15: 10, 22–34; Zakharova, 1987: 36–51).

In the late summer and autumn of 1859 the first group of deputies from the noble provincial committees arrived in St Petersburg. They represented around half the provinces, mainly in the less fertile regions. They included advocates of radical reform, in particular Unkovskii of Tver province, and Koshelev, who had been appointed to the Ryazan committee. The group also included conservatives, led by Shuvalov, who represented St Petersburg province. The deputies arrived in the capital expecting to be taken seriously and play a meaningful role in the preparation of the reform. Instead, they were outraged to discover that the initiative now lay squarely in the hands of the bureaucrats in the Editing Commissions. Their role was simply to supply information. At this point, 'liberals' and conservatives among the noble deputies found themselves on the same side, against the bureaucrats. They made a serious tactical error, however, in expressing their views in forthright terms in a petition to the tsar [*Doc. 17*]. They had misjudged the situation, not realizing that Alexander was firmly behind Rostovtsev and his plans. Some steps were taken to placate the noble deputies. But meetings between the deputies and the Editorial Commissions merely confirmed the extent of the disagreements between them over such matters as the size of the freed serfs' land allotments and obligations. Further joint action by the deputies was hindered, however, by the differences between them. They returned to the provinces frustrated, but in little doubt about where the balance of power lay between the provincial nobility and the central government (Emmons, 1968a: 234–65; Field, 1976a: 265–323).

Nevertheless, in late 1859, after the first group of deputies left St Petersburg, the Editing Commissions modified their proposals slightly in favour of the nobility. In particular, some reductions were made in the amounts of land to be allocated to the freed serfs. Zakharova has argued that this was a conscious concession to the nobility (Zakharova, 1987: 69–70). Field pointed to the absence of Rostovtsev, due to serious ill health, in weakening the Commissions' defence of their proposals (Field, 1976a: 252–3).

Another factor, as Hoch has demonstrated, was a serious banking crisis in 1859. This coincided with the planning of the redemption operation, under which the government would extend credit to the freed serfs to enable them to buy land. The redemption operation will be described in Chapter 8; it is necessary here to note the impact of the banking crisis. The crisis meant that the government was not able to offer any financial assistance to the peasants. Instead, the entire burden of payments for the land, together with the administrative costs and allowance for any defaults in payments, had to be borne solely by the peasants. Furthermore, the amount of land for which the government was able to make credit available was restricted. This meant that some peasants would lose part of the land they had used under serfdom. There was no question, moreover, of starting the redemption operation at once and making it compulsory for all nobles and peasants. In order to defer and spread out the amounts of credit that would have to be made available, peasants would not be able to start redeeming land for some years, re-demption would be voluntary for nobles, and peasants who performed labour services under serfdom would not be permitted to redeem land (Hoch, 1991).

FINAL HURDLES

The reformers in the Editing Commissions still had some obstacles to over-come. A major blow was Rostovtsev's death on 6 February 1860. He was succeeded as chairman of the Editing Commissions by the Minister of Justice, Victor Panin. He came from a leading aristocratic family, owned several thousand serfs, and was known for his conservative views on the reform. Alexander appointed him on the understanding that he would follow a testament left by his predecessor, would not make any changes to the membership of the Commissions, and would abide by the decisions of the majority. Like Rostovtsev, Panin was a loyal servant of the tsar, whom Alexander felt he could depend on. Indeed, Rostovtsev had recommended Panin's appointment on his death-bed for this very reason. Panin did try to alter the terms of the land settlement in the nobles' favour, but he did not succeed in making any significant changes to the draft statutes.

Panin's appointment raised the hopes of conservatives opposed to the reform the bureaucrats were drawing up, including many of the second group of noble deputies from the provincial committees, who arrived in St Petersburg in February 1860, many of whom came from fertile provinces where land was the nobles' principal concern. They hoped they could prevail on Panin to alter the terms of the land settlement in their favour to leave more, or indeed all, of the land in their hands. Thus, the idea of a landless abolition of serfdom had still not left the agenda. But, like their predecessors in 1859, the second group of deputies was disappointed, and returned home frustrated and empty handed.

In October 1860 the Editing Commissions sent the completed draft statutes to the Main Committee on the Peasant Question, now under the chairmanship of the Grand Duke Constantine Nikolaevich. The draft statutes met a mixed reception in the committee. A minority made a concerted effort to oppose them. Bludov proposed that peasant redemption of land be made compulsory. Gagarin argued that, instead of a government-organized redemption operation, the land question should be left to nobles and freed serfs to settle by 'amicable agreements'. (He clearly hoped that nobles would be able to use their power over the peasants to get their own way.) Muraviev and Dolgorukov tried to reduce the proposed sizes of the allotments for the freed serfs. The Grand Duke's personal diary reveals his growing exasperation with the committee members who spoke out against the proposed legislation, in particular Muraviev and Dolgorukov, and his immense relief when the draft statutes, with a few relatively minor changes, were approved [*Doc. 18*].

The final stage the draft statutes had to pass through before going to the tsar was approval by the State Council. This body was dominated by senior officials from aristocratic families. Alexander addressed the Council on 28 January 1861. He spoke strongly in favour of the proposed measure, and invited the State Councillors to offer their opinions, but demanded that they put aside 'all personal interests, [and] act not like estate owners, but like imperial statesmen invested with my trust' (Vernadsky, 1972, vol.3: 599–600). Nevertheless, several State Councillors proposed changes that were clearly in the interests of the nobility. A few were accepted. Gagarin provided a way for nobles to keep more of their land, and control over the freed serfs, with his 'free allotment' amendment (see Chapter 8). Other amendments included further reductions in the amounts of land to be allotted to the freed serfs under the standard procedures (Field, 1976a: 324–57; Zakharova, 1987: 91–101). The revised statutes, with the last-minute amendments, were formally signed into law by Alexander II on 19 February 1861.

CHAPTER EIGHT

THE TERMS OF THE ABOLITION OF SERFDOM

The legislation Alexander II ratified on 19 February 1861 was lengthy – around 360 pages of printed text – and very complicated, as befitted the scale and complexity of the task. A shorter Proclamation [*Doc. 19*], which introduced the reform and summarized some of its main points, was prepared for general consumption.

THE STATUTES ON THE ABOLITION OF SERFDOM

Serfdom was abolished not by a single decree, but by a number of statutes (Chistyakov, 1989; *PSZ*, 2nd series, 34, pt 1 [nos 36650–75, 19 February 1861]). The main act was the 'general statute on peasants who have emerged from servile dependence'. Other statutes dealt with more specific aspects of the reform, in particular: household serfs; estates with fewer than 21 male serfs; the redemption operation; the provincial officials and institutions which would implement the reform; and the procedures for implementation. To take account of regional diversity there were several 'local statutes'. The first dealt with by far the largest part of the empire where serfdom existed: the Russian provinces ('Great Russia'), southern Ukraine ('New Russia'), eastern Belorussia and part of the Ukrainian province of Kharkov. In much of this vast territory peasants held their land in communal and repartitional tenure (see Chapter 2). There were also local statutes for the other western parts of the empire: left-bank Ukraine ('Little Russia'), including the rest of Kharkov province; right-bank Ukraine ('The Southwestern provinces'); and Lithuania and western Belorussia. In most of these areas, which had been annexed from Poland in the seventeenth and eighteenth centuries, peasants held their land in hereditary, household tenure (see Chapter 2). Other statutes were enacted at various times for the Don Cossack territory, Bessarabia, Transcaucasia and Poland, as well as for factory and mining serfs throughout the empire (Kieniewicz, 1969: 170–9; Suny, 1979; Zaionchkovsky, 1978: 96, 215–27). These other reforms are not considered here for reasons of space. The further reforms of the state and appanage peasants of the 1850s–80s will be discussed briefly in Chapter 10.

The Statutes of 19 February 1861 set out a gradual process for the abolition of serfdom and transition to a new agrarian order. This process was divided into three stages: (1) a two-year 'transitional period'; (2) an indefinite period of 'temporary obligation', during which the freed serfs were guaranteed permanent use rights of allotments of land in return for fixed obligations; and (3) the 'redemption operation', which could be initiated by estate owners and would last for a further 49 years while the peasants paid for their allotments in instalments. At the end of this lengthy process – at some point after 1912 at the very earliest – the former serfs, or more likely their children or grandchildren, would be both legally free and would have become full owners of allotments of land without any further dues or payments. (The Statutes thus made a distinction between 'permanent use rights' and 'full ownership' of land. The former meant that peasants had the right to use – or cultivate – land with security of tenure. Full ownership rights included the right to buy and sell the land as well as use it. Full rights of ownership of peasants' allotments were to be retained by the noble estate owners during temporary obligation, but were transferred to the peasants at the start of the redemption operation.)

At each stage in the reform process the Statutes permitted nobles and their former serfs to reach voluntary agreements. But, the Statutes also laid down detailed instructions on the procedures to be followed. In the following account of the process, the main terms of the Statutes of 1861 will be summarized at each of the three stages as they affected the main features of serfdom: peasants' legal status; access to land; obligations to estate owners; and administrative and judicial authority over peasants.

THE TWO-YEAR TRANSITIONAL PERIOD

Immediately on the ratification of the Statutes on 19 February 1861 all serfs entered a two-year transitional period, during which their land allotments and seigniorial obligations (within certain limits) remained as they had been under serfdom. The freed serfs also remained subordinate to the estate owners' administrative and judicial authority, but new institutions of peasant self-government were set up at the local level. The one feature of serfdom that changed at once was the serfs' unfree legal status. All serfs became legally free and were no longer dependent on their estate owners. Legal freedom meant, among other things, that the now former serfs could no longer be bought and sold, relocated from one estate to another, or punished by their estate owners. Moreover, the freed serfs could marry, enter into legally binding contracts, buy and sell property, and initiate law suits without their estate owners' permission. The former serfs were given the legal status of 'free rural inhabitants', which put them on the same footing as the state peasants. Household serfs also received personal freedom, but were to remain dependent on their former owners during the two-year transitional period.

If the reform had consisted only in granting legal freedom to the serfs it would have resembled the abolition of serfdom in the Baltic provinces in 1816–19. The Baltic peasants had not been guaranteed access to land, and were condemned to a precarious, if free, existence (see Chapter 5). However, the reformers had learned the lessons of the Baltic emancipation and designed the reform of 1861 to ensure that, in most cases, freed serfs elsewhere in the empire would have guaranteed access to adequate quantities of land.

The reason for the two-year transitional period was to allow time for the preparation of the second stage in the reform process: temporary obligation. Special institutions and officials were created to manage these preparations and the part played in them by the local nobility. In each province a Bureau of Peasant Affairs was to be set up, including representatives of local and central government and the local nobility. Most important were the new 'peace mediators' (*mirovye posredniki*), who were to act as intermediaries between estate owners and freed serfs, dealing with disputes over the legislation and its implementation. Peace mediators' councils (*s˝ezdy*) were also set up.

During the second stage, relations between the freed serfs and their former estate owners – in particular the peasants' land allotments and the obligations they owed in return – were to be based on principles in the local statutes (see below) and recorded in legally-binding regulatory charters. These charters were to be drawn up for all estates by the estate owners during the transitional period. But, the charters were also to be approved by the peace mediators and the peasants. The charters were to be ready, and approved, for the start of temporary obligation on 19 February 1863.

The importance of the peace mediators at this critical time in the reform process was recognized by both the government and the nobility. While the reform was being prepared the provincial nobility had been anxious to elect the mediators themselves. Indeed, this had been the government's original plan. However, Nicholas Milyutin and the other enlightened bureaucrats did not trust local estate owners to choose men who would manage the transition to temporary obligation impartially, without favouring their fellow nobles and electors. The enlightened bureaucrats got their way. The Statutes of 1861 laid down a high property qualification for men eligible to serve as peace mediators, which could be reduced for men with higher education. Nobles in the civil service or armed forces were to be permitted to take leave to act in this capacity. The reformers' intention was to eliminate poor, uneducated and inexperienced nobles, whom they considered likely to defer to the wishes of their richer, better educated, and more powerful peers. (Wealthy nobles were used to getting their way in the provinces, if necessary by bribery.) In each province, the nobles were to compile lists of those eligible to serve as peace mediators, and then pass them to the provincial governor. Governors were then to select the peace mediators from the lists. On 22 March 1861 Minister of Internal Affairs Lanskoi sent a circular to all governors stressing the importance the central government attached to the post and the criteria for selection. Lanskoi directed the governors' attention to local nobles who were known for their 'unflinching sympathy for the reforms and good relations with the peasantry'. In case governors had still not got the message, the minister attached to each circular an extra list of 'educated and reliable nobles serving in St Petersburg but not necessarily personally known to the governor'. It is a further indication of the central government's attitude to the peace mediators that all appointments were subject to the approval of the Senate in St Petersburg (Ust'iantseva, 1994).

As well as setting peasants' land allotments and obligations for the period of temporary obligation, the regulatory charters were also to contain figures on serfs' allotments and obligations on the eve of the reform. The data on these in the charters are invaluable in tracing the impact of the reform (see Chapter 10). Several historians have considered this information to be more accurate than that in the 'Descriptions of Seigniorial Estates' compiled by the estate owners' provincial committees in 1858–59. In contrast to the 'Descriptions', the charters were approved by outside officials. In 1861–63, moreover, estate owners no longer had any motive to falsify the data, since the sizes of the freed serfs' allotments and obligations had already been decided and laid down in the Statutes (Litvak, 1972: 31–43) (see Chapters 3 and 7).

The peace mediators were also charged with setting up the new institutions of peasant self-government during the transitional period. Under serfdom, noble estate owners had, to a large extent, been legally responsible for the administration and dispensation of justice over the serfs on their estates. With the adoption of its second reform programme in late 1858, the government had committed itself to ending noble domination over the peasants once serfdom was abolished (see Chapter 7).

Village communities (*sel'skie obshchestva*) were to be formed from peasants who had lived on land belonging to individual nobles under serfdom. The new village communities did not necessarily coincide with the old village communes (the *mir* or *obshchina*), which continued to exist. Each new village community was to have its own assembly (*skhod*), and elected officials, including an elder, and could levy taxes on its members to enable it to carry out its functions. The main responsibilities of village communities were to be economic. In 'Great Russia' and other areas where peasants held their land in communal tenure, communities were to divide the land between member households and, under certain circumstances, periodically repartition it. The Statutes made different arrangements for the land in the western provinces, where peasants continued to hold their allotments in hereditary, household tenure. Everywhere village communities were to collect the obligations households owed in return for the use of their land. Communities were also to apportion and collect peasants' obligations, principally taxes, to the state. In addition, the new communities were to be responsible for issuing internal passports permitting their members to leave the villages. Temporary absences, and especially permanent departures, were to be permitted only under certain circumstances. Indeed, for the first nine years after 1861, the freed serfs were to remain on the land. Even after 1870, it would not be in communities' interests to allow wholesale departures, unless they were confident they could ensure those departing continued to pay their taxes and other obligations. The Statutes of 1861 retained and reinforced the long-standing principle of joint responsibility of peasant villages for their obligations (see Chapter 2).

A higher tier of local administration for the freed serfs was to be established for groups of neighbouring villages at the level of the township (*volost'*). Townships were also to have their assemblies, elders and other officials, and would be permitted to raise their own taxes. Townships' responsibilities were to include welfare and maintaining reserve granaries in case of harvest failures. They were also to be in charge of recruiting peasants for the army. Maintenance of law and order was to fall to townships and their officials. In addition, township courts were to be set up to deal with minor offences committed by peasants, and to settle disputes between them.

Thus, many of the administrative and judicial powers over peasants that had been vested in noble estate owners under serfdom were to be transferred to the new peasant institutions at village and township levels. Peasants were also to take over from nobles the responsibility for their welfare and provision in case of harvest failures. Ultimately, the freed serfs and their new village and township institutions were to be subordinate solely to the existing local and provincial government authorities. For the foreseeable future, however, nobles were to keep some authority over their former serfs. During the transitional period and the following stage of temporary obligation, nobles were to retain some police powers and to act as 'guardians' of village communities on their estates. The peasants' new institutions were also to be under the authority of the peace mediators and special institutions that were to be established to oversee the implementation of the reform, including the transition to the second stage.

TEMPORARY OBLIGATION

The second stage, temporary obligation, was due to start on 19 February 1863, when the regulatory charters were due to come into force. As has already been noted, the charters were to contain details of the land allotments estate owners were to grant to the peasants for their 'permanent use', and the obligations peasants owed the estate owners in return.

Land Allotments

The sizes of the peasants' allotments of land in the arable fields during temporary obligation were to be determined according to detailed instructions in the local statutes. For this purpose the local statute for 'Great Russia, New Russia and [eastern] Belorussia' divided this vast territory into three zones: non-black earth, black earth and steppe. These zones were then subdivided into 'localities' containing several provinces. The other local statutes also divided the areas they covered into localities. For each locality in the non-black earth and black earth zones of 'Great Russia', eastern Belorussia and part of Kharkov, maximum and minimum sizes were set for allotments of land per male peasant. The minimum sizes were one-third of the maximum. In the steppe zone, single statutory norms were set for each locality. In left-bank Ukraine, the minimum allotments were half the maximums, and the latter tended to be lower than in adjoining parts of the black earth zone of Russia (see Table 8.1). Peasants in right-bank Ukraine were to be granted the allotments recorded in the inventories of 1847–48 (see Chapter 5), and peasants in Lithuania and western Belorussia were to retain the allotments they held at the time of abolition.

Table 8.1   Sizes set for peasants' land allotments during temporary obligation

Region	Allotment sizes in desyatiny* per male peasant**		
	Minimum	Maximum	Statutory
Great Russia, eastern Belorussia and part of Kharkov province			
non-black earth	1.00–2.33	3.00–7.00	
black earth	0.92–2.00	2.75–6.00	
New Russia, steppe			3.00–12.00
Left-bank Ukraine	1.38–2.25	2.75–4.50	

* 1 *desyatina* = 2.7 acres or 1.09 hectares
** sizes varied by locality
Source: Zaionchkovsky (1978), pp.83–7.

The sizes set for peasants' land allotments in the local statutes took account of local soil fertility, population densities and agricultural practices. Peasants needed more land to support themselves in non-black earth areas than in more fertile, black earth localities. There was less land available in the densely populated central parts of both non-black earth and black earth zones of 'Great Russia', Belorussia and Ukraine than in the outlying steppe zone to the south. As well as these practical reasons, the arrangements for peasants' land allotments were designed to favour the noble estate owners. The prevailing market prices for land were higher in the central black earth localities, where peasants' land allotments were to be the smallest, than in the less fertile and outlying localities, where they were to be the largest. Thus, estate owners were to retain more land in areas where it was worth more. In addition, estate owners were allowed to reduce peasants' allotments to the minimum during the first nine years after 1861. Estate owners were also permitted to exchange peasants' existing allotments for land in other parts of their estates, thus giving them the opportunity to swap good peasant land for poor noble land. Furthermore, in all of Russia, eastern Belorussia and left-bank Ukraine, the maximum sizes laid down in the local statutes were smaller than the allotments some peasants had held under serfdom. In such cases, estate owners were to be permitted to take away ('cut off') the excess land from the peasants and keep it for themselves. Estate owners' rights to land were protected in another way. In the non-black earth and black earth zones of 'Great Russia' etc., estate owners were guaranteed to retain at least one-third of the productive land on their estates. If necessary, estate owners were to be allowed to 'cut off' parts of the peasants' allotments and reduce them to the minimum allowed in the Statutes. In the steppe zone estate owners were assured half the productive land on their estates. On the other hand, if peasants' existing allotments were smaller than the minimum size, then estate owners were either to increase them to the minimum, or demand lower obligations. The sizes set in the Statutes ensured that such cases would be fewer than those that would allow nobles to cut off parts of peasants' allotments.

The Editing Commissions had originally proposed larger allotments for peasants during temporary obligation, but these had been reduced in 1859–60. Part of the reason was the constraints imposed by the banking crisis, but also concessions made to the noble estate owners (see Chapter 7). A good example of a concession was the last-minute amendment made by Gagarin in late 1860 (see Chapter 7). This allowed estate owners to offer their former serfs small allotments of land – no less than a quarter of the maximum size laid down in the Statutes – free of charge, without any obligations in return, and as their full property. The motivation was not altruism, but to give peasants smaller allotments than they needed to support themselves. Thus, the peasants who took them would be likely to remain dependent on the estate owners, who could then take advantage of this.

All these provisions referred to arable land in the fields. Throughout the period of temporary obligation, peasants had only use rights of their allotments of field land. Ultimately, the land in the fields remained the property of the estate owners. During this second stage of the reform, however, peasants did have the right to buy ('redeem') their houses and garden plots from the estate owners, and thus acquire full property rights over them.

Nobles whose estates were inhabited by fewer than 21 male serfs were given greater flexibility in allotting land to temporarily-obligated peasants. Peasants on the estates of petty estate owners who had been allotted insufficient land were permitted to move on to state lands. Former household serfs were not included in the provisions for land allotments during temporary obligation. Their former owners were free to release them without land. A special levy was raised from the former household serfs to provide for those who could not fend for themselves.

Obligations

The temporarily-obligated peasants were to owe obligations to the estate owners in return for the use of their land. These obligations were to be set according to principles in the local statutes and recorded in the regulatory charters. Obligations had to take the form of either cash dues or labour services, and not combinations of the two. Moreover, estate owners were forbidden to demand additional obligations in kind, for example eggs and mushrooms, or labour. The reform encouraged the conversion of labour services into cash dues. During temporary obligation, peasants had to give estate owners only a year's notice to switch from labour to cash. Peasants could not, however, be converted from cash dues to labour. It was also made in the interests of estate owners to convert peasants from labour to cash dues, as the levels set for labour were much lower.

In the local statute for 'Great Russia' etc., the labour due for the use of a maximum allotment of land (in the non-black earth and black earth zones) and for a statutory allotment (in the steppe zone) was set at 40 days male labour and 30 days female labour a year. Three-fifths of these days were to be performed in the summer. Fewer days of labour were set for peasants with allotments below the maximum, but the number did not fall in proportion with the quantity of land. Peasants with a minimum allotment, one-third the size of the maximum, had to work for half as many days a year: 20 for men and 15 for women. Thus, the amount of labour per unit of land rose with smaller allotments.

The regulations for cash dues were more complex. For the purposes of setting the rates the local statute for 'Great Russia' etc. divided the territory into four parts. The annual dues for the use of a maximum allotment in the four parts were set at 12, 10, nine and eight roubles per male peasant respectively. The first part, with the highest dues, contained estates situated within 25 *versty* (16.5 miles) of the capital city of St Petersburg. The second part included the rest of St Petersburg province, Moscow province, and parts of the Central Non-Black Earth region around Moscow. Most of the black earth and steppe zones fell into the third part. The less fertile areas of central and western Russia and eastern Belorussia were in the fourth part and had the lowest dues. The cash dues to be paid by all peasants with land allotments below the maximum size were lower but, like the labour obligations, they did not fall in proportion to the sizes of the allotments. In the non-black earth zone, half the maximum level of dues was owed for the first *desyatina* of the allotment, a quarter for the second *desyatina*, and the remaining quarter for the rest. Thus, a peasant living near St Petersburg with a maximum allotment owed 12 roubles, while a peasant with a minimum allotment, one-third the size, owed six roubles, or half as much. In the black earth and steppe zones the disproportion was a little less: four-ninths of the dues were in payment for the first *desyatina*, and five-ninths for the rest.

The rationale behind the gradation between the four parts and the disproportionate weight given to the first *desyatina* of allotment land was made clearer in a clause allowing estate owners in all areas to petition for peasants' dues to be raised, by one rouble, if they lived near major cities or trading centres, or earned large incomes from sources other than arable farming. The point was that some peasants' incomes – and hence capacity to pay obligations to their estate owners under serfdom – varied substantially between regions and did not necessarily depend on the sizes of their land allotments. In the regions around St Petersburg and Moscow, for example, some peasants engaged in market-orientated agriculture. Others went in for non-agricultural pursuits, especially handicrafts, trade and wage labour. Under serfdom, the minority of entrepreneurial and successful serfs had been great assets to their owners as they could extract high dues from them.

Thus, the obligations set for peasants in return for use rights of their land allotments during the period of temporary obligation favoured the estate owners. That the peasants' obligations were to be highest in the less fertile areas, where their land allotments were to be largest, reflects the fact that under serfdom it had been the peasants' obligations, rather than the land, that were of greater value to the estate owners. Conversely, in the fertile, agricultural regions, the peasants' obligations, especially the labour services which predominated in such areas, were to be lower, but their allotments were also to be smaller, leaving more land in the hands of the estate owners. In these fertile regions it was the productive black earth, rather than the peasants' obligations, that was more valuable for the nobles. It would seem, therefore, that the levels of obligations set for the temporarily-obligated peasants were not in conformance with the market value of their allotments, but were veiled compensation to the estate owners for the loss of their serfs.

The arrangements for the second stage of the reform process, temporary obligation, were broadly similar to the government's first programme for reform laid down in the rescript of November 1857 [*Doc. 15*] and April programme of 1858 (see Chapter 7). They also resembled some earlier reforms on the peasant question (see Chapter 5), including those of the state and appanage peasants in the 1820s–40s (Druzhinin, 1946–58, vol.2: 551–66). The closest precedent, however, was the inventory reform in right-bank Ukraine in 1847–48. Indeed, the bureaucrats drew on this reform in preparing the abolition of serfdom (Zakharova, 1987: 83). Governor-General Vasilchikov of the southwestern provinces had been invited to St Petersburg to attend a session of the Main Committee in 1859 to share his experiences of the earlier measure (*RGIA, fond* 1180, *opis'* T.XV, *delo* 74, *listy* 16–23). In addition, the status of freed serfs during temporary obligation was to be similar in some respects to that of the 'obligated peasants' who, under the terms of the decree of 1842, concluded legally binding contracts concerning their land allotments and obligations with the estate owners [*Doc. 11*]. Some of these earlier reforms anticipated temporary obligation in strictly regulating the levels of peasants' obligations. All these measures, in contrast to the earlier Baltic emancipations, guaranteed peasants security of tenure of their land allotments. Temporary obligation went a stage further than the earlier reforms, however, in regulating *how much* land peasants were to be allocated. The need to appoint special officials (peace mediators) as intermediaries between estate owners and peasants was also a lesson learned from earlier reforms, especially the inventory reform. In right-bank Ukraine in 1847–48 the government had initially relied on the local Orthodox parish clergy. As Vasilchikov had reported in 1859, however, this had not been successful. Moreover, it was believed to have contributed to some of the disorders that followed the reform (Moon, 2001). A precedent for the administrative structure for the freed serfs set up in 1861, including the office of peace mediators, had been set by the slightly more complicated arrangements made for the state and appanage peasants in the 1820s–40s (Druzhinin, 1946–58, vol.2: 561–6).

According to the Statutes of 1861, temporary obligation could last indefinitely. It would come to an end only when the estate owner chose to initiate the third and final stage of the reform process: the redemption operation.

THE REDEMPTION OPERATION

During the lengthy, government-run redemption operation the peasants were to be able to buy – or 'redeem' – allotments of arable land. Once peasants had started to redeem their allotments they were to acquire full rights of ownership over them, and be called 'peasant-proprietors' (*krest'yane-sobstvenniki*). At the same time, the estate owners ceased to have any police powers, or act as guardians of village societies, on their estates. According to the Statutes of 1861 only peasants paying cash dues to estate owners were to be permitted to redeem their allotments under the government operation. This was amended in 1862 to allow peasants performing labour obligations to redeem their allotments.

As has already been noted, the initiative for starting the redemption operation lay solely with the estate owners. If they chose to initiate redemption, however, the peasants had no choice but to accept. Even in 1861, then, the state was reluctant to enact legislation compelling nobles to part with some of their land on top of the loss of their serfs. The terms of the redemption operation were, however, made favourable to the nobles to encourage them to opt for it, and thus transfer the peasants on their estates to the final stage of the reform process.

If estate owners decided to go ahead, the details of the land the peasants were to redeem and the payments they were to make, together with the peasants' allotments and obligations during temporary obligation, were to be recorded in formal, written agreements. Then, together with proof in cases when village communities had agreed to redemption, these agreements were to be sent to the peace mediators. The mediators were to verify the terms of the agreements, to ensure they were in line with the provisions of the Statutes, before sending them to the higher authorities for confirmation.

The allotments of land peasants were to be permitted to redeem under the terms of the Statutes were usually to be those they had been granted in permanent use during temporary obligation. Estate owners were to be allowed to reduce the allotments the peasants could redeem to the minimum sizes set in the Statutes, but only if the peasants agreed. Peasants were not to redeem their allotments individually but jointly in their village communities. All members were to be jointly responsible, moreover, for the redemption payments. Partly for this reason, restrictions on peasants leaving their villages and relinquishing their allotments were to continue during the redemption operation.

Since most peasants lacked the means to buy the land outright or to raise the money in loans, the government was to step in to act as intermediary. It would advance most of the sum set for redeeming the land to estate owners in bank notes and long-term bonds which, in most cases, would earn 5 per cent interest a year. However, any outstanding debts estate owners had to credit institutions, for example mortgages on their estates, were to be taken away from the amount advanced to them. If the allotments the peasants were to redeem were the maximum size, then the government would advance 80 per cent of the redemption sum to the estate owners. For allotments below the maximum, it would advance only 75 per cent. Peasants were to pay estate owners the remaining 20 or 25 per cent, in full, via the government.

The redemption sum set for the peasants' allotments was not to be based on current market prices for land, but was to be calculated from the cash dues the peasants were to pay estate owners for the use of their allotments during temporary obligation. In this way redemption was made attractive to the nobles. The peasants' dues were to be capitalized at a rate of 6 per cent a year by multiplying them by 16.67 (i.e. 100/6). The peasants were then to repay the government for the sum advanced to the estate owners in instalments – redemption payments – spread over 49 years, at an annual interest rate of 6 per cent: 5 per cent was to cover the interest paid on the bonds the government advanced to the estate owners, 0.5 per cent to repay the capital, and 0.5 per cent to cover the cost to the government of administering the redemption operation, and to establish a reserve fund in case of shortfalls in peasants' payments. The redemption operation thus resembled a nationwide, fixed-rate repayment mortgage scheme for the freed serfs.

To take an example to illustrate how the redemption operation would work in practice: the redemption sum for a peasant in Moscow province with a maximum allotment who paid dues of 10 roubles a year was to be calculated thus (where X = the redemption sum):

$$X = 10 \text{ roubles} \times \frac{100}{6} = 166.67 \text{ roubles}$$

20 per cent of the redemption sum, in this example 33.33 roubles, was to be paid to the estate owner by the peasant. The remaining 80 per cent of the sum, 133.34 roubles, was to be advanced to the estate owner by the government in bonds. The peasant was then to repay the government for the sum it advanced to the estate owner in redemption payments for instalments for 49 years.

The redemption operation was the mechanism the enlightened bureaucrats had designed to achieve the objective of a landed peasantry independent of the noble estate owners laid down in the government's second programme of December 1858 (see Chapter 7). There were precedents for the reformers to draw on. Both the 1803 decree on free agriculturalists [*Doc. 6*] and 1847 auctions law [*Doc. 13*] had permitted peasants to buy land from nobles, in the first case on the initiative of estate owners, and in the second if the estates of bankrupt nobles were sold at auction. In a few isolated cases, the government had stepped in to assist peasants with loans to buy their land, and freedom, under the terms of the 1803 law. But, it was made clear to peasants in 1847 that they could expect no assistance from the government. Moreover, under the terms of the auctions law, peasants had to find the total cost within 30 days. Many peasants who had the chance to buy their land and freedom under the terms of the laws of 1803 and 1847 simply did not have the means to take advantage of it (Moon, 1992: 89–93). What was new in the 1861 Statutes, therefore, was the mechanism set up by the government that turned a legal opportunity for the peasants to buy land into a realistic, if long-term, possibility.

THE PROCLAMATION ON THE ABOLITION OF SERFDOM

In addition to drawing up the detailed and lengthy Statutes, the government also had to explain what was about to happen to an expectant population, in particular noble estate owners and serfs. The vast majority of the serfs who were about to be freed could not read, and in any case lacked the education necessary to understand the complex legal terminology of the Statutes. Samarin took it upon himself to draft a proclamation with the assistance of Nicholas Milyutin. Their draft was quite long, and gave a detailed explanation of the terms of the reform and previous legislation on the peasant question. Count Panin rejected Samarin and Milyutin's draft proclamation on the grounds of length and the 'bureaucratic language' in which it was written, but his main objection was that it contained categorical statements about the rights of the newly freed serfs. Instead, Panin prevailed on a senior clergyman, Metropolitan Filaret Drozdov of Moscow, to compose a new proclamation. Like Panin, Filaret was a conservative who had doubts about the reform and feared its consequences. It was Filaret's proclamation that was read out to the population by parish priests all over the empire (Mel'gunov, 1911: 156–60; Semenov, 1891, vol.3, pt 2: 773–8, 883, 811–25).

Filaret's Proclamation [*Doc. 19*] was written in the high-flown, grandiloquent style that was customary for such documents. It was a cautiously worded document, reflecting the attitude of its author. It began by explaining that Alexander II had seen it necessary to enact the reform in the interests of the welfare of the enserfed peasants and the good of the fatherland. The decision was justified with appeals to the tsar's predecessors and to God. The nobility was praised for its loyalty and self-sacrifice in readily agreeing to the reform (despite what had actually happened between 1856 and 1861). The proclamation went on to summarize the main terms of the Statutes, but it concentrated on the immediate changes and the preparations for temporary obligation. The redemption operation was referred to only briefly. The final part of the proclamation called on the peasants to remain in complete obedience to the authorities and estate owners. Filaret supported this appeal by citing appropriate passages from St Paul's letter to the Romans (Wortman, 2000: 70–1). Far from being accessible and readily comprehensible to peasants who lacked formal education, however, the

Proclamation obscured rather than explained the reform. It met with scathing criticism from some intellectuals. Ivan Aksakov wrote that it was written in 'ugly language, as if in Tatar'. Ivan Turgenev, unaware of the Proclamation's actual author, wrote to Herzen that it: 'was evidently written in French and translated into clumsy Russian by some German' (Mel'gunov, 1911: 161). It is interesting to compare the text of the Proclamation with the clear and concise introduction to the actual Statutes [*Doc. 20*]. The latter, which was published but not read out to the population, gives a rather better summary of the terms of the abolition of serfdom.

CONCLUSION

The Statutes of 1861 thus laid down a complex procedure for the abolition of serfdom, and for the gradual transformation of the freed serfs into temporarily-obligated peasants and eventually, by means of redemption, into peasant-proprietors who were fully independent of the noble estate owners. The legislation made various concessions to practicalities and the interests of nobles, for example the sizes of the peasants' land allotments, and thus fell short of the enlightened bureaucrats' original aims. Overall, the legislation of 1861 was a compromise, albeit an unbalanced one, between the interests of the three main parties concerned: the government, the noble estate owners, and the peasants who were being freed from serfdom.

CHAPTER NINE

RESPONSES AND IMPLEMENTATION, 1861–63

The Proclamation and Statutes on the abolition of serfdom were published on 5 March 1861, and copies dispatched to towns and villages all over the empire. They met with varying responses from different sections of the government and society.

THE TSAR, HIS BROTHER AND THE GOVERNMENT

On 19 February 1861 the Grand Duke Constantine Nikolaevich recorded in his diary how he witnessed his brother, Alexander II, sign the Proclamation and the Statutes. 'From today...', he wrote, 'begins a new history, a new epoch for Russia. God grant that it will be for her greater glory. ... A revolution and sundry nonsense were predicted for today, but the city was as quiet and peaceful as always.' On 5 March, the day the reform was announced in St Petersburg, Constantine described how the tsar was cheered by his guards officers and people on the streets of the capital city. (Zakharova, 1994: 306, 309). Not everyone was as optimistic about the prospects for the reform as the Grand Duke, nor as dismissive about the possibility of disorders. Alexander II deliberately delayed the announcement until Sunday 5 March. One reason for the delay was that time was needed to print and distribute copies of the Proclamation and the Statutes. The tsar also seems to have hoped that the preparations for the Lenten fasting and abstinence, in particular from alcohol, which began on 6 March, would put people in a suitably solemn and restrained mood when they heard the Proclamation.

The government and military high command had made extensive preparations in case disorders broke out in St Petersburg. Troops were placed on high alert on both 19 February and 5 March. Infantry, cavalry and artillery units were stationed near the tsar's Winter Palace, and horses were kept at the ready in case Alexander II needed to make a quick get away. The authorities were so concerned about the possibility of trouble in the capital that sealed orders had been sent out in advance to senior government officials and military chiefs telling them how to act in such an eventuality. In spite of the tension, the Proclamation of the reform passed peacefully in St Petersburg. Nevertheless, the anxious mood of the governor-general of St Petersburg on the day of the announcement can be gauged from his nervous reaction to a dull thud that sounded like a gun shot, but was in fact caused by blocks of snow falling from the palace roof.

In addition, the authorities had made detailed preparations to deal with any trouble that might break out in the villages when the serfs heard the terms of their 'emancipation'. The Ministry of War had reviewed the disposition of troops in the provinces to ensure there were sufficient to put down any disorders. The tsar had dispatched a senior military officer from his personal suite to each province, armed with extensive powers, to oversee the announcement and implementation of the reform, and deal with any unrest. The government also turned to the Russian Orthodox Church with a request that parish priests, who were charged with reading out the Proclamation, use their influence to instill due respect for the authorities in their peasant parishioners. The government's concern for possible disorders was shared by noble estate owners, some of whom fled their estates for the cities in fear of an uprising by the freed serfs (Emmons, 1968b: 52–3, 291; Zaionchkovsky, 1978: 102–10). The effectiveness of the government's preparations in the provinces will be discussed shortly.

The announcement of the abolition of serfdom was quickly followed by changes in government personnel. On 21 April 1861 Alexander II removed Lanskoi from his post as Minister of Internal Affairs and Nicholas Milyutin from his position as acting deputy minister. Thus, two of the men who had worked hardest to see the reform through from its tentative start in the mid-1850s to its promulgation in early 1861 were dismissed at a stroke. Neither man was disgraced. Lanskoi was given the title of Count. Nicholas Milyutin was promoted to serve on the Senate and granted leave to spend time in western Europe. The new Minister of Internal Affairs was Peter Valuev. He had previously enjoyed a reputation as a reformer, but more recently had become associated with the conservatives Panin (who had succeeded Rostovtsev as chairman of the Editing Commissions) and Michael Muraviev (under whom he had served at the Ministry of State Domains). Valuev went on to remove some of the provincial governors who had most strongly supported the government's programme in the late 1850s. The reason for all the dismissals was that the tsar was seeking to placate the nobility. Many nobles had been offended not just by the abolition of serfdom, but especially by the way the tsar had allowed the bureaucracy to sideline the nobles' provincial committees and impose its programme (see Chapter 7). Shortly after his dismissal, Nicholas Milyutin wrote to Cherkasskii: 'They have removed Lanskoi and me from the Ministry without waiting for our initiative. We were informed that this was necessary for reconciliation with the nobility, and it seems they seriously think that such a modest sacrifice will console the noble class...' The changes of personnel did not mark the end of reforms under Alexander II, however, nor were they followed by wholesale appointments of conservatives inclined towards the nobility. In late 1861 and early 1862 the tsar appointed other enlightened bureaucrats to key posts, including Dmitrii Milyutin as Minister of War (Emmons, 1968a: 328–30; Lincoln, 1977: 62–74; Saunders, 1992: 241–5).

THE INTELLIGENTSIA

Many radical Russian intellectuals agreed that the reform did not meet the needs, as they saw them, of the peasants. When first news of the abolition of serfdom reached London, Herzen and his associate Nicholas Ogarev initially welcomed the measure in their *émigré* newspaper *The Bell*. But their attitude changed when they discovered the terms of the reform, and when they heard about the massacre of peasants at Bezdna in April (see pp. 91–3). Ogarev went on to publish a series of articles in which he gave a detailed, and highly critical, assessment of the Statutes [*Doc. 23*]. In July 1861 *The Bell* coined the slogan 'Land and Liberty'. It was quickly taken up by radicals inside Russia, who adopted it as the name for a short-lived organization set up to campaign for these aims.

Some radicals went on to argue that since, in their view, the reform was inadequate, then the form of government that had drawn it up needed to be changed. Thus, they demanded an end to the autocratic principle of government. Koshelev called for an elected assembly in a pamphlet published abroad in early 1862. Herzen and Ogarev made similar demands in *The Bell*. Calls for a representative assembly and a constitution were also made by radicals inside Russia writing in underground publications such as *The Great Russian*. The intelligentsia were not united on the issue of political reform. More moderate men such as Kavelin and Chicherin felt that calls for a liberal constitution for Russia were premature. On the other hand, some radicals went further. Peter Zaichnevskii in his proclamation 'Young Russia' envisaged the establishment of a socialist and democratic republic by means of violent revolution and the murder of the tsar (Emmons, 1968a: 369–75, 388–91; Saunders, 1992: 239–44). A more direct response to the reform was advocated by Nicholas Chernyshevskii. In the summer of 1861 he wrote a proclamation addressed 'to the nobles' peasants'. He subjected the terms of the reform to withering criticism, and called on the peasants to unite, organize themselves and rise up in revolt (Fedorov, 1994: 254–62, 495). The ferment among Russia's radical intellectuals provoked a hostile response from the authorities. The most outspoken people – including Chernyshevskii and members of 'Land and Liberty' – were arrested. But, the protests of the intelligentsia remained largely unknown to the peasants, and were disregarded by most nobles who learned about them.

THE NOBILITY

Some nobles responded to the abolition of serfdom – in a similar way to some radical intellectuals – by calling for political reform in a campaign of 'noble liberalism'. In the winter of 1861–62 'liberal' nobles in several provinces sent petitions and addresses to the tsar. The most extreme came from Tver province, where 'liberals' had made up a majority of the provincial committee in 1858–60 (see Chapter 7). The Tver nobles now called for an end to nobles' privileges, including exemption from taxation, and for men from other sections of society to have the right to serve in the government. Most dramatically, the Tver nobles called on the tsar to summon an elected assembly of representatives of the Russian people [*Doc. 24*]. Nobles in other provinces sent similar, but less far-reaching, petitions to the tsar. Alexander II rejected all the nobles' petitions. Behind the scenes, however, the bureaucracy was planning other reforms, including new, elected institutions of local government (see Chapter 11).

The nobles' motives were not simply liberalism for its own sake. Like the radical intellectuals, the 'liberal nobles' disagreed with the terms of the reform drawn up by the bureaucrats. Unlike the radicals, however, some nobles felt the reform was too favourable to the peasants at their expense. Nobles wanted to be able to elect representatives to a national assembly and participate in the government so that they could establish some control over the bureaucrats and prevent them riding roughshod over their interests again. Thus, the campaign of 'noble liberalism' of 1861–62 was a continuation of the disaffection with the bureaucracy among some deputies of the nobles' provincial committees who had been sidelined in St Petersburg in 1859 and 1860 (see Chapter 7).

Some of the representations nobles made to the government were more pragmatic. The Tver nobles also asked for the period of temporary obligation to be replaced by immediate redemption of peasant land financed by the state [*Doc. 24*]. This was clearly to the advantage of the nobles, especially as many feared for their financial security without their serfs. Many nobles, moreover, had little faith in the willingness or ability of the freed serfs to pay their obligations to them during temporary obligation, or to meet the cost of redemption (Emmons, 1968a: 331–93; Saunders, 1992: 239–44).

Noble demands for liberal reform in 1861–62 can be placed in a longer-term perspective. Part of the unwritten, and mostly unspoken, 'deal' between the Russian nobility and the tsars in the servile period had been that nobles accepted the autocratic principle of government in return for the tsars' support for serfdom and, more broadly, the nobility's pre-eminence in society. Thus, in response to the abolition of serfdom, some politically articulate nobles called for an end to the autocracy and the right to participate in the government, not only to prevent any further reforms that would undermine their position, but also as compensation for the loss of their serfs.

Not all nobles were hostile to the reform. A few – mostly idealistic young men – rejoiced at the abolition of serfdom. Some shared the unalloyed joy of the youthful Prince Peter Kropotkin (the future anarchist), who witnessed the acclamation of the tsar in St Petersburg on 5 March 1861 described at the start of this chapter (Kropotkin, 1930: 134–5). Other nobles who favoured abolition, including some 'liberal' members of the provincial committees of 1858–60, served as peace mediators (see Chapter 8 and p. 94). On the other hand, some conservative nobles complained about the actions of individual peace mediators and local officials, including provincial governors, whom they considered biased towards the peasants. This was one of the ways in which nobles sought to frustrate the implementation of the reform. The majority of nobles, however, simply tried to get the best deal they could as the reform process unfolded in the following months and years.

THE PEASANTRY

By far the largest section of society affected by the abolition of serfdom, of course, was the peasants who lived on nobles' estates and were about 'to emerge from servile dependence'. The government staged carefully orchestrated demonstrations at which delegations of peasants working in St Petersburg and Moscow thanked the tsar, presented him with the traditional bread and salt of hospitality, and shouted 'hoorah!' (Wortman, 2000: 72). The authorities were very well aware, however, that the terms of the reform would not meet the aspirations of most peasants. This was the reason for the preparations in case of disorders.

Some historians have argued that, on the eve of abolition, serfs hoped for complete freedom from the nobles, and that all of the land that currently belonged to the nobles would be handed over to them entirely free of charge. Indeed, it has often been argued that serfs believed that all the land actually belonged to them, but that it was they, the serfs, who belonged to the nobles. In this interpretation, moreover, serfs expected that, once freed from the nobles, they would be left completely alone to govern themselves and would no longer be obliged to pay taxes or supply recruits to the army. Such expectations would have been revolutionary, entailing the dismantling of the existing social, economic and political order in the empire. In the words of Irina Ignatovich: 'The reality [of the reform] cruelly disappointed peasants who were hoping to receive from the tsar genuine, full "freedom" [*volya*]' (Ignatovich, 1911b: 173). On the other hand, other historians have argued that serfs' hopes and expectations were more modest. They hoped to be freed from the nobles, but expected to be granted only the allotments of land they worked for themselves under serfdom. They may even have been prepared to pay for the land. Serfs expected their obligations to the nobles to be ended, but that those to the state would be reduced and brought into conformance with their ability to pay. There was little to distinguish these more modest hopes from the existing position of the state peasantry, with which many serfs were familiar. Such hopes and expectations were, therefore, reformist rather than revolutionary. Attempts to resolve these differing interpretations of serfs' agendas for reform – for that is how they are best understood – have included arguing that serfs' hopes and expectations became more radical over time, especially after the tsar's intention to abolish serfdom was made public in late 1857; that serfs in the central regions, where serfdom was oldest, had more modest hopes than those in outlying regions, where it was relatively recent; and that serfs who performed onerous labour services had lower expectations than those who paid cash dues and thus had greater control over their own lives. It seems most likely, however, that many serfs were pragmatic and opportunistic, and hoped and aspired simply for the best deal they could get (Moon, 1992).

When the abolition of serfdom was announced in early 1861, the first problem facing peasants on noble estates was working out precisely what it was they had been granted. Most peasants learned about the reform from the Proclamation [*Doc. 19*], which was read out by parish priests in village churches between early March and early April. Copies of the lengthy Statutes, which contained the details of the reform, were sent to all estates, but were not formally read out to the peasants. Even the partial explanation in the Proclamation of what was to unfold was obscured by its archaic language (see Chapter 8). Many observers noted that peasants' initial reactions to the Proclamation were a mixture of incomprehension and disappointment (Fedorov, 1994: 265–77) [*Doc. 21*]. It was not simply a matter of understanding what was in the Proclamation and the Statutes. Many peasants were deeply suspicious of any official pronouncements, as well as officials and nobles, as a result of generations of oppression and exploitation. Peasants feared being tricked or deceived, especially since most were illiterate and could not read the texts for themselves. Many peasants responded to the information on the reform they received through official channels in one of two ways. Some refused to believe that the Proclamation which had been read out to them by the priests was the real text that had been issued by the tsar. Instead they believed, or claimed to believe, that the priests had hidden the 'real' Proclamation. Some peasants went on and tried to find the 'real' documents. More widespread was the second response:

peasants did not doubt that the Proclamation and the Statutes which had arrived in their villages were genuine, but they did not, or claimed not to, believe that the priests had read or explained them properly. Some of the peasants who followed this line of reasoning sought out literate people whom they felt they could trust – mainly people on the margins of peasant society such as retired soldiers, migrant workers, low-ranking clergy and religious dissenters – to tell them the 'real' meaning of the legislation. Either way, peasants blamed the local nobles and officials. They believed, or claimed, that these people were trying to deceive them by concealing the 'real freedom' and substituting documents or interpretations that were much more advantageous to the nobles than the peasants. In the weeks after the promulgation of the abolition of serfdom many peasants engaged in a search for the 'real freedom' (Emmons, 1968b: 55–6; Zaionchkovsky, 1978: 111).

Examples of the first response occurred in a number of provinces. In some places, for example parts of the Central Black Earth and Lower Volga regions of Russia and in eastern Ukraine, fake 'golden charters' proclaiming the 'real freedom' circulated around the villages in the early spring of 1861. A few historians have suggested that some of these documents were the work of radical intellectuals. It is more likely that many had been produced by unscrupulous people hoping to make a quick profit by selling them to peasants who were looking for the alleged 'real' proclamation. One such document was read out to peasants in the village of Terny in Kharkov province by Prikhodko, a retired non-commissioned army officer. The fake decree, which contradicted itself, included provisions reducing but not abolishing labour services, and left estate owners with allotments of land similar to those given to the peasants. The fake decree included the memorable clause: 'The landowner must plough his land himself ... and if he does not know how to guide the plough, a peasant who happens to be passing, if the landowner asks him, must guide [it for him], but without laughing' (Emmons, 1968b: 59–61; Okun' and Sivkov, 1963: 497–8).

In April in several villages in Penza province, in the Mid-Volga region, peasants tried to find the decree containing the 'real' freedom. The parish priest of Bolshoi Izhmora, Kerensk district, wrote: 'the peasants completely disbelieved the Imperial Proclamation read to them ... and demanded from the priests some other proclamation [which was] marked, they said, with a cross in gold [and] which promised them freedom'. The peasants apparently assumed that the estate owners had bribed or otherwise persuaded the priests not to read out the real decree because, from their point of view, it was too favourable to the peasants (McCauley and Waldron, 1988: 114–15). Peasants in neighbouring villages in Kerensk and Chembar districts of Penza province approached their priests with similar demands. In Pokrovskoe, the peasants were more forceful. Five hundred peasants surrounded the house of Father Glebov, demanded the 'real decree', and beat him up when he did not give it to them. The peasants continued their search in the estate office, which they smashed up, beating up the village headman and estate clerk in the process. The house of the estate manager was next, but the occupant had the good fortune to be out at the time. The peasants did not find the 'real decree', but they made clear to the priest what they expected to be in it: 'We won't work [labour services], not for a day or a minute, the tsar won't demand taxes from us for twenty years, all the land [will be given] to us, [and] the forests, the meadows, the estate owner's buildings are all ours, and nothing for the master. Beat and throttle the lords and priests!'

The search for the 'real freedom' by peasants in Penza province did not come to an end when they failed to find the documents they thought had been concealed from them. Instead, they began to seek the 'real' freedom in the actual documents that had been sent to their churches and villages. An elderly retired soldier named Andrei Elizarov – but who called himself 'Count Tolstoi' – 'read' the Statutes and reinterpreted them in the spirit of the peasants' hopes and expectations. Thousands of peasants descended on the village of Chernogai and then Kandeevka to hear the good news. They were pursued by the local police, a detachment of soldiers, and General Drenyakin from the tsar's personal suite. There were a series of clashes between the two sides, which culminated in a tragic denouement in Kandeevka on 18 April. Unable to convince the 'stubborn' peasants of the actual meaning of the Statutes and persuade them to submit, the officials ordered the troops to open fire on the crowd. This only increased the resolve of the peasants, who shouted that they were prepared to die 'for God and the Tsar' to the last man, but they would not submit. The soldiers fired three volleys. Estimates of the casualties vary, but it seems probable that around 11 peasants were killed and several dozen wounded (Litvak, 1991: 193–4; Zaionchkovsky, 1978: 114–16).

Kandeevka was not the only village where peasants claiming to believe their interpretations of the Statutes were massacred by troops. Similar events unfolded in the village of Bezdna in the neighbouring province of Kazan. Drawing on a wide range of often contradictory sources, Field analysed the events and attitudes of the participants in the 'Bezdna affair' in April 1861 (Field, 1976b). What follows here can only be a brief summary of Field's imaginative reconstruction. The peasants in Bezdna and the surrounding villages were disappointed by what they heard when the priest read out the Proclamation. They decided that the priest's interpretation was false, and resolved to find someone who could read the Proclamation and Statutes 'properly'. Attention turned to Anton Petrov, who was a religious dissenter (either an 'Old Believer' or a member of a religious sect), and at least semi-literate.

Anton Petrov studied the text of the Statutes and tried to find the 'real' freedom. Various versions of what he subsequently told the other peasants were recorded in reports by different officials and Anton Petrov's own testimony after he was arrested. A number of statements were attributed to him: the tsar had already granted complete freedom (*volya*) to the peasants back in 1858, but the nobles and officials had concealed it from the peasants; the peasants were not to work for the estate owners or pay dues to them; nor were they to obey them or the authorities; all the land was given to the peasants, but (curiously) estate owners were to keep one-third of it. In other versions, Anton Petrov is alleged to have said that the nobles had murdered Nicholas I to stop him freeing the serfs, and that the true freedom would only be granted after the blood of Christians had flowed. Only the second part of this final statement turned out to be accurate. The basis for some of Anton Petrov's ideas can be traced. As he explained in his testimony, the notion that the tsar had in fact freed the serfs in 1858 was based on a misreading of a clause stating that the regulatory charters needed to declare how many (if any) serfs had been freed by estate owners since the last revision of the poll tax census in 1857–58. (Any such peasants were to be excluded from the land settlement.) It is a measure of either Anton Petrov's literacy or his desire to find the 'real' freedom that he interpreted this the way he did. Elsewhere, he allegedly took the percent sign (%) to be the seal of the Cross of St Anne (a tsarist order), which he maintained symbolized freedom.

As news of Anton Petrov's 'discovery' of the 'real' freedom spread, peasants from surrounding villages descended on Bezdna. The news also attracted the local police, provincial officials, a detachment of troops, and General Apraksin from the tsar's personal suite. The approach of the tsar's representative may have drawn more peasants to Bezdna, in the hope that he would confirm Anton Petrov's interpretation. The affair came to a climax on 12 April 1861, when a crowd of several thousand peasants seeking freedom confronted a handful of officials and around a hundred soldiers. The officials tried repeatedly, but without success, to persuade the peasants that Anton Petrov's version of the Statutes was false. Apraksin then ordered the troops to open fire on the unarmed peasants. In between the volleys, the peasants allegedly shouted out that they would not submit and that it was the tsar's blood they were shedding. When the smoke had cleared and the dust had settled, a hundred or more peasants lay dead and many more wounded. Anton Petrov, shaken and ashen-faced with fear, emerged from his house. He was taken away, interrogated, tried by summary court martial, and executed by firing squad a few days later.

The news provoked a furore in the provincial capital of Kazan. Some nobles welcomed the news of Apraksin's 'victory' over the 'rebels'. Students at Kazan University, however, held a requiem mass for the victims. One of

Plate 1   Tsar Alexander II (reigned 1855–81)
Photo: David King Collection

Plate 2 Ostankino Palace outside Moscow. It was built for Nicholas Sheremtev, one of Russia's wealthiest nobles, in 1792–98.
Photo: Novosti Photo Library

Plate 3   Peasant house in northern Russia in the Eighteenth century
Picture: Peter Newark's Historical Pictures

БОЖІЕЮ МИЛОСТІЮ

МЫ, АЛЕКСАНДРЪ ВТОРЫЙ,

ИМПЕРАТОРЪ И САМОДЕРЖЕЦЪ

ВСЕРОССІЙСКІЙ,

ЦАРЬ ПОЛЬСКІЙ, ВЕЛИКІЙ КНЯЗЬ ФИНЛЯНДСКІЙ,

и прочая, и прочая, и прочая.

Объявляемъ всѣмъ НАШИМЪ вѣрноподданнымъ.

Божіимъ Провидѣніемъ и священнымъ закономъ престолонаслѣдія бывъ призваны на прародительскій Всероссійскій Престолъ, въ соотвѣтствіе сему призванію МЫ положили въ сердцѣ СВОЕМЪ обѣтъ обнимать НАШЕЮ Царскою любовію и попеченіемъ всѣхъ НАШИХЪ вѣрноподданныхъ всякаго званія и состоянія, отъ благородно владѣющаго мечемъ на защиту Отечества до скромно работающаго ремесленнымъ орудіемъ, отъ проходящаго высшую службу Государственную до проводящаго на полѣ борозду сохою или плугомъ.

Вникая въ положеніе званій и состояній въ составѣ Государства, МЫ усмотрѣли, что Государственное законодательство, дѣятельно благоустрояя высшія и среднія сословія, опредѣляя ихъ обязанности, права и преимущества, не достигло равномѣрной дѣятельности въ отношеніи къ людямъ крѣпостнымъ, такъ названнымъ потому, что они, частію старыми законами, частію обычаемъ, потомственно укрѣплены подъ властію помѣщиковъ, на которыхъ съ тѣмъ вмѣстѣ лежитъ обязанность устроятъ ихъ благосостояніе. Права помѣщиковъ были донынѣ обширны и не опредѣлены съ точностію закономъ, мѣсто котораго заступали преданіе, обычай и добрая воля помѣщика. Въ лучшихъ случаяхъ изъ сего

Plate 4   The first page of the proclamation on the abolition of serfdom,
19 February 1861

Plate 5   Reading the legislation abolishing serfdom on the Prozorov estate, Moscow province, in 1861
Photo: Novosti Photo Library

Plate 6   Russian peasants at the end of the 19th century
Source: Peter Newark's Pictures

Plate 7   The Grand Duke Constantine Nikolaevich (1827–92)
Photo: Novosti Photo Library

Plate 8   Statue of Alexander II in Helsinki
Photo: Dr Melanie Ilic

the professors, Afanasii Shchapov, read a eulogy for the dead peasants. Shchapov was promptly sacked and jailed for a few months. News of the massacre at Bezdna reached Herzen and Ogarev in London, where they reported it in *The Bell*. The peasants who had been killed were portrayed as martyrs for the cause of freedom, and the perpetrators, together with the government, were denounced. Herzen's article concluded: 'Be strong in spirit, and remember the cry of the fallen martyrs of Bezdna, *Volya! Volya!* [Freedom! Freedom!].'

What distinguished the events at Bezdna and Kandeevka was not the actions of the peasants in interpreting the legislation in line with their hopes and expectations, but the over-reactions of the authorities in ordering troops to open fire, leading to many deaths. In villages all over Russia in the spring of 1861, peasants put forward their own versions of the reform, and insisted that these, and not what their priests had read out to them, were the 'real' freedom. In many cases, peasants backed up their 'understanding' of the reform by refusing to work for the estate owners or pay dues. For the most part, however, the authorities managed to 'restore order' by exhortations and corporal punishment, including mass floggings, rather than firing into crowds of unarmed peasants (Pushkarev, 1968: 205–6; Zaionchkovsky, 1978: 116–17).

What many peasants found difficult, or refused, to believe was that their obligations to the estate owners, especially the hated labour services, were to continue after serfdom had supposedly been abolished. For many peasants it was the obligation to work on estate owners' land, not an abstract relationship between serfs and nobles, that *was* serfdom. A district official in Kaluga province reported that some peasants asked him whether they still had to work for the estate owners. When he explained that they did, they replied: 'How is that? They tell us things will be better, but [labour services] will continue' (Fedorov, 1994: 272). The difficulty some peasants had in comprehending how labour services – the largest part of which were performed by men – could survive the abolition of serfdom led to a belief in some villages that the Statutes of 19 February 1861 were the 'women's freedom'. The reason for this was that the Statutes had abolished immediately all dues in kind, for example eggs, mushrooms, cloth and yarn, which by custom were collected or produced by women. Therefore, some peasants apparently believed that the tsar would issue another decree abolishing labour services, and thereby freeing the men (Fedorov, 1994: 386; Field, 1994: 40–1).

IMPLEMENTATION

The peasants' search for the 'real' freedom slowed markedly in the early summer of 1861. This coincided with the arrival in the villages of the peace mediators: the officials who were to oversee the implementation of the reform and prepare for the next stage. The peace mediators were more successful than many other officials had been in the spring in convincing peasants that the literal contents of the Proclamation and the Statutes were the real terms of the abolition of serfdom (McCauley and Waldron, 1988: 115–16; Pushkarev, 1968: 209, 211). To the extent that the peace mediators were successful in disabusing peasants of their misinterpretations, it may have been due to the calibre of some of the men appointed according to the strict criteria that had been insisted on by the enlightened bureaucrats (see Chapter 8). Although there was considerable diversity among the 1,700 noblemen who served as mediators, the majority were relatively young (under 40), well educated, and some were sufficiently well off not to be tempted by bribes from estate owners. Some mediators, indeed, were from the minority of nobles who were committed to the reform, and thus actively participated in trying to ensure it was implemented successfully (Ust'iant-seva, 1994). In spite of the efforts of the enlightened bureaucrats, however, other peace mediators took advantage of their positions to favour their fellow nobles against the peasants on their estates. The shortage of 'suitable' candidates who met the stringent selection criteria meant that many peace mediators were indifferent or hostile to the reform. The policy of actively seeking and appointing mediators who shared the objectives of the enlightened bureaucrats ended in May 1861 when Valuev was appointed Minister of Internal Affairs (Wildman, 1996: 10, 55–6).

The arrival of the peace mediators in the villages certainly did not mean that the implementation of the reform proceeded smoothly and without any more opposition from peasants. Some peasants took exception to the new institutions at village and township level that the mediators were responsible for setting up. The elections of elders of village communities and townships led to many disputes between peasants and mediators. Nevertheless, the new institutions were established in most areas by the end of 1861 (Zaionchkovsky, 1978: 123–9).

Even more contentious were the regulatory charters, which were compiled by estate owners and checked by peace mediators. These were the documents that laid down the land peasants would be allocated and the dues they would have to pay for it during temporary obligation [*Doc. 25*]. The information in the charters also provided the basis for calculating the amounts of land peasants would be allowed to redeem, and their redemption payments, during the final stage of the reform process. In a recent study, Allan Wildman called this point 'the defining moment' (Wildman, 1996). Peasants were well aware of the significance of the charters, and protested against attempts by estate owners to use them to take land away from them, deprive them of the best land or access to meadows, pasture, woodland and water sources, or to increase their dues [*Doc. 22*]. Peasants protested in a variety of ways against conditions in the regulatory charters they did not like, and against the ways estate owners and officials, including peace mediators, tried to impose the charters on them. Dissatisfied peasants sent petitions to higher authorities, including the Minister of Internal Affairs and the tsar himself. Peasants in a township in Balashov district, Saratov province, in the Lower-Volga region, sent a petition to the Grand Duke Constantine Nikolaevich. They complained that the estate owner, Prince Vasilchikov, had ordered that land be cut off from their township and tried to force them to sign the charters. When they refused, the estate owner left for the provincial capital and returned with the local peace mediator and a detachment of soldiers. At this point, Vasilchikov increased the amount of land he proposed to allot to the peasants, but the peasants still refused to sign. The officer in command of the detachment threatened the recalcitrant peasants with exile to Siberia and ordered several to be flogged. In their petition, the peasants explained to the Grand Duke that they suspected a trick by the estate owner and 'his accomplices' (Freeze, 1988: 170–9).

Many peasants who were not satisfied with the regulatory charters simply refused to sign them. On 3 January 1863 – 18 months after the peace mediators had started work and only a few weeks before all the charters were supposed to come into effect – Minister of Internal Affairs Valuev reported to the tsar that only 42 per cent of peasants had signed the charters. Peasants were refusing to sign even after the mediators had checked that the charters followed the principles laid down in the Statutes. This suggests that peasants were protesting not just against the allotments and dues the estate owners had entered in the charters, but against the terms of the reform itself. As has already been noted, many peasants seem to have expected, or hoped, to receive all the estate owners' land free of charge. Under the terms of the reform, however, peasants had to pay dues for the use of land allotments during temporary obligation. Some, moreover, had parts of their existing allotments taken away from them [*Doc. 25*]. This was the point, when the regulatory charters were ratified and implemented, that the 'cut offs' took place. There was some correlation between the percentages of peasants refusing to sign the charters and the amounts of land they lost. Both were highest in parts of the Central Black Earth and Mid- and Lower-Volga regions (see Chapter 10). Peasants did not seek only to maximize the size of their allotments. Some sought to minimize the amounts of land they were allocated in order to keep their dues to a minimum, since larger allotments came with higher burdens. In numerous cases where the terms in the regulatory charters were disputed by estate owners and peasants, the peace mediators assisted negotiations between them. In some cases, such as that on the estate of Prince Vasilchikov, estate owners made concessions in attempts to persuade the peasants to sign the charters. Even when peasants did not sign, however, peace mediators had the power to impose the charters. By the start of 1864, regulatory charters were in force on almost all nobles' estates (Wildman, 1996; Zaionchkovsky, 1978: 129–36, 158).

Some peasants refused to sign the regulatory charters because they had not yet lost hope in the prospect of the 'real freedom'. The two-year transitional period before the implementation of the charters and the start of temporary obligation became the basis for a widespread belief, or claim, by some peasants that on 19 February 1863 – the second anniversary of the ratification of the Statutes of 1861 – the tsar would issue a second proclamation. This proclamation, allegedly, would contain the 'real freedom' many peasants had hoped for. This date became known among peasants as 'the promised hour' (*slushnyi chas*'). Wildman noted that many peasants 'expressed the fear that if they signed the charters they would be delivering themselves back into serfdom and would forfeit the privileges the Tsar intended to grant them after two years' (Wildman, 1996: 27). The authorities became concerned that this belief would not only slow the process of implementing the charters, but could also provoke a new round of peasant disturbances. For this reason, on several occasions, Alexander II explicitly denied there would be another proclamation [*Doc. 26*]. In the event, however, the 'promised hour' came and went without any massive upheavals (Emmons, 1968b: 63–5; Field, 1994: 45–8).

POPULAR MONARCHISM

The peasants' responses to the abolition of serfdom – in particular the persistent hopes that the tsar would grant them 'full freedom' from the nobility and all the land – raise important questions about peasant attitudes to the tsar. The belief that the nobles and officials were concealing the 'real freedom' in the spring of 1861 was typical of a recurring popular belief that the tsar was on the side of the peasants, but the 'boyars' – in this case the nobles and officials – were preventing him from achieving his aim of helping them. Some historians, both Soviet and Western, have argued that this apparent peasant faith in the tsar was 'naive', as it was divorced from a reality in which successive tsars had actively supported the exploitation and oppression of generations of peasants. Moreover, the terms of the reform of 1861 did not, and any such reform was never likely to, meet the aspirations of the peasantry. Scholars taking this view of peasant attitudes to the tsar have tended to stress their ignorance, superstition, and very low level of awareness of the reality of the political structure of the autocracy.

More sophisticated analyses of peasant attitudes to the tsar, such as Field's study of the Bezdna affair, have suggested that peasants may not have been as politically naive as they have sometimes been portrayed. Field suggested that the peasants at Bezdna and elsewhere may have been claiming their belief in the tsar's benevolence in order to conform to the authorities' perceptions of them as childlike and devoted to their 'little father' the tsar, but gullible and easily led astray. Thus, Field implied, the peasants at Bezdna were trying to put forward their ideas about the sort of reform they were expecting by presenting them as the alleged real wishes of the tsar. The peasants' apparent intention was to try to attain some concessions from the authorities in their interests. Indeed, some highly educated nobles, for example those of Tver province in their address to the tsar in early 1862, adopted a similar strategy [*Doc. 24*]. In the case of the peasants, by claiming to be acting out of loyalty to the tsar they could plead they had been motivated by devotion to the tsar and had not rebelled against the authorities, hence the title of Field's book: *Rebels in the Name of the Tsar*. The massacres at Bezdna and Kandeevka are examples where this strategy went badly wrong. In other cases, however, peasants did extract some, mostly limited, concessions (Field, 1976b: 92, 208–15; Perrie, 1999).

CONCLUSION

People in the various groups involved or interested responded in various ways to the reform and its implementation. The numbers of people in the government, the nobility, intelligentsia and peasantry who actively supported the measure were quite small. Many more were at best indifferent or at worst hostile. It would be a mistake, however, to overstate the degree of active opposition to the reform. The most outspoken opponents were radical intellectuals, but they were few in number and, at this stage, had very little influence on anyone other than secret policemen. Even the peasant opposition should not be exaggerated. In spite of the apparently large numbers of disturbances and their wide geographical distribution, peasants who actively opposed the reform were a tiny minority of the total peasantry (Zaionchkovsky, 1978: 141). Most peasants, together with most estate owners, sought simply to get the best deal they could out of the reform.

CHAPTER TEN

THE REFORM PROCESS, 1863–1907

Over the years 1863–1907, as a result of the reform process set in motion by the Statutes of 1861, the freed serfs passed through successive stages of temporary obligation and the redemption operation. In addition, the government intervened to make minor alterations to the terms of the reform, and brought the process to a slightly premature end in 1907.

TEMPORARY OBLIGATION

The second stage in the reform process began when the regulatory charters were implemented. In most cases this was in early 1863. The charters contained detailed and relatively reliable data on the sizes of peasants' land allotments and their obligations to estate owners both during temporary obligation and on the eve of the reform [*Doc. 25*]. These can be compared to assess the consequences of the reform.

Land allotments

The land allotments allocated to temporarily-obligated peasants by noble estate owners were, on average, smaller than those the peasants had worked for themselves under serfdom. The land peasants lost – known as the 'cut offs' – was retained by estate owners. In the early twentieth century, many historians stated that the total amount of the land taken away from the freed serfs at the start of temporary obligation throughout the empire amounted to only 4.1 per cent of their previous holdings (Anisimov, 1911; Robinson, 1932: 87–8). This figure is misleading for two reasons. First, it included the western provinces, where peasants gained land following a revised reform in 1863 (see p. 107). Peasants in Russia and left-bank Ukraine lost 13.1 per cent of their land (Anisimov, 1911: 94). Second, the overall figure of 4.1 per cent for 'cut offs' was based on a comparison of figures on peasants' allotments in 1877–78 with data from the 'Descriptions of Seigniorial Estates', which were compiled by the estate owners themselves in the late 1850s and seem to have understated the sizes of peasants' allotments (Zaionchkovsky, 1978: 156; see also Chapter 3). In more recent decades, historians have produced new figures on the extent of the 'cut offs' based on the data in the regulatory charters. In most, but not all, cases their calculations suggest that the magnitude of the 'cut offs' was greater than previously thought. In Russia and left-bank Ukraine the former serfs lost an average of around 20 per cent, not 13 per cent, of their former allotments. This average conceals considerable differences between regions, provinces and villages, and between peasants who performed labour services and those who paid dues to estate owners. Not all peasants lost land. In most regions relatively small proportions – typically between 5 and 15 per cent – gained land. Larger proportions – as many as 43 per cent in the Central Black Earth region – received allotments that were the same size as those they had used under serfdom. Nevertheless, many freed serfs – an absolute majority in some regions – did end up with smaller allotments (Litvak, 1991: 152–70; Zaionchkovsky, 1978: 156–9).

The loss of land by peasants was a direct result of the Statutes of 1861. If peasants' allotments on the eve of the reform were larger than the maximum sizes laid down by the Statutes, then the excess was 'cut off' by the estate owner. Peasants who had had large allotments included some of those who paid dues, because nobles who demanded dues tended to allocate most of or all the land on their estates to the peasants. On the other hand, estate owners who required their serfs to work for them retained a substantial part of the land for themselves to cultivate with serf labour (see Chapter 2). Peasants in outlying regions had larger allotments than those in the central regions as a result of the lower population densities, and consequent greater availability of land, in peripheral areas. Thus, many peasants who paid dues and lived in outlying provinces lost substantial parts of their land in the early 1860s (Zaionchkovsky, 1978: 158). For example, in the Central Black Earth region – where labour services prevailed – and in the more densely populated provinces of Tula, Tambov and Kursk, peasants lost only between 12.6 and 15.7 per cent of their previous holdings. In the more outlying and slightly less heavily settled province of Voronezh in the same region, however, they lost an average of 26.7 per cent of their land. The substantial 'cut offs' in Kostroma province, on the edge of the Central Non-Black Earth region, and in the Northwest and Northern regions reflected both the prevalence of dues, and hence larger allotments, and the relatively low population densities (Table 10.1). A further cause of 'cut offs' was the provision in the Statutes that estate owners retain a minimum proportion of their estates – a third in the Russian provinces. Thus, on smaller estates where there was insufficient land to meet the needs of both estate owners and peasants, the reform gave precedence to the former (Litvak, 1991: 160).

Table 10.1 Percentage changes in peasant land allotments and obligations at the start of temporary obligation (according to regulatory charters)

Region/Province	Land allots	Obligations*		Region/Province	Land allots	Obligations*	
		per head	per des. of land			per head	per des. of land
Central Non-Black Earth				**Central Black Earth**			
Vladimir	-15.70			Voronezh	-26.70	-13.50	18.40
Kaluga	-10.90			Kursk	-15.70	-8.60	16.30
Kostroma	-32.00			Orel	-16.50	-13.50	10.80
Moscow	-14.20	-9.80	8.50	Ryazan	-16.80	-9.60	15.30
N. Novgorod	-17.10			Tambov	-13.10	-4.90	9.80
Smolensk	-16.00			Tula	-12.60	-15.70	2.40
Tver	-22.00			**Region**	**-16.30**	**-11.25**	**10.80**
Region	**-20.00**						
				Mid-Volga			
Northwest				Kazan	-11.50		
Novgorod	-28.50	-18.10	16.70	Simbirsk	-26.80		
Pskov	-22.70	-20.50	10.90				
St Petersburg	-33.40	-37.80	18.90	**Lower-Volga**			
Region	**-27.70**	**-24.10**	**16.00**	Samara	-41.30		
				Saratov	-42.90		
N. Urals							
Perm	-12.10			**S. Urals**			
Vyatka	0.40			Orenburg	-17.70		
				Ufa	-14.10		
North							
Vologda	-40.90						

* Dues only.

Data from regulatory charters are not available for some provinces. Figures for some provinces are based on incomplete data.

Sources: Kashchenko (1995), pp.110–11, 145, 159–60, 169–77; Degtiarev et al. (1992), pp.78–80; Litvak (1991), pp.157–75; Zaionchkovskii (1968), p.240. Where data conflict between sources, preference has been given to the most recent.)

The scale of the 'cut offs' was also very high in provinces where large numbers of peasants opted to take the small, free allotments – no less than a quarter of the maximum size laid down in the Statutes – permitted under Gagarin's last-minute amendment (see Chapters 7 and 8). Although the free allotments averaged only around one *desyatina* in size – much less than was needed to support their owners – over half a million male peasants opted to take them. They were popular in more outlying areas to the east and south, especially in the Mid- and Lower-Volga and Urals regions and in Southern Ukraine. The take-up of free allotments affected the total amounts of land lost by peasants in these areas. After allowing for the free allotments, the extent of the 'cut offs' due to other provisions of the Statutes in Simbirsk and Saratov provinces, in the Mid- and Lower-Volga regions, was 14.5 and 17.4 per cent respectively. This compares with 26.8 and 42.9 per cent if the free allotments are included. The high take-up of the free allotments also made substantial contributions to the proportions of land peasants lost in Penza and Samara provinces, also in the Mid- and Lower-Volga regions, in Perm, Orenburg and Ufa provinces in the Urals regions, and in Ekaterinoslav province in Southern Ukraine. So many peasants took the free allotments in Samara province that it threatened the incomes of some owners of smaller estates. The reason free allotments were so popular in outlying regions was that rents and prices for land on the open market were relatively low because of the abundance of land relative to the population. Peasants calculated that they could rent or buy the additional land they needed more cheaply on the open market than under the terms of the reform. What many peasants did not anticipate, however, was the rapid increase in rents and land prices after 1861. Those peasants who could not afford to rent or buy more land suffered great hardship. For this reason the free allotments came to be known as 'beggars' allotments' (Druzhinin, 1978: 54–5; Litvak, 1991: 163–5; Zaionchkovsky, 1978: 155–6).

Of the minority of peasants who gained land at the start of temporary obligation, some did so because their allotments on the eve of the reform were smaller than the minimum norms laid down in the Statutes. In such cases estate owners were required to allot them more land. On other estates nobles allocated peasants larger plots – even if the peasants did not need them – so that they could demand higher dues in return. This phenomenon was particularly widespread in the non-black earth regions, where the land was not very fertile and so of less value to estate owners than in black earth regions (Degtiarev et al., 1992: 78; Kashchenko, 1995: 173–4; Zaionchkovsky, 1978: 162).

As well as changes in sizes of peasants' allotments, there were also changes in the quality of their land and the types of land to which they had access. Many estate owners took the opportunity of the reform to relocate peasants on their estates, allotting them poor land and keeping the best for themselves. Estate owners in most regions tried to retain control of much of the meadows, pastures, woodland and water sources on their estates. Since peasants needed access to these lands to cut hay, graze livestock, gather timber and firewood, and collect water, estate owners could demand extra payments or labour in return (Kashchenko, 1995: 178–9; Zaionchkovsky, 1978: 159–60).

Obligations

The start of temporary obligation also saw changes in the levels of obligations peasants were required to work or pay estate owners for the use of their land allotments. Temporarily-obligated peasants who performed labour services did better than those who paid dues. Under the terms of the Statutes of 1861, labour services were restricted to maximums of 40 days a year for men and 30 for women. This was much lower than under serfdom. Many serfs, especially in the Central Black Earth region where labour services had predominated, had worked three or even four days a week for much of the whole year. This amounted to as much as 150–200 days a year. After 1861, therefore, some peasants' labour services fell by three to five times (Litvak, 1972: 320).

The Statutes included provision for peasants performing labour services to transfer to dues. This was advantageous for estate owners but disadvantageous for peasants, since the levels of dues in the Statutes were much higher than those for labour services. After a brisk start, the pace of transfers from labour to dues slowed. In the Central Black Earth region, almost half the peasants who had performed labour services under serfdom had their obligations commuted to dues by 1866. In 1881, however, 15 per cent of peasants in the region who had worked for their estate owners under serfdom still did so (Litvak, 1991: 173–4).

The experience of peasants who paid dues to estate owners under both serfdom and temporary obligation was different. Since the dues laid down in the Statutes depended on the sizes of peasants' allotments, and in most cases these decreased, many peasants' dues per head fell when the regulatory charters were enforced. For example, in Moscow province – in the Central Non-Black Earth region where dues were the prevailing form of obligations – average dues per head fell by nearly 10 per cent. In the Northwestern region, where dues also predominated, the average fell by nearly a quarter. In the Central Black Earth region, where a minority of peasants paid dues, the reduction amounted to just over 10 per cent. However, because peasants' allotments had, on average, fallen by more than the level of their dues, many peasants paid more per unit of land during temporary obligation than they had under serfdom. For example, average dues per *desyatina* of land rose by 8.5 per cent in Moscow province, by 16 per cent in the Northwestern region, and by 10 per cent in the Central Black Earth region (see Table 10.1).

Estate owners found ways of extracting additional obligations from peasants. They rented out part or all of the land that had been cut off from their allotments after 1861. Estate owners also demanded payment for access to the meadows, pastures, woodland and water sources they had retained. Some estate owners required peasants to pay these rents in labour rather than money (Litvak, 1972: 278, 320 and see Chapter 11).

THE REDEMPTION OPERATION

The redemption operation was the third and final stage in the reform process. During this stage peasants – now known as 'peasant-proprietors' – acquired full ownership of their allotments by making redemption payments over 49 years to the government. These were to pay for the compensation – the redemption sum – that the government advanced to the estate owners at the start of the operation. In the Russian provinces, where communal tenure prevailed, peasants redeemed their land in communes, and were jointly responsible for the payments. According to the Statutes of 1861, redemption was voluntary for estate owners but, if they decided to opt for it, compulsory for the peasants.

In the years after 1861 nobles steadily, but unevenly, transferred the peasants on their estates from temporary obligation to redemption. By the start of 1864 around 10 per cent of former serfs had begun to redeem their land. The proportion reached two-thirds by 1870. During the 1870s, however, the pace of transfers fell (Zaionchkovsky, 1978: 165–9). In the 1860s, the rate of transfers to redemption was higher in the fertile, black earth regions – where labour services predominated – than in the non-black earth regions – where most peasants paid dues. The reason for the regional difference was economic. The levels of labour services under temporary obligation were so low that it was in estate owners' best interests to move to redemption quickly in order to get their hands on the compensation, which was set at quite generous levels. On the other hand, the levels of dues in most non-black provinces during temporary obligation were fairly high. Thus, estate owners had no real incentive to rush to initiate redemption. The situation changed in the 1870s. Some estate owners in the black earth provinces realized it was more profitable to postpone redemption. Instead, they converted the peasants on their estates from labour services to dues, but then made them pay their dues by working on their land rather than delivering cash (Druzhinin, 1978: 67; Litvak, 1972: 177–80). In 1881 over a million and a half male peasants – 15 per cent of the freed serfs – were still temporarily obligated to estate owners. Temporary obligation was finally brought to an end by a decree issued on 28 December 1881 by the new tsar, Alexander III. Transfer to redemption was made compulsory for all temporarily-obligated peasants with effect from 1 January 1883. Even so, in practice, transfers dragged on into the 1890s (Fedorov, 1994: 459–63, 513; Litvak, 1991: 177; Zaionchkovsky, 1978: 205–8;).

Both estate owners and peasants tried to use the procedures for the redemption operation to their advantage. The start of redemption gave estate owners another opportunity to alter peasants' allotments. In the fertile Central Black Earth region some estate owners exchanged peasants' existing allotments for poorer quality land. Peasants responded by reducing the amount of land they were to redeem – and hence their redemption payments – by rejecting inferior plots. On the other hand, in the less fertile Central Non-Black Earth region some estate owners tried to enlarge the allotments the peasants were to redeem in order to increase the amount of compensation they would receive (Litvak, 1991: 177–80). Even after the start of redemption, moreover, some estate owners required the peasants to work for them in order to pay off the share of the compensation – 20 or 25 per cent of the redemption sum – that they owed them directly. Peasants also learned to use the provisions for their benefit. It will be recalled that peasants only had to pay the 20 or 25 per cent of the redemption sum to their estate owners if they agreed to their proposals. In the 1860s, almost half of redemption transactions had the agreement of the peasants. In the 1870s, however, the proportion fell to between a quarter and a third, and thus the peasants avoided having to pay their share (Gerschenkron, 1965: 741; Litvak, 1991: 177–80; Zaionchkovsky, 1978: 165–8).

The historical literature on the impact of the abolition of serfdom usually presents the level of the redemption payments as very high or ruinous for the peasants, and the sums the peasants had to redeem (i.e., the compensation paid to the nobles) as more than the open market value of the land (Druzhinin, 1978: 73–8; Robinson, 1932: 95; Shakhovskoi, 1911: 104). Closer analysis suggests a modified, if muddled, picture. In fact, many peasants' redemption payments to the government were less than the dues they had paid estate owners during temporary obligation. In the Central Black Earth region peasants paid, on average, between 19 and 24 per cent less per unit of land in redemption payments than in dues during the previous stage in the reform process (Litvak, 1972: 403). In the North-western region the average fall in peasants' payments per unit of land was between 5 and 15 per cent (Hoch, 1994: 71–2). Some peasants were also making payments to the estate owners for the part of the redemption sum they owed them directly. Nevertheless, taken as a whole, the freed serfs' payments for their land were lower under redemption than temporary obligation.

Most historians have argued that the sums set for redemption by the peasants were higher than the current open market prices of the land they were redeeming. Indeed, this was built into the system. Since redemption sums were calculated on the basis of peasants' previous obligations to the estate owners, which in non-black earth regions were often based at least in part on earnings from non-agricultural activities, there was no direct connection between the redemption sums and land prices. In practice, therefore, peasants were redeeming their dues to the estate owners rather than the market price of their allotments. Moreover, back in 1859, the legislators had been so concerned that the redemption operation would be paid for in full by the peasants that they had erred on the side of caution. They provided for a large 'reserve fund' to pay for the administrative costs and to protect the treasury against arrears, and they set the interest rate at the high level of 6 per cent a year (see Chapters 7 and 8). According to figures calculated at the start of the twentieth century, on average, peasants in Russia and left-bank Ukraine were overcharged for the land they redeemed by 90 per cent in the non-black earth provinces and 20 per cent in the black-earth provinces. Allowing for the larger area of land redeemed in the non-black earth regions, this works out at an average 'overcharge' of 47 per cent. The overcharge was greater in non-black earth regions because the peasants' dues were of greater value to their former owners than the relatively infertile land. In black earth regions, however, since the fertile land was of greater value, the need for hidden compensation for the loss of dues was less pressing (Gerschenkron, 1965: 738–40; Zaionchkovsky, 1978: 197; Table 10.2).

Table 10.2   Redemption payments and market prices for land (according to Lositsky)

Region	Allot land (000s des.)	Value of land at open market prices 1854–58	1863–72	Value of land according to redemption value	Redemption value as % of market prices, 1863–72
Russia and left-bank Ukraine					
(a) non-black earth	12,186	155	180	342	190
(b) black earth	9,841	219	284	342	120
Total	22,027	374	464	684	147
Western provinces	10,141	170	184	183	100
TOTAL	**32,168**	**544**	**648**	**867**	**134**

All prices in millions of roubles.
Source: Gerschenkron (1965), p.738.

More recently, two American economic historians have endeavoured to work out whether the freed serfs were indeed overcharged for their land allotments during the redemption operation. Evsey Domar's calculations revealed that peasants may have been required to pay as much as four times the market price for the land. He was careful, however, to note serious problems in the data. He also presented several qualifications to his findings, including a realistic, if cautious, statement that they might not be valid at all (Domar, 1989)! Paul Gregory accepted that the amounts set for the redemption sums in the Statutes of 1861 were above the market prices for land in the early 1860s. He calculated that land prices increased so quickly in the following years, however, that by 1879 they were higher than the sums set for the peasants to redeem. In other words, the 'negative equity' in the redemption operation had been wiped out by land price inflation within two decades of the reform (Gregory, 1994: 52–3).

Peasants quickly ran up arrears in their redemption payments. The government took some steps to ensure peasants paid and defaulters were punished. On a number of occasions, however, the government rescheduled the payments, that is spread them out over an even longer period, and reduced the total amount the peasants owed. In December 1881, for example, the government reduced the compensation estate owners received, initially to 80 per cent of the original sum, but raised to 88.5 per cent in 1883. The level of peasants' redemption payments was reduced at the same time (Robinson, 1932: 95–6, 150, 167–8; Zaionchkovsky, 1978: 205–8). In spite of the undoubted problems some peasants experienced in making the redemption payments, throughout the whole period of the redemption operation, peasants paid an average of 95 per cent of the total amounts due each year. Hoch calculated that they had repaid the entire cost of the operation to the treasury by 1906 (Hoch, 1994: 42–8).

THE END OF THE REFORM PROCESS

In the first decade of the twentieth century the government of Nicholas II took three steps that brought the reform process to an end. In 1903 the government abolished joint responsibility of peasant communities for their redemption payments and taxes. In November 1905 – during the revolution of that year – the government cut the redemption payments due in 1906 by half, and cancelled the remaining payments with effect from 1 January 1907 [*Doc. 28*]. Furthermore, on 5 October 1906 the government granted all peasants the right of freedom of movement (Crisp, 1989: 49–57). It had been the loss of this right at the end of the sixteenth century that had been a major step towards the enserfment of the peasantry. Thus, by 1907, the reform process had come to an end, and serfdom had finally been eradicated in the Russian Empire.

COMPARISONS

The impact of the abolition of serfdom on the former serfs in the Russian provinces and left-bank Ukraine – in terms of the amounts of land they were allocated and what they had to pay for them – can be compared with peasants on nobles' estates in the western provinces, where the reform was revised in 1863, and with the state and appanage peasants, who were the subjects of further reforms in the 1850s–80s.

The Western Provinces

In 1863 the imperial Russian government revised the terms of the abolition of serfdom of 1861 for the western part of the empire: right-bank Ukraine, Belorussia and Lithuania. In these areas the nobles were mostly Polish and the peasants mainly Ukrainian, Belorussian or Lithuanian. The reason for the revision of the reform was political. Another Polish nationalist revolt had broken out in Russian Poland. On 22 January 1863, in an attempt to gain peasant support, the Polish rebels issued a proclamation transferring all the land then in their use to the peasants. The questions of payments by the peasants and compensation for the nobles were deferred. The Russian government responded by revising the terms of its reform in an attempt to outflank the rebels, punish the Polish nobility for its disloyalty, and win the peasants over to its side (Kieniewicz, 1969: 155–79). Under the revised terms, larger quantities of land were allotted to the peasants at a lower cost than had been laid down in 1861. In Belorussia and Lithuania, peasants received an average of 24 per cent more land. In right-bank Ukraine, the increase amounted to 18 per cent. Land was also granted to the significant numbers of landless peasants in the western provinces. Overall the peasants got back all, and more, of the land that had been 'cut off' as a result of the 1861 legislation. The peasants' traditional rights of access to estate owners' meadows, pastures, woodlands and water sources (known as 'servitudes') were also guaranteed (Bircher, 1996: 54–67). Moreover, the second stage of the reform – temporary obligation – was brought to an immediate end, and all peasants were transferred to redemption. The peasants' redemption pay-ments – and hence the nobles' compensation – were reduced by 64 per cent in Belorussia and Lithuania and by 48 per cent in right-bank Ukraine (Zaionchkovsky, 1978: 142–8).

Thus, the peasants in the western provinces not only got a better deal in 1863 than two years earlier, but they also received a much more favourable settlement than their counterparts in the rest of the Russian Empire. This can be illustrated by figures on the relationship between the redemption sums and open market prices for the land. If the freed serfs in Russia and left-bank Ukraine were overcharged by 47 per cent, then in the western provinces the sums the peasants had to redeem were the same as the prices they would have paid on the open market (Table 10.2).

The Appanage and State Peasants

Beginning in the late 1850s, the government carried out further reforms of the appanage and state peasants (peasants who lived on land of the imperial family and the state) (see Chapter 5). These reforms aimed to equate the status of these categories of peasants with the freed serfs. Since there were no Russian nobles to be compensated and appeased, however, the former appanage and state peasants ended up with a better deal than the freed serfs in the Russian part of the empire. The appanage peasants were granted personal freedom in 1858. The reform was taken further in 1863. The appanage peasants' land allotments and the dues they paid for them were recorded in regulatory charters, which were compiled by local officials of the Appanage Department and verified by peace mediators. Peasants on appanage land did not have to go through a stage of temporary obligation, but were transferred to redemption in 1865. The redemption operation for former appanage peasants, like that for former serfs, was to last for 49 years (Gorlanov, 1986: 91–101).

Kiselev's reforms of the state peasants in the 1830s and 1840s had already granted them personal freedom (see Chapter 5). Two decrees in 1866 transferred the state peasants to a status similar to temporary obligation. They were given security of tenure of their allotments, and their dues were regulated. Both were recorded in documents similar to regulatory charters, which were drawn up by local officials of the Ministry of State Domains. Only in 1886 was a redemption operation set up to enable the former state peasants to redeem their land by making payments to the state for 44 years (Druzhinin, 1946–58, 2: 566–70).

In comparison with the freed serfs in Russia, the former appanage and state peasants did not lose large amounts of land in 'cut offs'. Moreover, since on average they already had larger holdings than peasants on nobles' estates, they ended up redeeming more land. In all regions of the empire, on average, former state peasants ended up with the largest allotments and freed serfs the smallest. In the Russian provinces, average allotments per male peasant were 6.23 *desyatiny* for former state peasants, 4.81 *desyatiny* for former appanage peasants, and 3.38 *desyatiny* for freed serfs. In addition, the former serfs' redemption payments were higher per unit of land than those of the former appanage and state peasants. Nevertheless, like the former serfs, both groups of peasants ran up arrears, had their payments rescheduled, and neither redemption operation ran its full course. The remaining redemption payments of the former appanage and state peasants were written off, at the same time as those of peasants on noble estates, in November 1905 (Druzhinin, 1978: 87, 109, 116–17; Robinson, 1932: 89–92) [*Doc. 28*].

CONCLUSION

Thus, of all the peasants in the Russian Empire, the former serfs on nobles' estates in Russia and left-bank Ukraine received the least favourable settlement as the reform process unfolded in the decades after 1861. The reasons for this were political and financial. The government offered Russian and Ukrainian noble estate owners adequate compensation for the land they allocated to their former serfs under the terms of the reform (and, in practice, also for the loss of the obligations they had received from their serfs). Since the government was unable to extend financial aid to the freed serfs, they had to bear the full cost of this compensation. The peasants on noble estates in the western provinces received a better settlement than their counterparts in Russia and left-bank Ukraine because, in the view of the government, the Polish estate owners of the region had forfeited the right to adequate compensation by their disloyalty in 1863. In the case of the appanage and state peasants, who also received a better settlement, there were no noble estate owners to compensate. There were also differences between former serfs on different estates and in the various regions of Russia and left-bank Ukraine. In addition, the settlement changed over the course of the reform process. In terms of the sizes of their land allotments and the dues or payments they owed for them, the former serfs were worse off during temporary obligation and better off during the redemption operation.

CHAPTER ELEVEN

THE IMPACT OF THE ABOLITION OF SERFDOM

The impact of the reform on the rural economy and society of the Russian Empire has to be seen in the context of wider developments in the decades after 1861. The reform and its aftermath also had an impact on the attitudes of the Russian public, including radical intellectuals.

THE WIDER CONTEXT

The abolition of serfdom was not, of course, the only influence on rural Russia in this period. The late nineteenth and early twentieth centuries saw broader changes in the Russian Empire. The abolition of serfdom was one – arguably the most important – of a whole series of 'great reforms' enacted by Alexander II in the 1860s and 1870s, including reforms of local government and the law courts (see p. 118), education, censorship, finance and military recruitment (see Chapter 6) (Eklof et al., 1994; Rieber, 1971).

Another factor that had a profound influence on rural Russia was the rapid growth in the population. The total number of inhabitants of the Russian Empire grew from 74 million in 1858, to 128 million in 1897, and to 178 million in 1914. Around 80 per cent of the population were peasants, and roughly 40 per cent of peasants were former serfs or the descendants of serfs (Moon, 1996c; Vodarskii, 1973: 103). The rapidly growing rural population put ever increasing pressure on peasants' allotments. Some of the pressure was relieved by migration from the villages of the European part of the empire to Siberia and other peripheral areas. Other peasants moved to the empire's expanding towns and cities (Anderson, 1980). The greater movement of people was facilitated by the construction of a national network of railways from the 1860s, culminating in the Trans-Siberian railway at the turn of the twentieth century (Marks, 1991). Urbanization and improvements in communications were accompanied by the expansion of the markets, both domestic and international, for agricultural and other goods. From the 1880s, moreover, the Russian Empire began to industrialize at an unprecedented rate (Gatrell, 1986; Gregory, 1994).

The relationship between the abolition of serfdom and these other areas of change is difficult to untangle. There is no doubt that the pace of social and economic changes in rural Russia was faster after 1861 than before. The extent to which the changes were *consequences* of the reform is debatable. Many of the developments – such as population growth, internal migration and the growth of the market – were building on trends and processes that preceded the reform (Gatrell, 1994; Kolchin, 1999: 105–6).

ESTATE OWNER–PEASANT RELATIONS

The abolition of serfdom led to a slow process of untying the bonds between noble estate owners and their former serfs. Many estate owners, however, tried to reproduce, as far as possible, the previous, servile relationship. Some of the ways in which estate owners managed to continue compelling peasants to work for them have already been mentioned: they converted peasants' dues under temporary obligation and, later, the part of the redemption sum peasants owed them directly into 'labour payments' on their lands; they demanded labour from the peasants in return for access to the land 'cut off' from their previous allotments, and to meadows, pastures, woodland and water sources (see Chapter 10). Estate owners rented out additional land to peasants in exchange for labour. Many peasants who had taken the 'beggars' allotments' also found themselves tied into new dependent relationships with their former owners in order to get access to the extra land they needed. In addition, some estate owners lent peasants money, and then required them to pay off the interest and capital by working for them. Peasants who fell into arrears in payments due to estate owners were also required to repay their debts in labour. This practice of working off dues, rents, interest and arrears – which closely resembled labour services under serfdom – became known as *otrabotka*, literally, 'working off'. Another practice that developed after 1861 was 'sharecropping': estate owners 'rented' land to peasants in return for a share of the crop (usually half) that the peasants grew on it. To some extent, sharecropping resembled the dues in kind that some peasants had rendered under serfdom. All these phenomena became known – both by contemporary critics of the reform and some historians – as vestiges or remnants of serfdom. To some extent, indeed, they were consequences of the terms of the reform. The gradual pace of the process set in motion in 1861 encouraged elements of the old, servile system to linger. Moreover, the 'cut offs', 'beggars' allotments', and continued obligations of peasants to estate owners all gave rise to the persistence of dependent or semi-dependent ties between former serfowners and former serfs (Anfimov, 1961; Mironov, 1996: 341–5).

Not all changes in relations between estate owners and peasants in the decades after 1861 resembled the previous, servile bonds. By the 1890s three-quarters of peasants who rented land paid in money rather than in labour or a share of the harvest. At this time it was estimated that peasants in the European part of the Russian Empire rented some 50 million *desyatiny* of land, in addition to the 123 million *desyatiny* they had been allotted as a result of the reform (Willets, 1971: 120). Peasants also bought land from nobles. They did so jointly as village communities or associations as well as individually. In 1883 the government set up the Peasant Land Bank to make loans available at reasonable rates of interest to assist joint purchases of land. The total amount of land that had been bought by peasants in the European part of the empire increased from 6.5 to 23.5 million *desyatiny* between 1877 and 1905. A further 10 million *desyatiny* were purchased by peasants between 1905 and 1914. Both rents and prices for land increased in these decades, in part as a result of the additional demand for land generated by the growing population (Gatrell, 1986: 112–15; Robinson, 1932: 268–72). Thus, a capitalist, monetized market in land involving former serfs and estate owners did develop, albeit unevenly, following the reform.

In addition, a capitalist, monetized market in labour developed after 1861. To some extent this was in response to the growing pressure on the land caused by the increase in the rural population. There was an increase in the numbers of wage labourers among former serfs. Moreover, capitalist farming evolved in the late nineteenth century. But, most former serfs who worked for wages did not do so for neighbouring estate owners, and most capitalist farms were not in the old heartlands of serfdom. Many peasants who worked as agricultural labourers did so on a seasonal basis in the outlying steppe regions of southeastern Russia and Southern Ukraine. It is significant that in these peripheral regions serfs and serfowners had made up small minorities of the rural population before 1861. The combination of fertile land and access to markets for agricultural produce via ports made capitalist agriculture viable in these regions. A shortage of local labour pushed up wages, and attracted migrant labourers from central Russia and Ukraine (Burds, 1998; Mixter, 1991). Large numbers of former serfs also found work as wage labourers in the Russian Empire's growing and indus-trializing towns and cities. Most of the factory owners who hired them, however, were not nobles who had invested in industry, but came from a variety of social backgrounds, including merchants, townsmen and even peasants (Bradley, 1985; Economakis, 1998; Gatrell, 1986: 84–96, 128–39).

Thus, the decades after the abolition of serfdom witnessed parallel developments in the evolution of relations between estate owners and freed serfs. Remnants of the old, servile relationships still persisted – in the forms of labour rents and share-cropping – while newer relationships – based on monetary exchanges for land and labour – also emerged. The former proved most resilient in the Central Black Earth and Mid-Volga regions of

Russia and in parts of Ukraine. In these areas the land was fertile, agriculture was by far the largest sector of the economy, and labour services had prevailed on nobles' estates before 1861. The newer developments, associated with the spread of capitalism, were most widespread in peripheral regions and in the Central Non-Black Earth and Northwestern regions. The common factor between these areas was the existence of large markets: for example, Moscow and St Petersburg in the Central Non-Black Earth and Northwestern regions respectively, and ports, such as Odessa on the Black Sea, in peripheral regions. The proximity of markets made it worthwhile to produce goods, both agricultural and non-agricultural, for sale rather than just local consumption (Anfimov, 1961: 190–3; Gatrell, 1986: 139–40, 231–2).

The parallel developments in the economy of rural Russia in the aftermath of the abolition of serfdom were reflected in contemporary debates between Populists, who argued that the basis of the rural economy was remaining unchanged, and Marxists – notably Lenin – who argued that capitalism was developing in Russia and penetrating the rural economy (Gatrell, 1986: 12–27). The debate over the form and extent of changes in the economy of rural Russia in the decades after 1861 has continued among historians to the present day (Anfimov, 1980: 3–9; Shanin, 1986: 103–73).

PEASANT AGRICULTURE

In contrast to the reforms of the appanage and state peasants in the first half of the nineteenth century (see Chapter 5), the abolition of serfdom of 1861 was not accompanied by government programmes to encourage peasants to adopt different, more 'advanced', methods of cultivation. Indeed, the traditional view of peasant agriculture in the decades after 1861 among historians is that the decision by the reformers to retain peasants' communal organizations and communal land tenure had a conservative or retarding impact on the development of Russian agriculture since they discouraged individual enterprise (Gerschenkron, 1965: 755). There is evidence to support this view. The most radical changes in agriculture in the Russian Empire in the decades after the abolition of serfdom took place in peripheral regions where serfdom had never been well developed. On the other hand, in much of central Russia – the heartland of serfdom – most village communities persisted with their customary methods of farming the land, in particular strip farming in open fields and the three-field crop rotation (see Chapter 2).

Recent research, however, has suggested that the traditional view of communal institutions acting as a barrier to agricultural development is too categorical. Russian peasant agriculture in the decades after 1861 was not static (nor had it been under serfdom). While many peasants persisted with their customary methods, the growth in population led peasants to bring more land into cultivation to produce the extra food they needed. Some of the newly cultivated arable land was rented or bought. Part, however, had previously been used as meadows and pastures to feed livestock. This led to a greater emphasis on growing crops than animal husbandry. Another way of feeding more mouths from limited amounts of land was to grow potatoes, as they generated more calories from the same area of land as grain. Some village communities made further changes, adopting more productive crop rotations, growing new varieties of crops, improving the land by using fertilizers or draining it. The increasing urbanization and industrialization of the Russian Empire from the late nineteenth century had an impact on peasant agriculture. Some peasants who lived in the hinterland of large cities specialized in growing fruit and vegetables or dairy farming, and then sold the produce in urban markets. The spread of the railway network brought more villages into market relations both with towns and cities and with other regions of the empire (Gregory, 1994: 37–54; Moon, 1999: 118–55).

Later in the nineteenth century, central and local government did attempt to foster rural 'development', mainly through agricultural co-operatives. They met with mixed success, however, not least because agronomists were too eager to try to impose their 'scientific' ideas on the peasants without due regard for the peasants' experience and ideas (Kotsonis, 1999).

PEASANT LIVING STANDARDS

In the late nineteenth century most contemporary observers, for example the Populist Stepniak, believed that peasant living standards in the Russian Empire were in decline, and that this was a result of the terms of the abolition of serfdom [*Doc. 27*]. This alleged decline was attributed to the peasants' inadequate land allotments, high dues and redemption payments, and also to the retention of communal land tenure and village communes which, it was believed, contributed to the persistence of inefficient agricultural techniques. When these were coupled with a rapidly rising population and increasing taxes, the result was 'land hunger', growing arrears in peasants' payments, widespread poverty and famine. This view was shared by most historians for a century or so after 1861. Writing in the 1930s, for example, Geroid Tanquary Robinson gave a graphic portrayal of 'the hungry village'. 'Serfdom was gone, but poverty remained' was his stark conclusion (Robinson, 1932: 94–116).

In recent decades historians have seriously challenged the whole idea that there was a 'crisis' in peasant living standards after 1861. In the process they have suggested an alternative assessment of the terms of the reform. One of the most positive assessments has come from Hoch. He found much of the existing literature on the subject lacking. He drew attention to the fall in the level of the payments due from the freed serfs at the start of the redemption operation (see Chapter 10). Furthermore, he denied that rapid population growth had 'disastrous consequences' for the Russian peasantry. He noted that, after allowing for exports, grain production and consumption per head of population increased in the late nineteenth and early twentieth centuries. He went so far as to conclude: 'The fundamental realignment of agrarian class relations in Russia during the 1860s, an immediate result of autocratic policy, produced direct, measurable benefits to the formerly servile peasantry...' (Hoch, 1994: 74).

A key to resolving the debate has been suggested by Stephen Wheatcroft's judicious analysis of regional variations and changes over time. Based on detailed analysis of grain production, rural wages, land prices and rents, tax burdens and government relief measures, he reinterpreted the traditional argument for crises in agriculture and peasant living standards. He identified 'indicators of real crisis' in the Central Black Earth and Volga regions, among rural wage labourers, and in the years 1891–93 and 1905–8. On the other hand, he also pointed to the long-term improvement in grain production per head of the population, indicating that, on average throughout the empire, there was an improvement in the food supply (Wheatcroft, 1991).

THE POSITION OF THE NOBILITY

Much of the historical literature on the impact of the abolition of serfdom has concentrated on the peasants. It is also important, of course, to look at the impact on the nobility. The traditional view has been that, in spite of the gradual nature of the reform process, the compensation the nobles received and the ways in which they continued to exploit peasants after 1861, the Russian nobility was in decline in the decades after the reform. Nobles lost not only their serfs and substantial amounts of land, but also the way in which they had run their estates. Increasing numbers of nobles sold what was left of their land and moved to towns and cities. In Blum's words: 'the emancipation of the serfs in 1861 opened a calamitous last stage in the history of the Russian nobility, during which the pillars upon which its power and privilege had rested crumbled one by one' (Blum, 1977: 79). The end of the old noble way of life in the countryside was immortalized in literature by Anton Chekhov in his play *The Cherry Orchard*, published in 1904. In the play, the widowed noblewoman Ranevskaya is forced to sell her beloved cherry orchard to repay her debts. Poignantly, the orchard is bought by a merchant named Lopakhin, who is the son of a former serf from the estate.

This notion of decline has been challenged by historians since the 1970s. Seymour Becker went furthest. He concluded that the landowning nobility did not simply decline after the end of serfdom, but adapted rationally and, to a large extent, successfully to the changing circumstances (Becker, 1985: 171–8). The loss of land by the nobility as a direct result of the reform is, of course, undeniable. The immediate loss in land allotted to the freed serfs left nobles with a little under 90 million *desyatiny* (Becker, 1985: 32). The compensation nobles received in redemption sums was generous when compared with current market prices for land (see Chapter 10). However, a few qualifications need to be made. The element of over-compensation was cancelled out by land price inflation by the end of the 1870s (see Chapter 10). Nobles would thus have benefited in the long-term by retaining their land since it was an appreciating asset. As part of their compensation, nobles received interest-bearing, long-term bonds. Nobles who could not, or did not wish to, wait until the bonds matured could sell them for cash on the open market. But, if they did so, they received only around 70 per cent of their face value. Before giving nobles their compensation, moreover, the government recovered any outstanding debts, in particular mortgages on estates. This amounted to quite a large part of the compensation. Some estimates put it as high as 75 per cent, others at around 40 per cent (Munting, 1992: 25; Emmons, 1968a: 421).

The decline in noble landownership continued throughout the post-reform decades as many nobles sold off more land. Total noble land-holdings in the European part of the empire (excluding the Baltic provinces) fell from just under 90 million *desyatiny* to 77 million by 1877. By 1905 they had fallen further to 51 million *desyatiny*, and in 1914 to 41 million *desyatiny* (Becker, 1985: 32). To some extent, this decline mirrored the rise in peasant landownership in this period (see p. 112). However, nobles sold land to merchants as well as peasants. Nobles with an eye to the future invested the profits from the sale of their estates in bonds or shares, which generated an income for them to live on (Lieven, 1992: 95). Some nobles sold only parts of their estates. Others gave up landowning altogether. In 1861 80 per cent of nobles owned land. By 1905 the proportion had fallen to 40 per cent. The noble flight from the land was most marked among lesser nobles in the relatively infertile provinces of the Central Non-Black Earth region (Munting, 1992: 26). Nobles who did not own land lived off incomes from other sources. As in previous centuries, many made a living from military or civil service. Significant numbers worked in the professions or in other occupations, but relatively few became industrialists (Becker, 1985: 171–2; Lieven, 1992: 123–4, 185–6).

Nobles also sought incomes from their estates without selling them. Many rented out part or all of their land, mostly to peasants. It has been calculated that nobles rented out more land than they sold in the decades after the abolition of serfdom. It has also been estimated that, on average, it was more profitable for nobles to rent out their estates than to farm the land directly themselves (Munting, 1992: 27–8). Nevertheless, a minority of nobles did farm their land. Indeed, some nobles bought land from others to increase their landholdings. Some estate owners continued to rely on peasants to provide the labour, albeit now remunerated, as well as the implements, and hence the agricultural technology. Thus, some noble farmers' operations continued to resemble those of the peasants. On the other hand, there were a relatively small number of nobles who set out to run their estates in new, 'improved' ways. They were engaging in what was, for the Russian nobility as a whole, a new venture (Manning, 1982: 11–24). In comparison with most peasants, these 'improving' noble farmers used more complex crop rotations, cultivated a wider variety of crops, employed more agricultural machinery – for example reaping and threshing machines – and hired more labour. Nobles were able to do these things, of course, because they had greater access to money for investment than peasants. The results could be quite impressive. Noble farmers, on average, attained higher yields and put a larger part of their produce on the market than peasants. Large-scale cultivation of cash crops, for example tobacco and sugar beet, and processing such crops on an industrial scale, was also carried out by some more profit-minded nobles. These trends in noble agriculture were most marked in peripheral regions near ports and other areas with ready access to large markets (Gatrell, 1986: 98–140; Munting, 1992: 28–40 and 1979).

A few nobles engaged in farming partly for non-economic reasons, seeing it as an opportunity to 'raise' the economic and cultural level of the peasants. The academic chemist Alexander Engelgardt was exiled by the authorities from St Petersburg in 1871 on suspicion of stirring up radical student protests. He chose to live on his family estate in Smolensk province, where he endeavoured to use his expertise to find more efficient ways of cultivating the land. He was particularly interested in new crop rotations, new crops (for example, clover and flax) and chemical fertilizers. Engelgardt became very closely involved with the local peasants, and wrote a series of long letters about his experiences which were published in the journal *Notes of the Fatherland* (Frierson, 1993). A fictional example of an enthusiastic noble farmer who sympathized with the peasants is Constantine Levin in Leo Tolstoy's novel *Anna Karenina*. To some extent, Levin was based on the author and his experiences on his estate of Yasnaya Polyana, Tula province, in the Central Black Earth region.

The overall trend in Russian agriculture, however, was towards peasant rather than noble farming. Fewer nobles were cultivating their estates than opted to give up agriculture and sell or rent their land to peasants. According to one set of estimates, in the 1850s nobles produced a quarter of total crop production in the Russian Empire, and half the amount that was sold on the market. In 1916, however, the equivalent proportions had fallen to only 11.3 and 20.6 per cent (Munting, 1992: 37).

Although many Russian nobles felt let down by the government in 1861, they were not completely abandoned in their efforts to find new ways of supporting themselves and new roles in society. Two of the other 'great reforms' – those of local government and the courts – were designed, at least in part, to appease the nobility. Some nobles had responded to the abolition of serfdom by demanding liberal reforms, including the right to participate in the government by electing a representative assembly in St Petersburg (see Chapter 9). Alexander II was not prepared to concede any of his autocratic powers in the centre. In 1864, however, he legislated for the creation of elected councils (*zemstva*) at provincial and district levels. The electoral systems were weighted heavily in favour of the nobles and against other inhabitants, in particular peasants. The *zemstva* were to complement the existing institutions of local government, and were to concentrate on social and economic matters such as public health, transport and schooling. The *zemstva* gave nobles an opportunity to make new roles for themselves in local affairs. The judicial reform, also enacted in 1864, addressed the concerns of many nobles by replacing the old, slow and closed courts with new, more efficient open courts, with juries and barristers, similar to those in contemporary Great Britain and North America (Emmons, 1968a: 399–402; Lincoln, 1990: 90–117).

Following the death of Alexander II in 1881 (see p. 120), his son and successor, Alexander III, significantly revised some of the 'great reforms'. His measures have been characterized as 'counter-reforms'. Some of the changes directly affected the provincial nobility. In 1885 Alexander III established the Noble Land Bank. The bank lent nobles money at relatively low rates of interest (4–4.5 per cent) against their estates. This gave them another way of earning income from their land, of which many took advantage. By 1914 total noble mortgage debt exceeded 1,400 million roubles. Many used the money they borrowed for current consumption, to subsidize their lifestyles. Thus, noble indebtedness, which had been wiped out at the start of the redemption operation, once again increased. Becker has argued, however, that nobles' debts did not reach excessive proportions. Total noble debt in 1914 represented only 20 per cent of the total value of noble land. Some nobles, moreover, made more productive use of the money they borrowed by investing it (Becker, 1985: 47–53). Other 'counter-reforms' enacted by Alexander III concerned local government. In 1889 the new office of 'land captain' (*zemskii nachal'nik*) was created to supervise the institutions of peasant self-government set up in the 1860s. (The post of peace mediator had been abolished in 1874.) Land captains were appointed by the government from men nominated by the local nobility. Thus, nobles regained some of the control over the peasants they had lost after 1861. In addition, a revised *zemstvo* statute of 1890 altered the franchise, raising further the representation of nobles. The statute also, however, increased the dependence of *zemstva* on the central government. Indeed, the main aim of the 'counter-reforms' was not so much to promote the interests of the provincial nobility, but to reassert the authority of the autocratic government (Wcislo, 1990: 83–118).

PUBLIC OPINION

One of the reasons the government was on the defensive in the late nineteenth century was the growing opposition from sections of the public that was fuelled, in part, by negative perceptions of the situation in rural Russia in the wake of the abolition of serfdom. In spite of the relatively generous settlement that nobles received, many were unhappy with the end of serfdom, and the end of the old ways of life that it entailed. Many nobles, especially the older generation, struggled to come to terms with the new situation in which they found themselves (Manning, 1982: 6–8). Nor did peasants, most of whom had been disappointed by the reform in 1861, become reconciled to it. After the outburst in the spring of 1861 (see Chapter 9) peasant protest continued, albeit at a low level, throughout the following decades. Increasingly, peasant protests centred on the question of land (Anfimov, 1984: 191–222; Zaionchkovsky, 1978: 202–4). Judging from periodic rumours that spread around the villages, many peasants seem to have hoped that the tsar would announce a new land reform, allocating them more land free of charge (Frierson, 1993: 179, 228–38). Older interpretations of peasant protest after 1861 argued that peasants were motivated by growing impoverishment. If, as many historians now suggest, peasants on average were experiencing improved standards of living in the late nineteenth century, then it would suggest that a combination of disappointment with the terms of the reform and rising expectations may well have been major factors behind continuing peasant discontent.

Russian intellectuals – many of whom became increasingly radical in the late nineteenth century – stepped up their criticism of both the terms of the reform and the political system that had produced it. Most radical intellectuals believed that peasant living standards were in decline following, and as a result of, the terms of the abolition of serfdom [*Doc.* 27]. A whole movement – the Populists – grew up to advocate what they saw as the interests of the peasants. To varying degrees, moreover, Populists idealized the peasantry and the customs of village life. In the 1870s young radical intellectuals attempted to make contact with the peasants – and spread their radical and revolutionary ideas to them – by going to live among them in the villages. The result, however, was mostly suspicion and incomprehension by the peasants, and disappointment among the now less naive radicals. In 1876 Populists formed an underground organization called 'Land and Liberty' to campaign for revolutionary social and political change. In particular, it advocated a wholesale transfer of land from nobles to peasants without compensation. If the members of 'Land and Liberty' broadly agreed on aims, they disagreed on tactics. 'Land and Liberty' soon split between some members who promoted educating peasants and gradualism and, on the other hand, those who believed the only way forward was terrorist attacks on leading figures in the government. On 1 March 1881 revolutionary terrorists assassinated Alexander II (Saunders, 1992: 311–43). The 'tsar-liberator' went to his grave unable to comprehend why his subjects were not more grateful for all he had tried to do for them (Mosse, 1958: 163). There was a fundamental gulf, however, between the sort of reform Alexander, as an autocrat, was prepared to enact, and the much greater changes that Populists, liberals and others were demanding.

CONCLUSION

Much of the literature on the impact of the abolition of serfdom, both by contemporaries and historians, has concentrated on what they saw as the 'defects' of the reform and the problems that ensued. Most attention has focused on the amounts of land that were taken away from the peasants after 1861 and the growing land shortages among peasants. More recent appraisals of the reform have tended, for the most part, to be less critical and more balanced. It is clear that the impact of the reform varied over time, especially between the stage of temporary obligation and the redemption operation, also by region, and between the different sections of the population – principally nobles and peasants – who were involved. To some extent, the land shortages experienced by many peasants in the decades after 1861 were due not so much to the terms of the land settlement, but to the rapid increase in the rural population. Allotments that might have been adequate to support the peasant population in the early 1860s soon became inadequate. Nevertheless, any attempt to present a positive interpretation of the impact of the abolition of serfdom has to contend with the fact that the post-reform Russian state struggled to deal with challenges of modernity. In addition to the impact of the reform on rural society and the economy, moreover, the end of serfdom and the other 'great reforms' wetted the appetites of Russians for more, and more far-reaching changes.

PART THREE CONCLUSIONS AND ASSESSMENT

CHAPTER TWELVE

ABOLITION AND AFTERMATH

In 1905–7 and 1917–18, throughout much of the territory of the Russian Empire, there were two massive peasant revolutions. During both revolutions, acting with growing confidence and decisiveness, peasants seized land that remained in the hands of nobles and other non-peasant owners. Peasants also seized agricultural implements, machinery and draught animals. And they tried to drive landowners out of rural areas by threats, arson, assaults and murder. Revolutionary actions by peasants were widespread in the Central Black Earth and Volga regions and in Ukraine, where land shortages were most acute, but the peasant revolution was not limited to impoverished areas. In 1905–7 the tsarist authorities tried to stem the tide of rural revolution by making concessions. This was the occasion of Nicholas II's decision to put an end to outstanding redemption payments with effect from 1 January 1907 [*Doc. 28*]. The authorities also used force and, by the end of 1907, had managed to suppress the first peasant revolution. A decade later, in March 1917, after the abdication of Nicholas II and the collapse of the tsarist regime, peasants once again erupted in revolution. The new Provisional government vacillated rather than take action to settle the land question. In marked contrast, the day after Lenin and the Bolshevik Party seized power in October 1917, the new Soviet government issued the 'Decree on Land'. This gave legal sanction to the land seizures that had been taking place since the spring, and prompted a further wave of peasant action to take over the land (Perrie, 1990, 1992).

The peasant revolutions of 1905–7 and 1917–18 would seem to suggest that the terms of the abolition of serfdom of 1861, in particular the land settlement, had completely failed to replace serfdom with a viable social and economic order in rural areas. Indeed, at the time, this was the view of most revolutionaries. Lenin wrote that '1861 gave birth to 1905' (Perrie, 1993: 32). Lenin and other revolutionaries were not, of course, writing as historians, but were attacking the tsarist regime. Most revolutionaries argued that the reform of 1861 had been too favourable to the nobles and too burdensome for peasants. The peasant-orientated Socialist Revolutionary Party demanded that all land be 'socialized', that is transferred to common ownership, without compensation for its previous owners (Perrie, 1976). Many historians have also made a direct link between what they have seen as the limitations of the 1861 reform and the peasant revolutions of the early twentieth century (Acton, 1990: 50–1; Shanin, 1986: 92). All attempts to make a direct, causal link between the abolition of serfdom and the rural revolutions, however, rely too heavily on hindsight. Just because the reform of 1861 was followed around half a century later by two peasant revolutions does not necessarily mean that one caused the other.

Closer analyses of the revolutions of the early twentieth century have shown that peasants joined in revolutions that had been started earlier, mainly in the cities, by other sections of the population, in particular the new industrial working classes and professional middle classes, for wider reasons than discontent with the terms of the abolition of serfdom. On both occasions, therefore, peasants were taking advantage of breakdowns in authority created by the outbreak of revolutions to settle their grievances and take control of their own lives by direct action. Thus, the peasant revolutions that began in 1905 and 1917 were the result of a broader range of factors than the terms and consequences of the reform of 1861.

In both 1905 and 1917 the wider revolutions were precipitated by military defeats – by Japan in 1904–5 and by Germany in the First World War that broke out in 1914 – which were more decisive and humiliating than the defeat in the Crimea in the 1850s. The ultimate causes of both revolutions, however, can be traced to the extreme reluctance of the tsar and his government to share power and work effectively with representatives of the population to tackle the wide range of social and economic problems inside the empire – including the land question – as well as the external threats from the empire's enemies. Autocracy, especially an autocracy headed by the ineffectual Nicholas II, was no longer a viable system of government for a vast empire experiencing the pains of economic and social 'modernization' and trying to maintain its international status in competition with more economically developed and more effectively governed rivals. Thus, by the early twentieth century, autocracy – like serfdom in the mid-nineteenth century – was found wanting. Unlike serfdom, however, the tsarist government was unwilling to deal with the problem by reform. In October 1905, in an attempt to divide the revolutionary opposition to the regime, Nicholas II very reluctantly announced that a legislative assembly, the State Duma, would be elected. The tsar regretted his moment of weakness, and his subsequent intransigence ensured the failure of the 'constitutional experiment'.

In spite of the deadlock with the State Duma, the tsarist government did make one last attempt to answer the peasant question. The revolutionary demand for land to be transferred to the peasants without compensation was unacceptable to the government. Peter Stolypin – Prime Minister from 1906 to 1911 – imposed an alternative solution: the break-up of the peasants' village communes. Peasants' communal institutions and practices had been retained and reinforced in the Statutes of 1861. The authors of the Statutes had seen village communes, and the Russian practices of communal land tenure and joint responsibility for taxes and other obligations, as forces for stability in the uncertain atmosphere that would follow the end of serfdom. However, the future of village communes and communal practices, which were believed by many to inhibit economic development, was the subject of continued debate in governmental and intellectual circles after 1861. Indeed, a change of direction was planned before 1905, and joint responsibility had been abolished in 1903. The peasant revolution of 1905–7 spurred the government to further reform. The role played by village communes in organizing land seizures demon-strated that they could be a force for revolution rather than stability (Macey, 1987).

Stolypin's reforms of 1906–11 permitted individual peasant households to leave their village communes, convert their land allotments from communal property to their own individual property, and consolidate their scattered strips of land in one place. It was Stolypin's aim that the 'separators' would become prosperous, yeoman family farmers with a stake in the existing order, who would thus become a force for stability in the villages. In his often-quoted words, his reform was 'a wager on the strong'. The outbreak of the First World War in 1914 and revolution in 1917 prevented the land reforms from having the time Stolypin believed they would need to achieve their aims. Historians have endlessly debated the results, and potential results, of the reforms. Attention has focused on the numbers of peasant households who petitioned to separate and those who completed the process of leaving the communes. The numbers do not tell the full story, however, since peasants, as ever, used the legislation for their own purposes, regardless of Stolypin's intentions. The events of the peasant revolution of 1917–18 suggest that the mass of the peasantry did not support the reforms. 'Separators' and their land were forcibly brought back into the communes. The most recent historian of the reforms has concluded: 'Con-ceived as a broad measure to modernize peasant farming and create a loyal peasantry, the final verdict on the Stolypin Reform must be that it was too narrowly conceived to be able to deliver this result' (Pallot, 1999: 247).

Thus, between the mid-nineteenth and early twentieth centuries, the tsarist state was indeed unable to create a viable social, economic and political order in the villages where most of its subjects still lived. On the other hand, by the eve of the First World War and the revolutions of 1917, the Russian Empire, the problems, challenges and threats it faced, both internal and external, had changed a great deal since the 1850s. To condemn the reform process devised by the enlightened bureaucrats in the late 1850s because, on the one hand, it fell short of the political goals of revolutionaries who were dedicated to the overthrow of the tsarist state and existing social order and, on the other hand, because it failed to contribute to the survival of a still largely agrarian autocracy beyond the second decade of the twentieth century seems rather harsh. It would perhaps be more appropriate to assess the reform of 1861 in the contexts of the problems the reformers themselves set out to address, what was possible in practical terms at the time, and in comparison with similar reforms in east-central Europe.

One of the motives of the reformers was to create the conditions for economic development along the lines of Western capitalism. Was this achieved? Economic development continued at a slow pace in the 1860s and 1870s, but took off in the last two decades of the nineteenth century, when the Russian Empire experienced unprecedented rates of industrial development. In part, the pace of industrialization was the result of state policies directed at heavy industry and infrastructure. It was also a result of growing demand for consumer goods from peasants who, on average, were experiencing a steady improvement in their living standards.

The terms of the reform of 1861 that hindered economic development – in particular the large debt transferred to the freed serfs at the start of the redemption operation and the restrictions on the mobility of the freed serfs enforced by village communes – can be explained by the reformers' concerns for financial and social stability. The Russian state was virtually bankrupted by the Crimean War and faced a banking crisis in 1859. Thus, the reformers had little choice but to compel the freed serfs to pay for the land that was transferred to them from the nobility and to restrict the amount of land the freed serfs could redeem. The redemption operation, including joint responsibility of communes for their redemption payments, was devised within these constraints.

Official concerns about the prospect of a massive peasant revolt, that had been brought into sharp focus by the unrest in Estonia in 1858, had a two-fold influence on the reformers. On the one hand, they persuaded them to ensure that the freed serfs had access to adequate quantities of land, and the opportunity in the medium term to acquire land as property. On the other hand, concern for social stability was part of the reason why the reformers decided to retain the restrictions on peasant movement, and replace the authority of the nobles with village communities, lest greater mobility and freedom made peasants more, rather than less, volatile. Were the reformers successful in averting the feared peasant revolt? Peasants certainly complained about the terms of the reform in the wave of disturbances, such as the incidents at Kandeevka and Bezdna, in the spring of 1861. They continued to protest about the land they lost after 1861, and that they had to pay for it. But, the freed serfs did not rise up in revolt *en masse* for almost half a century, by which time the situation in the villages had changed considerably for a range of reasons, some of which were linked only indirectly to the abolition of serfdom. In particular, by 1905 the rural population had more than doubled, putting pressure on the land that even the most farsighted enlightened bureaucrats did not anticipate. Recent research strongly suggests that average peasant living standards were improving in the decades after 1861. This has pointed to another link between the reform and peasants' propensity to rebel that the enlightened bureaucrats can hardly have anticipated. Some historians are now moving towards reinterpreting the peasant revolutions of 1905–7 and 1917–18 in part as revolutions of rising expectations (Burds, 1998: 176–85; Channon, 1992: 117).

The authors of the reform of 1861 were also concerned to mollify the nobles who were about to lose their serfs and part of their land. If the terms of the reform had transferred more land to the freed serfs with less, or no, compensation for noble estate owners, then the state might have faced another noble rebellion with much greater support than the Decembrist revolt of 1825. Were the reformers successful in averting mass noble disaffection? Provincial nobles and their deputies grumbled in 1859–60. Some agitated for a constitution to limit the powers of the tsar and his bureaucrats in 1861–62. And liberal nobles in the *zemstva* demanded political change in later decades. But, for the most part, Russian nobles accepted the compensation they received for the loss of part of their land, and in practice for the loss of their serfs, and did not try to overthrow the tsar. Indeed, after 1861, the nobility lacked the influence to have a major impact on the government (Emmons, 1968a: 414–23). This was a reflection of the long-term decline in the political importance of the Russian nobility since Peter III had dispensed with compulsory noble state service in 1762.

The reformers who drew up the Statutes of 1861 faced a more serious political constraint than opposition from the nobility. They needed to devise a reform that would meet as many of their objectives as possible, but which was also acceptable to a tsar who, while recognizing the need for reform, was cautious and conservative. In persuading Alexander II, the enlightened bureaucrats were greatly assisted by the strength of their arguments and the support of three key people: Rostovtsev, the Grand Duke Constantine Nikolaevich and Grand Duchess Elena Pavlovna.

One of the strongest arguments for reform, if not the decisive one, was the connection made by Dmitrii Milyutin in early 1856 between serfdom and the weakness of Russia's military forces that had been exposed in the Crimean War. He argued that serfdom needed to be abolished in order to prepare the way for reform of the system of recruitment. On his appointment as Minister of War in November 1861, Dmitrii Milyutin immediately drew up a comprehensive plan of reform. The culmination was the Military Service Reform of 1874. The Russo-Turkish War of 1877–78 came a little too soon, however, and 'exposed the limits of the military reforms that had been enacted after the Crimean War debacle'. Nevertheless, Russia's reformed armed forces performed better than the pre-reform army (Bushnell, 1994: 144, 156). The Russian Empire emerged victorious on the battlefield in 1878. But, it had not regained sufficient standing as a European power to impose the peace settlement it wanted in order to expand its influence in the Balkans. The British and Austrian governments strongly objected. Bismarck, the Chancellor of the increasingly powerful German Empire, brokered a new settlement that curtailed the growth of Russian influence. The Russian Empire was more successful in expanding its interests in Central Asia, but could not overcome the concerns of Great Britain, which was worried about the potential threat to its empire in India. Russian expansion in the Far East was also successful in the medium term, until it came up against a Japan that was modernizing its economy and military power more quickly than Russia (Seton-Watson, 1967: 438–59, 579–97).

The limitations in the foreign policy achievements of the post-reform Russian Empire cannot, of course, be attributed mainly to the Statutes of 1861. A more appropriate benchmark by which to assess the terms of the reform would be similar reforms to eradicate serfdom that were enacted in east-central Europe, where serfdom had also survived into the nineteenth century. In most states the main principles were similar: over time peasants were granted personal freedom from nobles, and access to, or ownership of, land. But, there were differences in the amounts of land peasants received and how much they had to pay for it. Blum concluded that the terms of the 1861 reform in the Russian Empire, together with those in Prussia between 1807 and 1850, were among the least generous to the peasants. One of the most generous settlements for the freed serfs was in the Austrian Empire in 1848–49. In the Austrian lands, the state paid half the nobles' compensation, and in the Hungarian lands, the state took on the entire burden. It is worth bearing in mind, however, that the reform process in the Austrian Empire had begun in 1781 with what amounted to a landless abolition of serfdom. As in the Baltic provinces of the Russian Empire after the landless abolitions of 1816–19, further laws had been required to ensure peasant access to land. The most favourable settlements for peasants came in the former Polish lands, where the peasants were the beneficiaries of the struggle to win their support between the governments of Russia, Austria and Prussia, on the one hand, and Polish nationalists on the other (Blum, 1978: 383–400; Kieniewicz, 1969).

Thus, it is possible to reach a more measured assessment of the abolition of serfdom in the Russian Empire. In terms of what the enlightened bureaucrats set out to achieve in the late 1850s, making allowance for the financial and political constraints in which they had to operate, and in comparison with similar reforms in east-central Europe, the reform of 1861 can be seen as moderately successful in the medium term. Indeed, it could be argued that it was just about the best settlement that was possible in the circumstances. Maureen Perrie concluded that Alexander II's 'great reforms', including the abolition of serfdom, 'may well have postponed [revolution from below] for half a century', and that they 'must be ranked among the most successful achievements of the traditional autocratic system in Russia' (Perrie, 1993: 32–3). Emmons went further, arguing that the abolition of serfdom was 'probably the greatest single piece of state-directed social engineering in modern European history before the twentieth century' (Emmons, 1968a: 414).

Another comparison would also suggest that the abolition of serfdom in 1861 can be considered a modest success. In the Soviet Union in 1929–30, a little over a decade after the downfall of the tsarist regime in 1917, Stalin and the Communist Party imposed their solution to the 'peasant question': forced collectivization of peasant agriculture. The immediate consequences were as follows: the violent suppression of massive resistance to the new collective farms by peasants who believed they were worse than serfdom (Viola, 1996); the forcible deportation of over four million peasants who were branded as 'kulaks', several hundred thousand of whom died; a devastating famine in 1932–33 that resulted in several million more deaths; and the collapse of agricultural production below the levels of 1913 that had barely been made good by the end of the 1930s (Davies et al., 1994: 68, 106, 114).

PART FOUR DOCUMENTS

This proclamation ended compulsory state service by noblemen, which had existed in principle since the sixteenth century. Noble military and civil service, together with education, had been rigorously enforced by Peter the Great at the turn of the eighteenth century.

[The proclamation began by noting the circumstances (i.e., war) which had compelled Peter the Great to enforce military and civil service for noblemen and education for their sons. It noted how nobles had often found the obligation to be 'burdensome and intolerable'. On the other hand, Peter III went on to proclaim:]

We see with satisfaction, and any true son of the fatherland must acknowledge, that incalculable good has come from [compulsory state service and education]: boorishness harmful to the general good has been eliminated; ignorance has been replaced by common sense; useful knowledge and assiduity in service; an increase in the numbers of proficient and courageous Generals in military service; and [it] has provided experienced and suitable people in civil and political service. To conclude..., noble thoughts have taken root in the hearts of all true Russian patriots, [who have shown] Us unlimited loyalty and love, [and] great ardour and estimable zealousness in Our service. Therefore, We do not consider it necessary to enforce service in the way it has been required until now.

And thus We, in view of the aforementioned circumstances, by the power given to Us by the Almighty, as a favour from Our Imperial Majesty, from henceforward and for all time ... grant freedom and liberty to the entire Russian well-born Nobility, who may continue service in Our Empire, and in other European Powers allied to Us, in accordance with the following regulations:

1. All Nobles currently in various [branches] of Our services may continue [to serve] for so long as they wish and their condition allows them. However, military [servicemen], neither during a campaign, nor three months prior to the start of one, are not to dare to seek permission to retire from service. ...

3. [Noblemen] who have been in retirement for some time, or after military [service] have been in civil or another [branch] of Our services, [who] wish anew to enter military service, such [men] will be admitted at the same ranks [as they held or hold in civil service] if they are worthy of them. ...

9. However, as We are decreeing fundamental and unequivocal regulations for the entire well-born Nobility for all time, so in this conclusion We, by

Our Imperial word, in the most solemn manner, confirm this [i.e., the abolition of compulsory noble state service] forever ... [Peter III also bound his legitimate descendants to uphold his proclamation.]

On the other hand, We trust that the entire well-born Russian Nobility, aware of Our ... generosity to them and their descendants, will be induced not to depart from their most humble loyalty and fidelity to Us, neither to hide from service, but with fervour and desire to enter [service], and honestly and proudly continue [to serve] to the utmost, no less will they assiduously and earnestly instruct their children in decorous arts, for all those who never serve anywhere will spend all their time in sloth and idleness, and their children will not be able to apply any useful sciences for the good of their fatherland. We command all Our loyal subjects and true sons of the fatherland to disdain and disparage such [people] as detrimental to the general good, and neither will they be admitted to Our Court, or be tolerated at public assemblies and ceremonies.

PSZ, 1st series, vol.15 (1758–62), pp. 912–15 (no.11444, 18 February 1762) (extracts).

DOCUMENT 2   **PETER III'S DECREE ON THE SECULARIZATION OF THE ESTATES AND PEASANTS OF THE RUSSIAN ORTHODOX CHURCH, 21 MARCH 1762**

This decree brought the considerable landed wealth of the Russian Ortho-dox Church under direct state control. The peasants on former church lands were thus converted from the equivalent of serfs of the church to state peasants. The reform had been prepared by Empress Elizabeth in the 1750s, and was revised by Catherine the Great in 1764.

Our Dear Aunt ... Empress Elizabeth, who is now asleep with God, combining piety with the good of the fatherland, and wisely differentiating between abuses which have begun to occur [on church estates], the prejudices of sincere dogmatists of the faith, and the true foundations of our Eastern Orthodox Church, chose to free the monks ... from worldly and temporal cares. And as a consequence of this, she deigned [in 1757] to ratify a statute concerning the management of bishops' and monasteries' estates [which is] useful for the whole state. ... We have commanded that this statute ... be implemented with immediate effect. ...

1. For the management of all estates ascribed to the Synod, Bishops, monasteries, cathedrals, churches and hermitages a College of the Economy has been established under a department of Our Senate in Moscow, and an Office of this College [has been established] in St Petersburg with the appropriate instructions from Our Senate. And it has been commanded ... to appoint a Staff Officer in every province ... to manage and supervise

[these estates] and to protect the peasants from any maltreatment ...

2. Henceforward, in addition to the ... poll tax, and in place of all previous dues extracted from them by Bishops' houses, monasteries, cathedrals, churches and hermitages, all peasants ... will be obliged to pay a single levy of one rouble per head according to the number of males recorded in the latest revision [of the poll tax census] ... [This was the same as the levy paid by court and state peasants.] And for [the payment of this levy] the arable land which they plough ... is given to the [former church] peasants. ...

PSZ, 1st series, vol.15 (1758–62), pp. 948–53 (no.11481, 21 March 1762) (extracts).

DOCUMENT 3 PUGACHEV/PETER III'S 'DECREE' ABOLISHING SERFDOM, 31 JULY 1774

The rebel leader Emelyan Pugachev issued this fake 'decree', in the name of Peter III in the Mid-Volga region.

By God's grace, We, Peter III, Emperor and Autocrat of All the Russias, etc., etc., etc.

It is declared for the information of all the people.

By this personal decree with our monarchical and paternal mercy, We grant to all who formerly belonged to the peasantry, in subjection to the estate owners, the status of faithful subjects of our own crown, and We reward them with the ancient cross and prayers, heads and beards, with freedom and liberty and eternal cossackdom, without demanding recruit levies, the poll tax and other monetary dues, and with possession of the land, with forests, hayfields, fisheries and salt lakes, without payment or dues ... and we free all of them from all the taxes and oppressions formerly imposed on the peasants ... by the nobles and the bribe-taking judges. ... And we wish you the salvation of your souls and a peaceful life on earth, for which we endured from the aforementioned villainous nobles a wandering exile and no little distress.

And as now Our name flourishes in Russia by the power of the almighty hand, then We command ... those who formerly were nobles on their hereditary and service estates, those opponents of our power and disturbers of the Empire and destroyers of the peasantry [are to be] caught, punished and hanged, and treated in the same way as they, having no Christianity in them, treated you, peasants. On the extermination of [these] opponents and villainous nobles, everyone can enjoy a quiet and peaceful life, which will last forever.

Perrie, M. (2000) '"They Would Probably be Spared": The Fate of "Good" Nobles in the Pugachev Revolt', in Reid, E. (ed.), *Edinburgh Essays on Russia: Celebrating 50 Years of Russian Studies*. Nottingham: Astra Press, p. 55 [with minor alterations].

DOCUMENT 4   ALEXANDER RADISHCHEV, *A JOURNEY FROM ST PETERSBURG TO MOSCOW*, 1790

Alexander Radishchev (1749–1802), a radical nobleman whose family owned serfs, published a book under the guise of a traveller's account in which he attacked serfdom ('slavery') from which this extract is taken.

But nothing is more harmful than to see forever before one the partners in slavery, master and slave. On the one side there is born conceit, on the other, servile fear. There can be no bond between them other than force. And this ... extends its oppressive autocratic power everywhere. But the champions of slavery, who, though they hold the sharp edge of power in their hands, are themselves cast into fetters, become its most fanatical preachers. It appears that the spirit of freedom is so dried up in the slaves that they not only have no desire to end their sufferings, but cannot bear to see others free. They love their fetters, if it is possible for a man to love his own ruination. I think I can see in them the serpent that wrought the fall of the first man. The examples of arbitrary power are infectious. We must confess that we ourselves, armed with the mace of courage and the law of nature for the crushing of the hundred-headed monster that gulps down the food prepared for the people's general sustenance – we ourselves, perhaps, have been misled into autocratic acts, and, although our intentions have always been good and have aimed at general happiness, yet our arbitrary behaviour cannot be justified by its usefulness. Therefore we now implore your forgiveness for our unintentional presumption.

Do you not know, dear fellow citizens, what destruction threatens us and in what peril we stand? All the hardened feelings of the slaves, not given vent by kindly gesture of freedom, strengthen and intensify their inner longings. A stream that is barred in its course becomes more powerful in proportion to the opposition it meets. Once it has burst the dam, nothing can stem its flood. Such are our brothers whom we keep enchained. They are waiting for a favourable chance and time. The alarm bell rings. And the destructive force of bestiality breaks loose with terrifying speed. Round about us we shall see sword and poison. Death and fiery desolation will be the meed [*sic*] for our harshness and inhumanity. And the more procrastinating and stubborn we have been about the loosening of their fetters, the more violent they will be in their vengefulness. Bring back to your memory the events of former times. Recall how deception roused the slaves to destroy their masters. Enticed by a crude pretender [Pugachev], they hastened to follow him, and wished only to free themselves from the yoke of their masters; and in their ignorance they could think of no other means to do this than to kill their masters. They spared neither sex nor age. They sought more the joy of vengeance than the benefit of broken shackles.

This is what awaits us, this is what we must expect. ... Beware!

Radishchev, A. N. (1790/1966) *A Journey from St. Petersburg to Moscow*. Ed. R. P. Thaler, trans. L. Wiener. Cambridge, MA: Harvard University Press, pp. 152–3.

DOCUMENT 5   **PAUL'S PROCLAMATION ON SERFS' LABOUR SERVICES, 5 APRIL 1797**

Paul issued this proclamation on the day of his coronation.

We announce to all our loyal subjects: The Law of God ... in the Ten Commandments teaches us to dedicate the seventh day to Him. For this reason, We decided to receive the sacred consecration and coronation on Our Dynastic Throne on the day when the Christian Faith is celebrated. We consider it Our duty before the Creator ... to insist on the strict and absolute adherence to this law throughout Our empire. I order each and everyone to observe that no one, under no circumstances, is to dare to force peasants to work on Sundays. Six days a week are left for rural labours. They should be divided equally between the peasants for themselves and for the work which is due to estate owners. With good order, this will be sufficient to satisfy all economic needs.

PSZ, 1st series, vol.24 (1796–98), p. 587 (no.17909, 5 April 1797).

DOCUMENT 6   **ALEXANDER I'S DECREE ON FREE AGRICULTURALISTS, 20 FEBRUARY 1803**

Alexander I issued this decree after Count Sergei Rumyantsev sought permission to free some of his serfs and sell them land.

Finding that, on the one hand, existing laws [of 1775 and 1801] permit freeing peasants and ownership of land as property by freed [peasants]; and, on the other, that in many cases, confirmation of such landownership may be advantageous to estate owners and be conducive to the improvement of agriculture and other branches of the State economy, We consider it just and useful, both for Count Rumyantsev and for all estate owners who wish to follow his example, to permit the following...:

1. If any estate owner wishes to free his ... serfs, individually or in whole settlements, and, at the same time, grant them an allotment of land...; then, after reaching mutually acceptable agreements with them, he must present these in a petition through the Provincial Marshal of the Nobility to the Minister of Internal Affairs for examination and Our approval. ...

2. Such agreements, made by an estate owner and his serfs and registered

in the deeds, are sacred and inviolable. After the estate owner's death, his legitimate heir, or heirs, are bound by all rights and obligations in these agreements.

3. In case of a breach by one or other party of these conditions, then the Offices for complaints will investigate and proceed on the basis of general legislation on contracts and deeds, with the following observation: if a peasant or a whole settlement does not fulfil its obligations, then the families together with the land will be returned to the estate owner to be under his ownership as before.

4. Peasants and settlements freed with land by estate owners according to such agreements, if they do not wish to transfer to other social estates [e.g., townspeople], then they may remain on their own land as agriculturalists and will become a special category of free agriculturalists [part of the state peasantry]. ...

6. Peasants who have been freed by estate owners and who own land as property are liable to the poll tax on the same basis as serfs, to fulfil the recruiting obligation in kind [i.e., by supplying men]; and while fulfilling local obligations on the same basis as other state peasants, are not liable to pay dues [*obrok*] to the treasury. ...

8. Once they have fulfilled the agreements [i.e., paid off the sum agreed with the estate owner for the land], these peasants acquire the land as property. They will have the right to sell, mortgage, and bequeath it to their heirs, [as long as they do not] divide it into allotments of less than eight *desyatiny* [about 22 acres]. Likewise, they have the right to buy more land, and to move from one province to another. [These changes must be made] with the full knowledge of the [provincial] Chambers of the Treasury in order to transfer [peasants'] tax and recruiting liabilities. ...

PSZ, 1st series, vol.27, pp. 462–3 (no.20620, 20 February 1803) (extracts).

DOCUMENT 7   DECEMBRISTS' PLANS TO ABOLISH SERFDOM, 1823–25

The Decembrists were radical army officers, and a few civilians, who formed secret societies after the end of the Napoleonic Wars in 1815. They staged abortive revolts in St Petersburg in December 1825 and near Kiev in January 1826. Among the leaders were Paul Pestel and Nikita Muraviev, who drew up detailed plans for reform, including the abolition of serfdom.

(a) *Extract from Paul Pestel's 'The Russian Law', 1823–25*
6. The Nobility
To own other men in property, to sell, pawn, give away, inherit men like things, to use them according to one's own caprice without their prior

consent and exclusively for one's own profit, advantage, and at times whim, is shameful, contrary to humanity, contrary to the laws of nature, contrary to the Holy Christian faith, contrary, at last, to the will of the Almighty Who had declared in the Scriptures that all men are equal in His eyes and that only their deeds and virtues make for the differences between them. And for this reason there can no longer be in Russia the right for one man to possess and call another his serf. Slavery must be definitively abolished and the nobility must forever, without fail, renounce the vile privilege of owning other men. ... Destruction of slavery and serfdom is enjoined to the Provisional Supreme Administration [the ruling body the Decembrists hoped to establish in Russia] as its most sacred and unfailing command in the shortest time, by the most energetic and effective measures, it will be called [to account] before the throne of the Almighty and to eternal shame.

(b) Extracts from Nikita Muraviev's Draft Constitution, 1824
10. All Russians are equal before the law. ...
13. Serfdom and slavery are abolished. The slave who touches Russian soil becomes free. No distinction is recognized between commoner and nobleman, for it is against our faith, according to which all men are *brothers.* ...
23. The right to property, pertaining only to *things* [i.e., not people] is sacred and intangible.
24. The estate owners' lands remain their possession. The peasants' houses, gardens, all their agricultural implements, and livestock are recognized to be the property of the peasants.

Raeff, M. (ed.) (1966) *The Decembrist Movement.* Englewood Cliffs, NJ: Prentice-Hall Inc.,
pp. 150–1, 105, 106.

DOCUMENT 8	THE ANNUAL REPORT OF THE CHIEF OF THIRD SECTION (THE SECRET POLICE) TO NICHOLAS I FOR 1839

The Chief's annual reports included sections on the mood of the peasantry and rural disturbances, and sometimes also offered advice on policy.

With every new reign and with every major event in the court or in the affairs of the state ... news spreads around the common people of an impending change in the internal administration, and the idea of freedom for the peasants is aroused; as a consequence of this, disorders, murmurs and dissatisfaction occur, and [in fact] took place last year. [Such events] pose a danger that, although distant, is terrible. Thus, on the occasion of the wedding of the Grand Duchess Maria Nikolaevna [Nicholas I's daughter], news has spread that the peasants will be freed. The rumours are always the same: the tsar wants it [freedom for the peasants], but the boyars are resisting. This is a dangerous matter, and to conceal this danger would be a crime. The simple people now are not as they were 25 years ago. Clerks, thousands of petty officials, merchants and retired soldiers, who have a common interest with the people, have spread many new ideas to them, and have blown a spark into their heart which may one day flare up.

The people constantly talk about how all the non-Russians in Russia ... are free, but only the Russians, the Orthodox, are unfree, in spite of the Holy Scripture. That the cause of this whole evil is the masters, i.e., the nobles! On them is heaped the whole misfortune! That the masters deceive the tsar and slander the Orthodox people in his presence etc. They even bring in texts from the Holy Scripture and prophesies based on interpretations of the Bible that foreshadow the emancipation of the peasants, [and] vengeance on the boyars, whom they compare with Aman and Pharaoh. In general, the whole spirit of the people is directed towards one aim, towards freedom, and meanwhile, in all parts of Russia, there are idle people, who stir up this idea, and in recent years the persecution of the Old Believers has turned them against the government so that their retreats have become centres of this evil. ... In general serfdom is a powder keg beneath the state, and it is all the more dangerous because the army is made up of these same peasants, and that now a large mass of landless nobles has emerged from officials who are inflamed with ambition and, having nothing to lose, welcome any disorder. The reforms of the appanage peasants [peasants on the estates of members of the imperial family] and the protection that has been granted them have had the effect of arousing even greater loathing for serfdom. In this regard, soldiers released on indefinite leave draw attention to themselves. The best of them remain in the capital cities and towns, while men who are lazy or of bad behaviour have dispersed around the villages. Having lost the habit of peasant labour, without any property, [and] alien to their home villages, they provoke hatred against the landowners with their tales of Poland, the Baltic provinces and, in general, could have a harmful influence on the mind of the people. The best of the soldiers on indefinite leave will not be able to counteract this harmful influence, because opinions which stir up passions are readily accepted.

The opinion of sensible people is that, without announcing freedom for the peasants, which could lead to disorders by its suddenness, it would be possible to start to act in this spirit. Now the serfs are not even considered members of the state, and do not even swear allegiance to the sovereign. They stand outside the law, for the landowner can banish them to Siberia without trial. It would be possible to start by ratifying by law all the arrangements that already exist on well organised estates. This would not be anything new. Thus, for example, it would be possible to establish township administrations, selection of recruits by lot or by a general court of township elders, and not according to the whim of landowners. It would be possible to determine measures of punishment for faults and subject serfs to the protection of general laws; and most importantly of all, to divide Russia into zones, according to the quality of the soil, the climate and the state of industry... and then set the number of working days for the master according to the land occupied by the peasants, and set dues in the same way.

It is necessary to start some time and with something, and it is better to start gradually, carefully, than to wait until it starts from below, from the people. A measure [of reform] will be successful only if it is undertaken by the government itself, quietly, without noise, without loud words, and if a prudent gradual approach is followed. But, that it is necessary and that the peasantry is a powder keg, is agreed by all.

Morokhovets, E. A. (ed.) (1931) *Krest'yanskoe dvizhenie 1827–1869* (2 vols). Moscow and Leningrad, vol.1, pp. 31–2 (extracts).

DOCUMENT 9   **SECRET MEMORANDUM BY ANDREI ZABLOTSKII-DESYATOVSKII 'ON THE SERF CATEGORY IN RUSSIA' TO THE MINISTER OF STATE DOMAINS, COUNT PAUL KISELEV, 1841**

Zablotskii-Desyatovskii (assistant minister in the Ministry of State Domains which administered the state peasants) wrote this memorandum after a tour of noble estates in central Russia on the orders of Kiselev.

[Following a survey of relations between noble estate owners and the peasants on their land, Zablotskii-Desyatovskii concluded 'serf labour is less productive than freely-hired' labour]. This conviction is shared by the peasants, who have created a saying about a lazy labourer: 'you are working as if for the estate owner', and by the estate owners themselves. 'There is no doubt', Titov, the marshal of the nobility of Zaraisk [district, Ryazan province] told us, 'that free labour is better. It is wrong to think that our peasant, once free, will become even lazier. It is not true! A free person knows that without work there will be nothing to eat, and that is why he will work diligently. Here is my own experience: 20 *versty* [about 12 miles] from my Zimenki (the estate we were visiting) I own unsettled land, which is cultivated by my own peasants, but not as labour services, but for hire on the basis of voluntary agreement. The same peasants who idle while working labour services, are uncommonly diligent there, [they are] prepared to work on a holiday, as long as they are not driven to, and they take care of the place so [well], that they are even afraid to anger the elder.'

Zablotskii-Desyatovskii, A. P. (1882) *Graf P. D. Kiselev i ego vremya* (4 vols) Spb, vol.4, p. 327 (extracts).

*Nicholas I made the speech from which this extract is taken to the State
Council when he introduced the decree on 'obligated peasants' [see Doc. 11].*

Before attending to the matter for which we have assembled [the decree on
'obligated peasants'], I consider it necessary to acquaint the Council with
my views on this subject and with the motives by which I have been guided.
There is no doubt that serfdom in its present condition in our country is an
evil, apparent and obvious to everyone, but to touch it *now* would be even
more harmful. The late Emperor Alexander [I] at the start of his reign
intended to grant freedom to the serfs, but then gave up his idea as utterly
premature and impossible to implement. I have also resolved never to do it,
considering that if the time when it will be possible to undertake such a
measure is still very far off, then at the *present* time any thoughts about this
would be nothing other than a criminal encroachment on public tranquillity
and the good of the state. The Pugachev riot showed how far mob violence
can go. The most recent events and endeavours of this sort have until now
always been happily brought to a halt, which, of course, in future will also
be a special and, with God's help, successful concern of the government.
However, it is impossible to conceal from ourselves that now ideas are not
as they were before, and that it is clear to any sensible observer that the
present state of affairs cannot continue forever. The reasons for this change
in ideas and troubles which are occurring more frequently at the present
time I cannot but attribute to two reasons above all: *first*, to the careless-
ness of landowners themselves, who give their serfs higher education, which
is incompatible with their status and, as a result, they develop a new range
of ideas which make their position even more burdensome; *second*, to the
fact that some landowners, although thank God a very small number, forget
their noble duty and abuse their power, and marshals of the nobility, as
many of them have reported, cannot find the means to prosecute such
abuses in the law, which does almost nothing to limit seigniorial power.
However, if the present situation is such that it cannot continue, and if, at
the same time, decisive methods to end it are also impossible without
general upheavals, then it is necessary at least to prepare the way for
gradual transition to a different order and, without being frightened by any
change, to discuss calmly the [likely] benefits and consequences. Freedom
must not be given, but a way must be cleared for a transitional status,
which will include the inviolable preservation of patrimonial property in
land. I consider this my sacred obligation and an obligation to those who
will come after me, and the means, in my opinion, are fully presented in the
draft decree now laid before the Council. First, it is not a *new* decree, but

only a sequel and, so to speak, development of the law on free agriculturalists which has existed for forty years [*Doc. 6*]; second, it removes, however, the harmful principle of that law – the alienation of estate owners' landed property, which, on the contrary, all desire to see for ever as the inviolable [property] of the nobility – an idea from which I will never deviate; third, it expresses directly the ... conviction of the government that land is the property not of the peasants who are settled on it, but the estate owners – a subject of paramount importance for future calm; finally, fourth, without any great upheavals, without even any appearance of innovation, it gives every loyal estate owner the means to improve the position of his peasants and, without placing on anyone the obligation of compulsion, or infringing in any way the right of property, it leaves everything to the good will of each and to the inclination of his heart. On the other hand, the draft [decree] leaves the peasants bound to the land on which they are registered, and in this way avoids the inconveniences of the statutes which are in force until now in the Baltic provinces – statutes, which led peasants to a very pitiful condition, converted them to landless labourers and prompted the local nobility to request precisely what is now proposed here. Meanwhile, I repeat that everything must proceed gradually and cannot and must not be done suddenly and at once. The draft contains some main principles and first instructions. It reveals to everyone, as I have already said, the means to follow, under the protection and with the aid of the law, the inclination of one's heart. In protection of the interests of the estate owners is placed their good will and own solicitude, and the interests of the peasants will be protected every time by the examination of the agreements [between estate owners and peasants], not only by the local authorities, but also by the central government, with the approval of the autocratic power. It is impossible to go further now and in future to embrace the rest, [which] could become a very wide and separate development of these main principles. ...

Gershenzon, M. O. (ed.) (1910) *Epokha Nikolaya I*. Moscow, pp. 61–3.

DOCUMENT 11   **NICHOLAS I'S DECREE ON OBLIGATED PEASANTS, 2 APRIL 1842**

This decree allowed estate owners to conclude agreements with their serfs assigning them the use of plots of land in return for fixed obligations. These 'obligated peasants', like the 'free agriculturalists' [see Doc. 6] would become part of the state peasantry.

In [the decree of 20 February 1803] ... estate owners were permitted to convert their peasants to free agriculturalists, with the concession to them of seigniorial land in return for compensation determined by mutual agreement. Desiring, in the general view of state benefit, that with the conclusion of such agreements, the land belonging to the estate owners, as the patrimonial property of the nobility, be preserved from alienation from noble ownership, We acknowledge the right to elucidate the [decree of 1803] ... to allow those estate owners who wish to conclude agreements ... with their peasants ... on such a basis that ... estate owners retain the right ... of full patrimonial ownership of the land..., but the peasants [shall] receive from them plots of land for use in return for fixed obligations. In compiling such agreements, estate owners can exact further conditions from the peasants, by mutual agreement with them, on the following rules, which were examined by the State Council and ratified by Us:

1. The peasants' obligations for the estate owners can be determined in agreements by money dues, produce, cultivation of seigniorial land, or other work.

2. In case the peasants do not fulfil the obligations they accepted in the agreement, they are to be compelled to by the local police, under the leadership of the district marshal of the nobility and ... the provincial administration.

3. Peasants, according to proper approval of the agreements concluded between them and the estate owners take the name of obligated peasants.

4. The recruiting obligation in villages of obligated peasants is performed according to the usual order. ...

5. Reserves [of grain in the event of bad harvests] and aid in case of fire are [to be] established at the expense of the obligated peasants..., under the supervision of the estate owners, if the estate owner does not wish to take these obligations onto himself. ...

6. Estate owners are to set up in villages of obligated peasants an estate office and ... [are to] supervise the village police, the implementation of laws on village services and amenities, [and] ... the dispensation of justice in cases of misdemeanours ... by the obligated peasants ... and disagreements between them. ...

7. [Estate owners] concluding agreements with peasants on estates mortgaged to credit institutions ... must have the agreement of those institutions. Estates of obligated peasants can ... be mortgaged anew to credit institutions, in proportion to the permanent income, determined by the area and quality of the land and the methods of cultivating it. ...

8. Estate owners and obligated peasants [shall] keep the agreements concluded between them as inviolable for ever, having, however, the right under special particular conditions to make changes in the allotment of land and obligations for a fixed time with mutual agreement, and if the estate is mortgaged, then with the agreement of the credit institution, in all cases not otherwise than with the preliminary agreement of the government.

9. Agreements which are concluded on this basis by the personal desire of estate owners ... are to be presented ... for OUR examination and ratification.

PSZ, 2nd series, vol.17, pp. 261–2 (no.15462, 2 April 1842).

DOCUMENT 12   ALEXANDER KOSHELEV'S ARTICLE 'VOLUNTARISM IS BETTER THAN COMPULSION', 1 NOVEMBER 1847

The article, whose author was a slavophile noble, was published in the journal 'Agricultural Gazette'. The editor, Andrei Zablotskii-Desyatovskii, shared the sentiments expressed [see Doc. 9].

We often repeat this proverb ['voluntarism is better than compulsion'], but rarely ... do we think about its real meaning. ...

Take a look at labour obligations. The peasant arrives as late as possible, looks around and about as often and as far as possible, and works as little as possible – the work isn't his business, but a day to kill. For the lord he works three days and for himself also three days [a week]. On his own days he works more land, manages to do all his household work, and still has a lot of free time. [Peasants'] work for the lord ... drives the zealous supervisor to despair or anger. You punish [the peasants], not because you want to, but ... because [it is] the only possible way to make progress with the work. Now compare this with work by [gangs of hired labourers]. Here everything goes without a hitch, ... they work for less time than a peasant performing labour obligations, they rest more ..., but they get two or three times more work done. Why? Voluntarism is better than compulsion. ...

In our houses we have many servants, but few helpers. ... In other countries, even in St Petersburg in the houses of foreign merchants, [there is only] one servant, nevertheless everything is clean [and] put away; he alone serves fifteen, twenty people at table. ... Why? Because he receives good pay, i.e. that which would be deserved by two or three of our unfree servants. Because if he does not carry out all his master's demands, [and] anticipate his wishes, then he will be dismissed, and a more zealous servant taken on. ... One man does the work of three. Why? Voluntarism is better than compulsion. ...

We often hear complaints about the drunkenness of the Russian people. And how, dear readers, can they not be drunkards! What is the main effect of drunkenness? That when drunk everything seems more attractive. As the liquor warms a man up, he feels that everything around him becomes transformed ... and he enters another sort of world. He forgets his woes, becomes bolder, lives another sort of life, takes the attitude that the devil may care, as the saying goes. How can we blame our serfs if, from time to time, they want to taste another life. Drunkenness is a necessary consolation in their position, and woe unto us when they ... stop drinking.

Only habit, only eastern ... laziness prevents us from freeing ourselves of our serfs. Almost all of us are convinced of the superiority of free labour over labour obligations, free labour over forced, but we stick with the worse while knowing better. ...

Koshelev, A. I. (1884) Zapiski. Berlin: B. Behr's Verlag, appendices, pp. 11–14.

DOCUMENT 13   NICHOLAS I'S 'AUCTIONS DECREE', 8 NOVEMBER 1847

This decree granted serfs of estates sold at public auction for debts the right to buy the estates and their freedom. It proved very controversial as it allowed serfs to buy their land and freedom without the permission of the estate owners. It was effectively repealed in 1849.

1. When a populated estate on which debts are secured to the treasury, private [individuals] or credit institutions is designated for public sale, then the peasants who belong to such an estate are to be granted the right to buy themselves [i.e., their freedom], together with the land..., by paying the highest bid at the auction or, in the event that there are no buyers, the full valuation. But, in the latter case, if the valuation is less than the sum of the debt secured on the estate..., then the peasants are obliged to take it upon themselves to guarantee payment of the debt in full.

2. Purchase under the aforementioned conditions is allowed only of the whole estate ... or, if it is sold in parts, of each part in its entirety, jointly by all the peasants of that estate or part thereof.

3. For the purchase to take place, ... at the end of the auction or, in the event that there are no buyers, at the end of the term [laid down for the submission of bids], the local Provincial Administrative Board must be informed of the purchase price..., and the ... Board ... is to inform the peasants of the purchase price via the local police, who are to get the peasants to sign a document confirming the date of the announcement. All the actions of the police, in announcing the purchase price to the peasants, getting their response, and the payment of the designated sum, must be held in the presence and under the supervision of the Marshal of the Nobility and the District Attorney.

4. The peasants are obliged to pay the purchase price in full, without expecting any assistance from the treasury, within 30 days of the announcement of the price to them, to the Provincial Administrative Board. ...

5. If the peasants turn down the right of purchase or, having expressed the

wish to pay the purchase price, do not pay it within the time allowed, then the estate is sold to the highest bidder at the auction. ...

6. After paying the purchase price, the peasants are to be given the deeds, but do not have to pay the stamp duty.

7. Peasants who purchase [redeem] themselves are to be admitted to the state peasantry, and are to acquire the right of ownership of the land and all other property belonging to the estate which they have purchased. But, peasants who have acquired land in this manner have the right to transfer [it] to others, by means of sale, exchange or other transactions, only on the decision of the village commune and with the authorization of the Ministry of State Domains. The peasants must retain, for every revision soul [male peasant], a total of two *desyatiny* [5.4 acres] of homestead, garden, arable and meadow land. The peasants must not secure any debts on this area of land.

8. Peasants who have become state peasants in this manner are liable to all state peasants' taxes and obligations, besides dues [*obrok*], for which reason they are to be designated non-*obrok* [state peasants].

PSZ, 2nd series, vol.22, pp. 841–2 (no.21689, 8 November 1847).

DOCUMENT 14   **ALEXANDER II'S SPEECH TO THE MARSHALS OF THE NOBILITY OF MOSCOW PROVINCE, 30 MARCH 1856**

This speech is often seen as signalling the start of the process that led to the Statutes abolishing serfdom in 1861. The speech circulated in two versions. The first contained the words the tsar actually said, which were written down at the time by some of the marshals. The second was corrected afterwards (presumably by the tsar or his aides).

Version 1.

There are rumours that I want to announce ... the emancipation of the serfs. This is unjust, and as a result there have been a few cases of insubordination by peasants to estate owners. You may say that to everyone, to the right and to the left. I said the same thing to the marshals [of the nobility] who came to me in [St] Petersburg. I will not say to you that I am completely against [emancipation]; we live in such an age that it must come about in time. I think that you are of the same opinion as I am: therefore it is much better that this happens from above than from below.

Version 2.

I have heard that rumours have spread among you of My intention to abolish serfdom. To deny such unfounded talk about such an important subject, I consider it necessary to announce to all of you that I do not intend to do so now, but of course, and you yourselves understand, that the present order of owning souls [i.e., serfs] cannot remain unchanged. It is better to start to abolish serfdom from above, than to wait for that time when it starts to abolish itself from below. I ask you to think about the best way to carry this out. Pass My words to the nobles for consideration.

Version 1: 'Dostopamyatnye minuty v moei zhizni. Zapiska Alekseya Iraklievicha Levshina', *Russkii arkhiv*, 1885, book 8, pp. 475–6. Version 2: 'Zapiski Senatora Ya. A. Solov'eva o krest'yanskom dele', *Russkaya starina*, vol.30 (1881), pp. 228–9.

DOCUMENT 15   ALEXANDER II'S RESCRIPT TO GOVERNOR-GENERAL V. I. NAZIMOV OF VILNO, GRODNO AND KOVNO (LITHUANIA), 20 NOVEMBER 1857

This document laid down guidelines for the nobility of the Lithuanian provinces, who were charged with drawing up proposals for reform. It formed the basis for the government's first programme for reform throughout the empire.

In the provinces of Kovno, Vilno and Grodno, special committees of the marshals of the nobility and other estate owners were founded to examine the inventory regulations that exist there. Now, the Minister of Internal Affairs has informed me of the good intentions expressed by these committees concerning the seigniorial peasants of these three provinces. Fully approving the intentions of these representatives of the nobility of [these] provinces, which conform to my views and wishes, I authorise the noble estate ... to proceed to compile draft [statutes], according to which the committees' intentions may be implemented, but not otherwise than gradually, in order not to violate the existing economic organisation of seigniorial estates. For this I command:

1. A preparatory committee is to be inaugurated in each of the provinces of Kovno, Vilno and Grodno, and then one general commission for all three provinces in the city of Vilno.

2. Each provincial committee, under the chairmanship of the provincial marshal of the nobility, is to consist of the following members:

(a) one from every district in the province, elected from their numbers by nobles who own populated estates in the district, and

(b) two experienced estate owners ... appointed directly by the governor.

3. The general commission is to consist of the following people:

(a) two members chosen by each provincial committee;

(b) one experienced estate owner from each province appointed by you [Nazimov]; and

(c) one member from the Ministry of Internal Affairs. The chairman of the commission is to be appointed by you from one of its members who belongs to the local nobility.

The provincial committees ... must proceed to the compilation of detailed draft [statutes] for each province, in conformance with the views of nobles' representatives, concerning the organisation and improvement of the way of life of the seigniorial peasants, while bearing in mind ... the following main principles:

1. Estate owners are to retain the right of ownership of all the land, but the peasants are to keep their household plots, which they are to acquire as their own property by means of redemption over a definite period; moreover, the peasants are to be granted the use of a quantity of [arable] land, according to local conditions, [adequate] to guarantee their way of life and to meet their obligations to the government and the estate owner, in return for [this land] they are either to pay dues or perform labour for the estate owner.

2. The peasants must be assigned to village societies, while the estate owners are granted [the powers of] manorial police, and

3. The future organisation of relations between estate owners and peasants must guarantee full and correct payment of state and local taxes and monetary dues.

The provincial committees are to develop these principles and apply them to local conditions in each of the three ... provinces. The Minister of Internal Affairs will inform you of his thoughts, which can serve as a guide for the committees in their work.

When they have completed their work the committees must report to the general commission. The commission is to discuss and examine all the proposals of the provincial committees and adapt them to the principles set forth above. [The commission] must [then] reach a final conclusion on this whole matter and draw up a general draft statute for all three provinces. ...

While charging you with overall supervision and direction of this important matter ... I authorise you to give the necessary instructions, both to the three provincial committees and the general commission, for the successful execution and completion of the work entrusted to them. The provincial governors must assist you in carrying out this duty. You are to forward the draft [statute] drawn up by the general commission, with your opinion, to the Minister of Internal Affairs for presentation to me for my consideration.

Thus creating the means for the noble estates of Kovno, Grodno and Vilno provinces to bring their good intentions to fruition on the basis of the principles I have laid down, I hope that the nobility will fully justify the faith I have placed on [them] ... by calling on [them] to participate in this important matter, and that with God's help and the enlightened assistance of the nobility, this matter will be concluded with fitting success.

You and the governors of the provinces ... are obliged to strictly observe that the peasants, while remaining in complete obedience to their estate owners, do not listen to any ill-intentioned suggestions or false rumours. ...

Fedorov, V. A. (ed.) (1994) *Konets Krepostnichestva v Rossii: Dokumenty, pis'ma, memuary, stat'i.* Moscow: Izdatel'stvo Moskovskogo Universiteta, pp. 85–7.

DOCUMENT 16   ROSTOVTSEV'S PROPOSED PROGRAMME FOR REFORM, 5 MARCH 1859

This document, which Rostovstov presented to the Editing Commisions, expanded on the government's second programme for reform that had been adopted in December 1858.

1. The problem ... of abolishing serfdom and ameliorating the condition of the peasants must be settled ... impartiality ... for both [estate owners and peasants], and in order to avert the emergence of any reasons for ... antagonism between [them] ...; in other words, in such a manner that Russia may attain ... insurance in the long term against disorders. ...
2. In addition to individual freedom, the peasants must have the chance to obtain sufficient land as property for their subsistence, for otherwise [their] lives would improve only in word and not in reality.
3. Homesteads alone [i.e., without arable land], especially in agricultural [regions]..., would not give [such a] provision.
4. Separate redemption of homesteads is only a half measure, which will not achieve its aim, and is dangerous. ...
5. Obligatory relations [between peasants and estate owners], especially labour services, are also serfdom, except that it is clothed in legal forms and therefore, for the peasant, all the more unbearable and inconsistent with the good intentions of the Sovereign to abolish serfdom and ameliorate the condition of the peasants.
6. Obligatory relations have entered the government's programme only as an inevitable transitional measure, but if our [Editing] Commissions succeed in their project to curtail it or even leave it out altogether, then in this way the amelioration in [the peasants'] condition would be consolidated in the transitional period as well.
7. The landed property which the peasants will be permitted to redeem should contain a homestead and enough land in a plot separate from the rest of the estate owner's land.
8. Estate owners must be compensated for the land they cede [to the peasants] fairly and, in so far as possible, without [leading to] loss and destitution.
9. The peasants' annual payments, both the interest and repayment of the capital [the redemption sum], must not be more than the average level of

their current obligations, otherwise there will be no amelioration in their condition.

10. The earlier the process of redeeming the land occurs, or at least starts, the more beneficial it will be (a) to the peasant, because land prices in Russia are continually rising, and (b) to the estate owner, because he needs money for the economic reforms that will follow without fail from the [reform] ...

11. Therefore, to speed up the process of redeeming the land and to balance the interests of estate owners and peasants, which may come into conflict, the government must ... act as a mediator, extending credit, providing guarantees, or organising monetary arrangements.

12. The issue of whether the peasants are to own the land they redeem communally or individually should be left to history, and measures should not be imposed by the government. ...

Semenov, N. P. (1889) *Osvobozhdenie krest'yan v tsarstvovanie Imperatora Aleksandra II: Khronika deyatelnosti komisii po krest'yanskomu delu* (3 vols) Spb, vol.1, pp. 86–9.

DOCUMENT 17 **PETITION FROM THE FIRST GROUP OF DEPUTIES OF THE NOBLES' PROVINCIAL COMMITTEES TO THE TSAR, 26 AUGUST 1859**

After the first group of deputies from the nobles' provincial committees arrived in St Petersburg in the summer of 1859, they were so angered by their reception by the government that they sent this petition to the tsar, who rejected it.

Throughout the immeasurable vastness of Russia, Sire, Your voice resounded calling the nobility to the great work of transformation for which Your reign will be celebrated.

The first born of the Russian land responded with zeal to Your call, and the nobility entrusted the Provincial Committees with the implementation of [its] obligation to compile draft statutes, which would put into practice the principles expressed, Sire, in Your rescripts.

The drafts of the provincial committees could represent only local needs, and You, Sire, understanding with keen insight the disadvantages of such uncoordinated work, enabled it to become smooth and fine by ordering that the committees, at their discretion, elect two deputies each <u>to sit in the Main Committee [on the Peasant Question] and give general consideration to the draft statutes for organising the lives of the peasants</u>. [Alexander II underlined this passage and in the margin wrote 'Never'.]

The necessity, correctness and logical nature of these measures, ordained by the lustrous thoughts of the Tsar, has aroused universal joy; but while the heart of the Tsar and the hearts of the people were uniting for the good of the fatherland, the bureaucracy was sowing seeds of discontent.

Having distorted in the Provincial Committees the deeds of the Tsar and the people, and having distorted for so many years the Tsar's best thoughts and trampled on his most noble feelings, could the bureaucracy tolerate a situation in which the Tsar would hear the voice of his people other than through its own untruthful lips?!

Sire! ... what have they done with Your order, which You solemnly deigned to announce to the nobility, and which was announced to the whole people? The bureaucracy, in order to express how little significance the [Provincial] Committees have in its eyes, have turned away one by one the deputies who were elected by the full complement of the Committees, and have granted, in violation of the most simple understanding of the organisation of consultative assemblies, members from the minority, which has sometimes been divided into two or three opinions, [the opportunity] to appoint their own deputies. ...

The deputies who arrived in St Petersburg were completely ignored. The minister of internal affairs [Lanskoi] did not bother to present them to Your Majesty or even to the Main Committee. Then they were suddenly sent an unsigned invitation to visit the Editing Commissions, and there Adjutant General Rostovtsev issued written instructions ... in which, without any regard for the normal system of announcing imperial commands, Your Majesty's orders were countermanded and the deputies were obliged to answer questions which the Editing Commissions considered necessary. ...

Our sorrow, Sire, cannot be expressed! We have seen several times in the course of the present matter the bureaucracy either counterpose one Imperial command against another or violate them, but their effrontery had never reached this point before.

Throughout the course of this matter the administrative authorities have continually scorned legality and justice; but they did so out in the provinces in the obscurity of office correspondence, whereas now they are doing it in front of the sovereign and Russia, in plain sight of everyone.

The proceedings of the Editing Commissions and all its administrative actions are filled with harmful and ruinous ideas; we can see them but we are powerless to expose them.

Striving from our whole heart to implement Your will, Sire, and to realise the ardent wish of the entire state, that the civil rights of the peasant estate be restored and their welfare consolidated, we not only were abandoned from our first step, but were stricken in the very root of our hopes.

Placed in this position, we have not, however, given ourselves up to despondency: we place all our hopes on Your help, Sire! While committing the culprits of violating Your commands and [their] oath to Your autocracy for Your justice, we most loyally request that You command that Your order, which was solemnly announced to the nobility, be fulfilled.

[The petition ended with a request that the 'Great Sovereign' allow all the deputies of the Provincial Committees to take part in the examination of the committees' drafts at a general meeting of the Main Committee under the chairmanship of the tsar or a member of his family.]

Semenov (1889) *Osvobozhdenie*, vol.1, pp. 615–17. The translation of some paragraphs has been adapted from Vernadsky (1972), vol.3, pp. 593–4.

DOCUMENT 18   **THE DIARY OF THE GRAND DUKE CONSTANTINE NIKOLAEVICH, CHAIRMAN OF THE MAIN COMMITTEE ON THE PEASANT QUESTION, 10 OCTOBER 1860–7 JANUARY 1861**

The entries in the Grand Duke's diary for this period, from which these extracts are taken, are dominated by his accounts of the meetings of the Main Committee, which was reviewing the Editing Commissions' draft statutes, and private discussions with committee members and his brother, Alexander II. The two men suffered a personal tragedy with the death of their mother, the dowager empress Alexandra Fedorovna, on 20 October 1860.

10 October 1860

On the first iron horse [*chugunka*] to the city, to the Marble [palace] ... discussed the peasant question with Chevkin [a member of the Main Committee]. Then I went to the [SS Peter and Paul] fortress and prayed intensely at the grave of Father [Nicholas I] and Adinya [his late sister Alexandra], and from there, having gathered my strength, to the Peasant Committee, which I chaired for the first time. First we read the Imperial Command, then I said a few words, then we read Rostovtsev's testament and started the discussion. We decided at once and irrevocably that we must strive to ensure that the peasants become property [i.e., land] owners. Here [Paul] Gagarin began to propose his idea concerning settling the matter solely by means of amicable arrangements [between nobles and peasants], without any limitations, and [Dmitrii Nikolaevich] Bludov [his idea] about ... compulsory redemption. There were rather heated discussions, and we quickly demonstrated the complete impossibility and unsoundness of these ideas, and they were conclusively rejected. ... [The meeting] finished at 3.30 ... I wrote a long letter about it all to Sasha [Alexander II], and after dining at 6.00 [went] home on the iron horse. We had only just left the city when the locomotive broke down. They had to send [someone] on foot to the city for another, return to the station, change the engine, so that we didn't arrive till 7.45 ...

2 November 1860

... From 1.00 until 6.30 the Peasant Committee. At first successfully, without disagreement. ... Then we began the frightful question of the [peasant's] *allotment*. Here Dolgoruk[ov] and Muraviev conducted frightful balderdash and finished by proposing one standard allotment. However we tried to show them the impossibility of putting this idea into practice, they became obstinate and wouldn't budge. ... The whole session was spent in long, unending arguments on this. This had an awfully melancholy effect on me, because I cannot see how we will get out of it. I was terribly wearisome and was almost unable to dine. ...

3 November 1860

... From 1.00 until almost 6.30 again the Peasant Committee. We discussed the allotment and in general the main principles of this matter. Three new systems are clearly visible: (1) Dolgorukov and Muraviev's system of standard allotments; (2) Gagarin's, the *status quo* for the transitional period, and then voluntary agreements; (3) Panin's, such balderdash, which no one understands. We asked them to lay out their systems in a letter, and then continued [reading the draft statutes] section by section and got quite far. ...

4 November 1860

... From 1.00 until 5.30 again the Peasant Committee. We continued reading section by section, but did not get very far, because we argued about regulating the [size of peasants'] farmsteads. We all agreed with the printed wording, except the scoundrel Muraviev, who wants to reduce them. ...

8 November 1860

... The rest of the day was spent in long, extremely wearisome, but important and interesting discussions about the peasant question, this afternoon with [deputy minister of state domains] Zelenoi (property) and Chevkin, and this evening with Samarin and Panin. These last two discussions were very interesting, and Panin was far from being as stubborn as they say he is. ...

10 November 1860

... Then again the Peasant Committee from 1.00 until 7.00. We argued a frightful amount about the right [of peasants] to leave the community during the period of temporary obligation, and about what would come next. I returned frightfully wearisome. ...

11 November 1860

All morning I felt tired from yesterday and was in a state of nervous agitation in anticipation of today's committee, because discussion of allotments was in prospect. ... The Committee lasted from 1.00 until 6.30. We argued a great deal and heatedly, but the essence of the matter passed. ...

30 November 1860
... From 1.00 until 6 again the Peasant Committee. ... Then we had a discussion about allotments. Muraviev was loathsome as always. Panin is still stubborn, but already making concessions. ...

1 December 1860
... From 1.00 until 5.30 again the Committee. We examined the whole local statute for Lithuania, without big arguments, except, of course, Muraviev, who is always equally vile. ...

7 January 1861
... From 1.00 until 6.30 again the Peasant Committee; I hope that [it is] the last. All examined the final version. Muraviev and Chevkin argued frightfully for a long time about the factory [peasants] and all were sick [of it]. Towards the end [Muraviev] announced that when the journal [of the committee] is signed, he will still give his separate opinion. But we did not allow this. From this a very unpleasant scene resulted. ...

Zakharova, L. G. (compiler) (1994) *1857–1861. Perepiska Imperatora Aleksandra II s Velikim Knyazem Konstantinom Nikolaevichem. Dnevnik Velikogo Knyazya Konstantina Nikolaevicha.* Moscow: TERRA, pp. 272, 278, 279, 282, 296.

DOCUMENT 19   ALEXANDER II'S PROCLAMATION ANNOUNCING
THE ABOLITION OF SERFDOM, 19 FEBRUARY 1861

The Proclamation announcing the abolition of serfdom was written in lofty rhetorical language by Metropolitan Filaret Drozdov of Moscow, a conservative cleric. It was read out in churches around the empire in March and April 1861.

By the Grace of God, WE, Alexander II, Emperor and Autocrat of All the Russias ... etc. announce to all OUR loyal subjects:

Called by Divine Providence and the sacred law of succession to OUR ancestral All-Russian throne..., WE vowed in OUR heart to embrace with OUR tsarist love and solicitude all OUR faithful subjects of every rank and social estate, from those who nobly bear swords in defence of the fatherland to the craftsmen who humbly wield the tools of their trade, from those who serve the state at the highest levels to those who plough the fields.

Investigating the condition of the ranks and social estates which comprise the state, WE saw that state law, while actively promoting the welfare of the higher and middle social estates by defining their obligations, rights and privileges, has not equally favoured the serfs, who ... have been hereditarily bound to the authority of estate owners, who are obliged accordingly to see to their welfare. Hitherto the rights of estate owners were broad and not precisely defined in law, wherefore tradition, custom, and the estate owners' good will prevailed. At best this produced good patriarchal relations of sincere solicitude and benevolence on the part of the estate owners and good-natured submission from the peasants. But owing to the decline of morals, an increase in the variety of relationships [between estate owners and peasants], and a lessening of the estate owners' direct paternal relations with their peasants, and because estate owners' rights sometimes fell into the hands of persons seeking only their own advantage, good relations weakened, and the way was opened to an arbitrariness that has been burdensome for the peasants and not conducive to their welfare, whence they have shown indifference to any improvement in their lives.

Such was perceived by OUR Predecessors..., and they took steps to improve the condition of the peasantry. But these steps were only partly successful, depending as they did on the good will and voluntary action of estate owners and applicable as they were only to certain areas. ... Thus, Emperor ALEXANDER I issued the law on free agriculturalists [1803, see *Doc. 6*], and ... OUR father NICHOLAS I the law on obligated peasants [1842, see *Doc. 10*]. In the western provinces peasants' land allotments and obligations were fixed by the inventory regulations [in 1847–48]. However, the laws on free agriculturalists and obligated peasants have been put into effect on a very small scale.

WE were therefore convinced that the task of improving the condition of the serfs is a legacy to Us from OUR Predecessors, and a destiny conferred upon Us ... by the hand of Providence.

WE began this task with an act of OUR trust in the Russian nobility, knowing of its great proofs of loyalty to the throne and its readiness to make sacrifices for the good of the Fatherland. WE left it to the nobility itself, according to its own wishes, to prepare proposals for a new way of organising the way of life of the peasants, whereupon the nobles offered to limit their rights over peasants and to bear the difficulties of a transformation that would entail losses to themselves. And OUR trust was justified. Through its representatives in the provincial committees, who had the faith of the nobles' societies of every province, the nobility voluntarily renounced any rights to the persons of the serfs. These committees, after collecting the necessary information, drew up proposals for a new way of organising the way of life of the serfs and their relationships with the estate owners. These proposals were quite varied, as could be expected from the nature of the task. They were checked, collated, put in proper form, corrected and supplemented in the Main Committee [responsible] for this matter. Thus, the new Statutes on seigniorial peasants and household serfs were compiled and were examined in the State Council.

Having called on God for assistance, WE resolved to implement this measure.

Pursuant to these new Statutes, the serfs are to receive in due course the full rights of free rural inhabitants.

The estate owners, while retaining their right of ownership of all lands belonging to them, are to grant the peasants, in return for a certain obligation, perpetual use of their homesteads as well as such quantity of field land and other lands according to the Statutes so that they may be secure in their livelihoods and [have the] ability to fulfil their obligations to the government.

In taking advantage of these land allotments, the peasants are thereby required to fulfil the obligations to their estate owners specified in the Statutes. In this condition, which is transitional, the peasants are designated temporarily obligated.

They are also to be given the right to buy their homestead, and with their estate owner's agreement they may acquire ownership of the field land and other lands assigned to their perpetual use. On acquiring ownership of this quantity of land, the peasants are freed from their obligations to the estate owners for the land thus redeemed, and will become free peasant proprietors.

A special statute defines the transitional status of houschold serfs, as appropriate to their occupations and needs. Two years after publication of this Statute they will receive complete freedom and certain temporary privileges.

In accordance with the general principles of the ... Statutes the future organisation of peasants and [former] household serfs is to be defined, a system for administering peasant affairs is to be established, and the rights granted to the peasants and [former] household serfs, as well as their obligations to the government and the estate owners, are to be specified in detail.

Although these Statutes, general, local and special supplementary regulations for certain particular localities, for small estate owners, and for peasants working in seigniorial factories and mills, have been adapted as far as possible to local economic needs and practices, nevertheless, to preserve the customary order, where it is mutually advantageous, WE leave it to the estate owners to reach voluntary understandings with the peasants and to conclude agreements concerning the extent of the peasants' land allotments and corresponding obligations, observing therein the regulations laid down for preserving the inviolability of such agreements.

Since this new arrangement, given the inescapable complexity of the changes required by it, cannot be introduced at once, but needs time ... of not less than two years, then during this period, to avoid confusion and to maintain the public and private good, the order hitherto existing on seigniorial estates should be preserved until, on completion of the necessary preparations, the new order will begin.

For the proper realisation of this, WE ... command:

1. A Provincial Bureau of Peasant Affairs be opened in every province, to which is to be entrusted oversight of the affairs of peasant communes settled on seigniorial lands.

2. Peace Mediators be appointed and district mediators' congresses set up in all districts to resolve misunderstandings and disputes arising in the implementation of the new Statutes.

3. Then set up mediation offices on seigniorial estates, which, while leaving the village communes in their present form, will open township administrations in major settlements and bring small villages under one township administration.

4. A regulatory charter be compiled, verified and ratified for every village commune or estate, in which shall be specified, on the basis of the local Statute, the quantity of land to be granted to the peasants in perpetual use and the extent of the obligations owed by them to the estate owner in return for this land and any other lands granted by him.

5. The terms of these regulatory charters are to be put into effect on each estate when they are ratified, and finally, for all estates within the two years from the day of publication of this Proclamation.

6. Until the end of this period [i.e., two years] the peasants and [former] household serfs are to remain in their former submission to the estate owners, and fulfil without fail their former obligations.

7. Estate owners will continue to keep order on their estates, with judicial and police powers, until the formation of the township administrations and the opening of the township courts.

Considering the inescapable difficulties involved in this transformation, WE place OUR hope above all in the goodness of Divine Providence, which protects Russia.

WE also rely on the valiant zeal for the common good of the nobility, to whom WE cannot fail to express, on behalf of Ourselves and the whole Fatherland, well-deserved recognition of their unselfish realisation of OUR designs. Russia will not forget that, prompted only by respect for human dignity and Christian love of [their] neighbours, they voluntarily renounced serfdom and laid the basis of a new economic future for the peasants. WE assuredly expect that they will nobly exhibit the utmost care in seeing that the new Statutes are implemented in good order, and in a spirit of peace and benevolence; and that every estate owner will see to completion on his own estate [this] great civic act of the entire [nobility], having arranged the affairs of the peasants settled on his land and of his [former] household serfs on terms advantageous to both sides, and he will thus give a good example to the rural population and an incentive to their exact and conscientious fulfilment of state regulations.

Mindful of such examples of the estate owners' generous solicitude for the good of the peasants, and of the peasants' recognition of this, WE are confirmed in OUR hope that mutual voluntary agreements will resolve most of the difficulties that are unavoidable when general regulations are applied to the varying circumstances of individual estates. In this way the transition from the old order to the new will be eased, and mutual trust, good accord, and a unanimous aspiration for the common good will be strengthened in the future.

To facilitate the execution of those agreements between estate owners and peasants by which the latter will acquire ownership of field land as well as their homesteads, the government will render assistance, on the basis of special regulations, by giving out loans or transferring debts encumbering estates.

And WE place OUR hope in the common sense of OUR people.

When word of the Government's plan to abolish serfdom reached peasants who were unprepared for it, partial misunderstandings arose. Some thought about freedom and forgot about obligations. But general common sense was not disturbed in the conviction that, according to natural reason, anyone freely enjoying the benefits of society owes in return to serve the good of society by fulfilling certain obligations, and, according to Christian law, every soul is subject unto the higher powers (Romans 13:1) and renders therefore all their dues, in particular tribute, custom, fear and honour (Romans 13:7); that rights legally acquired by the estate owners cannot be taken from them without a decent recompense, or through their voluntary concession; [and] that it would be contrary to all justice to use estate owners' land without bearing the corresponding obligations.

And now WE with hope expect that the serfs, as a new future opens before them, will understand and accept with gratitude the important sacrifice made by the ... nobility for the improvement of their way of life.

They will understand that, receiving the advantages of ownership and the freedom to conduct their own affairs, they owe it to society and to themselves to realise the beneficence of the new law by a loyal, judicious, and diligent exercise of the rights granted to them. The most beneficent law cannot make people happy if they do not themselves labour to build their happiness under the protection of the law. Prosperity is acquired and increased only by hard work, the judicious use of strength and resources, strict economy, and, overall, by an honest, God-fearing life.

The authorities who prepared the new way of life for the peasants and will manage its implementation must be vigilant that this is done legally, calmly, and in a timely way, so that the peasants are not distracted from their indispensable agricultural labours. May they carefully cultivate the land and gather its fruits, so that from a well-filled granary they may take the seeds for sowing the land [which they now] use in perpetuity or have acquired as property.

Make the sign of the cross, Orthodox people, and invoke with Us God's blessing on thy free labour, the pledge of thine own prosperity and of the public good.

Given at Saint Petersburg in the year of Our Lord one thousand eight hundred and sixty-one, and the seventh of Our Reign.

Fedorov (1994) *Konets*, pp. 211–16.

DOCUMENT 20   THE INTRODUCTION TO THE GENERAL STATUTE ON 'PEASANTS WHO HAVE EMERGED FROM SERVILE DEPENDENCE', 19 FEBRUARY 1861

Following this concise introduction, the rest of the General Statute and the other statutes on the abolition of serfdom greatly expanded on these basic points.

Introduction

1. Serfdom over peasants who are settled on seigniorial estates and household serfs is abolished forever according to the procedure laid down in the present Statute and [those] published with it.

2. ...peasants and household serfs who have emerged from servile dependence are granted the rights, both personal and property, ... of free rural inhabitants [i.e., state peasants]. They will obtain these rights according to the procedure and in the time periods laid down in the Statutes. ...

3. Estate owners, while retaining property rights over all the land belonging to them, will grant peasants, in return for prescribed obligations, permanent use of their homesteads and, in addition, in order to ensure their way of life and the fulfilment of their obligations to the government and estate owner, that quantity of field lands and other lands ... on the basis of principles laid down in the local statutes.

4. In return for the allotment of land..., peasants are obliged to render to the estate owner the obligations determined in the local statutes: in labour or money.

5. [These] obligatory agrarian relations between estate owners and peasants are determined by regulations set out in both this General and the special local statutes. ...

7. According to these principles, regulatory charters are to be compiled, in which must be determined the permanent agrarian relations between each estate owner and the peasants settled on his land. The compilation of these regulatory charters is entrusted to the estate owners themselves. [To allow time for] both the compilation and examination of [the charters], they will be put into effect two years from the day these statutes were ratified. ...

9. From the implementation of this Statute, estate owners are no longer required to bear: (1) the obligation to feed and care for peasants [in the

event of crop failures etc.]; (2) responsibility for payment by peasants of state taxes and obligations...; (3) the obligation to petition for peasants in civil and criminal cases. ...

10. Thereafter, the peasants themselves are entrusted with supervision of public provisions and welfare [in the event of crop failures etc.], and responsibility for correct payment of the state [and] local obligations, in-kind and monetary, to which they are liable. ...

11. Peasants are granted the right to redeem [and thereby acquire as] property their homesteads by means of payment of the prescribed redemption sum and in conformance with the regulations set out in the local statutes.

12. With the agreement of estate owners, peasants may, in addition to their homestead, acquire as property the field land and other lands which have been allocated to [them] for permanent use. ... With the acquisition as property by peasants of their allotment or part of it ... all obligatory agrarian relations cease between estate owners and ... peasants. ...

14. In order to facilitate peasant acquisition as property of lands that have been allotted to them for permanent use, in the event of voluntary agreement ... between estate owners and peasants or on demand by estate owners, the government will render assistance in the amount and according to the procedure determined in the special Statute on redemption. ...

15. Peasants who have emerged from servile dependence but are in obligatory agrarian relations with estate owners are called temporarily-obligated peasants.

16. Peasants who have emerged from servile dependence and have acquired land as property on the basis laid down in the Statutes are called peasant-proprietors.

17. Peasants who have emerged from servile dependence [are to] form village societies for economic matters, and are [to be] united in townships for local government and justice. In each village society and township, management of public affairs is [to be] given to the village commune and its elected [officials]. ...

18. Until obligatory relations between estate owners and peasants have ceased, the estate owner is granted [powers of] estate police and guardian-ship over the [village] society of peasants settled on his land. ...

19. Peasants and their societies' institutions are subordinate to the general provincial and district government.

20. To implement [these] Statutes ... and to resolve the special affairs arising from obligatory relations between estate owners and temporarily-obligated peasants in each province are to be established: (1) a provincial bureau for peasant affairs; (2) district mediators' congresses; and (3) peace mediators. ...

Chistyakov, O. I. (ed.) (1989) *Rossiiskoe zakonodatel'stvo X–XX vekov*, vol.7, *Dokumenty krest'yanskoi reformy*. Moscow: Yuridicheskaya literatura, pp. 37–40 (extracts).

DOCUMENT 21   REPORTS FROM THE PROVINCES ON THE RECEPTION OF THE PROCLAMATION ON THE ABOLITION OF SERFDOM

(a) Extract from a private letter from I. Nikitin in Voronezh to N.I. Ivanovich in St Petersburg, dated 13 March 1861, seized by the Third Section [secret police] in the St Petersburg Post Office.

On the 10 March the long awaited and eagerly anticipated imperial proclamation on the emancipation of the peasants was announced here. Undoubtedly you will ask: Well, what impression did it have on the people? [The answer is] absolutely none. The peasants understood ... only that they will have to wait another two years. In two years, they are saying, a lot of water can flow under the bridge. ... This indifference among the people at such a moment is very understandable for two reasons: firstly, they do not yet know how things will turn out, whether things will be easier for them now...; secondly, until now they are [so] used to this air that they are accustomed to breathing, that now, when they breath the new, fresher [air], they don't feel its life-giving force, they didn't even understand that there is a life-giving force in this new air.

(b) Extract from a Report by Collegiate Assessor Gubin to Governor V. A. Artsimovich of Kaluga, March 1861.

[The priest came to the lectern with the Proclamation.] The people greeted the appearance of the priest with a fervent prayer to the icons, accompanied by deep breaths; then followed a dead silence, and the reading of the Proclamation began. ... When [the point] ... about estate-owners' property rights to the land and the following point ... were read out, the peasants appeared sadder and sadder, and when the last point in that section ... [was read out], where the two-year period is set for the transition, all the peasants' faces displayed an inconsolable ... sadness, but among the braver and more spirited, discontent was apparent. ...

(c) Extract from a Report by Assessor Kondyrev of Tarusskii District Court to Governor V. A. Artsimovich of Kaluga, March 1861.

One cannot draw a positive conclusion about the extent of popular sympathy for the reform which is being carried out, both because they have still not completely clearly understood the current transformation, and because they have still not had time in their families and [communal] meetings to discuss all the proposals in the Statutes. But, from detailed observation it seems to me that the largest part of the peasants understood emancipation from servile dependence in a broader sense, that is that their obligations to the estate owners would be much lighter.

Fedorov (1994) *Konets*, pp. 266, 270, 273.

DOCUMENT 22   MEMOIRS OF PEACE MEDIATOR, NICHOLAS KRYLOV

Krylov (1830–1911) was a Peace Mediator in Alatyr district, Simbirsk province, in the Mid-Volga region. He had served on the Simbirsk Provincial Committee in 1858–60. His memoirs were published in the late nineteenth and early twentieth centuries.

Although the appropriate clause of the Statutes required estate owners to submit [their] regulatory charters within a year from the date they received the Statutes of 19 February 1861, it was a rare person that fulfilled this clause. The peace mediators had to travel around, remind, request and finally assist in the compilation of these charters. In the majority of cases, estate owners presented the charters after two and sometimes after three years.

Checking the charters on the spot, in the presence of the entire village assembly and trustworthy witnesses from outside, frequently gave rise to disputes between peasants and estate owners about the quality of the land, about the pastures..., ponds, cattle trails, and above all [about] accessible and inaccessible land. In the last case, a full session of the peace mediators' congress, in the presence of trustworthy witnesses, had to examine the nature of the disputed land, reach a decision and implement it. ...

In general, checking the allotments was not managed without curious incidents. Frequently it was accompanied by an acrimonious dispute between the estate owner and the peasants; sometimes mutual sharpness and laughter, occasionally... remarkable compliance by the peasants and unselfishness by the estate owners.

There were also village assemblies from which it was impossible to get any reasonable responses or demands. I remember one assembly of about five hundred people which said, as if prepared in advance: 'We won't agree to anything, but what his majesty has ordered, let it be!'

There was an assembly, also no less than five hundred people, which said: 'We don't need any land if it belongs to the estate owner, let it remain in the estate owner's [possession]. We have now become free, the tsar will order free land to be allotted to us.'

Or another response: 'We are not disobeying the tsar's command, but it's just that we can't live from that allotment, so there's no point in taking it! Near the cemetery our village has a whole *desyatina* [2.7 acres] of land, where three *arshiny* [about six feet] each would be enough to bury us if the lords have been given such a freedom by the tsar.'

Fedorov (1994) *Konets*, pp. 387–8.

DOCUMENT 23   NICHOLAS OGAREV'S ATTACK ON THE STATUTES IN ALEXANDER HERZEN'S *THE BELL*, 15 JULY 1861

The following extracts are from the opening and final paragraphs of the first part of Ogarev's searing indictment of the terms of the abolition of serfdom published in The Bell *on 15 July 1861.*

At that time [19 February 1861] it seemed that the government stood at the head of the emancipation of Russia; its standing was unusually bright and happy; [but] it lost it all at once, and finally hope in it, faith in it collapsed once and for all. After falling into blood [a reference to the massacre at Bezdna in April], it [the government] fell into a mire, and had to explain to the people that black is not black, that two is not two, that labour services are not labour services [a reference to a circular from the Minister of Internal Affairs explaining that labour services in the transitional period were different from those under serfdom]. What a lie and what impotence! The causes of this state of affairs are not hard to divine; there are two: (1) the government was *not sincere* in emancipating the people, i.e., in essence the sovereign did not want emancipation at all; (2) it was completely *without ability*, that is it did not know how to *understand* anything or to *do* anything. Every honest person must break with this government. Look at the new minister of internal affairs [P. A. Valuev]; we don't know him, we just see that from his first step he talks nonsense out loud. ...

With grief in the heart and profound sadness we must acknowledge that, besides allowing peasants to marry without the agreement of the land-owner, which they did anyway on estates where landowners were absentees, personal rights for the peasants *who have emerged from servile dependence* do not exist, because they *have not emerged* from servile dependence.
The heading *who have emerged is a lie.*
The old serfdom has been replaced by a new [serfdom].
In general, serfdom *has not been abolished.*
The people have been deceived by the tsar!

Kolokol, no.101, 15 July 1861, pp. 845, 848.

DOCUMENT 24   ADDRESS OF THE TVER NOBLE ASSEMBLY TO TSAR ALEXANDER II, FEBRUARY 1862

The 'liberal' nobles of Tver province, who had proposed a radical abolition of serfdom in 1859, responded to the abolition of serfdom by calling for more far-reaching reforms.

Having assembled for the first time since the legislation of 19 February

1861 [on the abolition of serfdom] was published, the nobility of Tver expresses its greetings to the Russian Tsar who undertook to free the peasants and to excoriate every injustice in the Russian land. The nobility of Tver solemnly avows its sincere affection for Your Imperial Majesty and its readiness to follow You on the pathway to prosperity for the Russian people. As proof of our readiness and complete trust in the person of Your Imperial Majesty, we have decided to make a sincere statement of our ideas for Your consideration, without any deception and concealment.

The proclamation of 19 February, which announced the people's freedom, improved the peasants' material welfare somewhat, but did not free them from servile dependency; nor did it eliminate all the arbitrariness caused by serfdom. The people's common sense cannot reconcile the freedom proclaimed by Your Majesty with the current obligatory ties to the estate owners, with the artificial separation of social estates. The people see that, in time, they can become free of labour obligations, but must forever pay dues, which are now shifted to the authority of those same estate owners, [now] called peace mediators.

Sovereign! We sincerely admit that we ourselves do not understand the Statute [on the abolition of serfdom]. Such enormous confusion puts [our] entire society in a hopeless situation, which threatens to destroy the state. What prevents elimination of this situation?

We not only do not regard the obligatory grant of landed property to the peasants as an infringement on our rights, but consider this the sole means to guarantee the tranquillity of the country and our own propertied interests. We ask that this measure be immediately implemented through the general resources of the state, without placing the entire burden on the peasants alone, who are less responsible than all other social estates for the existence of serfdom. The nobility, by virtue of its social privileges, has thus far been exempt from fulfilling the most important civic duties. Sire! We consider it a mortal sin to live and enjoy the benefits of the public order at the expense of other social estates. No order can be just if the poor man pays a rouble and the rich man not a single copeck. This could be tolerated only under serfdom, but it now places us in the position of parasites, who are completely useless to their fatherland. We do not wish to retain any longer such disgraceful privilege, and we do not accept responsibility for its further existence. We most loyally request Your Majesty's permission to assume a share of the state taxes and obligations, according to the wealth of each. Besides property privileges, we enjoy the exclusive right of providing men to govern the people. In the present day we deem this exclusive right unlawful and ask that it be extended to all social estates.

Most Gracious Sovereign! We firmly believe that You sincerely desire the well-being of Russia, and therefore consider it our sacred duty to state frankly that between us and Your Imperial Majesty's government there exists a strange misunderstanding that prevents the realisation of Your good intentions! ...

A convocation of elected representatives from all the Russian land represents the only means for a satisfactory solution that was outlined, but not achieved, by the Statute of 19 February [1861]. In presenting this petition to Your Imperial Majesty to consider convoking an assembly of the land, we hope that the Tver nobility's sincere desire for the general good will not be subjected to perverse interpretation.

Freeze, G. L. (ed.) (1988) *From Supplication to Revolution: A Documentary History of Imperial Russia*. New York and Oxford: Oxford University Press, pp. 104–5 [with minor alterations].

DOCUMENT 25   REGULATORY CHARTER FOR THE VILLAGE OF BARKINO, GORBATOV DISTRICT, NIZHNII NOVGOROD PROVINCE, WHICH BELONGED TO ESTATE OWNER AVDOTYA SEMENOVNA ERSHORA, COMPILED ON 15 FEBRUARY 1862

This is one example of the tens of thousands of regulatory charters drawn up for estates during the two-year transitional period that followed the Statutes of 19 February 1861. One-third of the peasants' land in the village was 'cut off'.

I

1. In the village of Barkino, according to the 10th revision of the poll tax census [1857–58] there are 44 male peasants.
None of them was freed after the revision.
2. Of this number, 5 are not eligible to be allotted land ... under article 8 of the Local Statute.
3. Therefore, on the basis of the Statute, 39 male peasants must receive the use of allotments of land.

II

1. Before the promulgation of the Statute ... the peasants had the use of 214 *desyatiny*, 1,212 *sazheny* of land [about 580 acres].
2. Of this, peasants' farmsteads made up five *desyatiny*, three hundred and sixty-six *sazheny* (including 1 *desyatina*, 266 *sazheny* of pasture in peasant use). ...
3. For the locality in which the settlement is situated, the Local Statute ... set a maximum size for allotments per male peasant of 4 *desyatiny*, and a minimum of 1 *desyatina* 800 *sazheny*: the maximum size of the allotment for the whole peasant community would be 156 *desyatiny*, and the minimum 52 *desyatiny*.
4. ...as the total amount of productive land on the estate, including forest, is 214 *desyatiny* 1,212 *sazheny*, then on the basis of the right granted to estate owners in article 20 of the Local Statute to retain one-third of the

total quantity of land [after allotting land to the peasants], then one hundred and forty-three *desyatiny* 8 *sazheny* is left in the permanent use of the peasants, and the rest of the land is liable to be cut off and transferred to the estate owner. ...

III

4. The pasture situated near the settlement remains in the use of the peasants.

IV

1. In return for being granted the use of [an allotment of] 3 *desyatiny* 1,600 *sazheny* of land per male peasant, on the basis of the Statute, dues (*obrok*) of eight roubles sixty-two and a half copecks a year are to be paid for each allotment, and for all 39 allotments – three hundred and thirty-six roubles thirty-seven and a half silver copecks a year. But, as the peasants paid dues of two hundred and seventy-four roubles and thirty-four copecks for the whole community before the promulgation of the Statutes, then, on the basis of article 170 of the Local Statute, they must continue to pay the same dues as before, which come to seven roubles three and a half copecks for every male peasant a year. ...

[The regulatory charter was signed by estate owner Eshora. It was checked and signed by local peace mediator Babkin, and ratified and signed by members of the district peace mediators' council.]

Fedorov (1994) *Konets*, pp. 374–5.

DOCUMENT 26   **SPEECH BY ALEXANDER II TO TOWNSHIP AND VILLAGE PEASANT ELDERS OF MOSCOW PROVINCE, 25 NOVEMBER 1862**

Following rumours among the peasantry that the tsar would announce a new freedom on 19 February 1863 ('the promised hour'), Alexander II made a number of speeches denying them.

Greetings lads! I am pleased to see you.

I gave you freedom, but remember, [it is] lawful freedom, not a licence to do what you want. Therefore, above all, I demand from you precise fulfilment of the prescribed obligations. In those places where the regulatory charters have not yet been compiled, I want them to be compiled quickly, by the date I appointed. Then, after they have been compiled, that is after 19 February next year, do not expect any new freedom or new privileges. Do you hear me? Do not listen to the rumours that are circulating among you, and do not believe those people who will try to convince you otherwise, but believe only my words. Farewell now. God be with you!

Fedorov (1994) *Konets*, pp. 415–16.

DOCUMENT 27   STEPNIAK ON 'THE RUSSIAN AGRARIAN QUESTION', 1888

'Stepniak' (alias Sergei Mikhailovich Kravchinskii) was a Populist and terrorist. He lived in exile after he assassinated General Mezentsev (the Chief of the Third Section) in 1878. This passage is taken from his book on the Russian peasantry published in 1888.

The Emancipation Act of February 19, 1861..., followed in 1866 by a second Act, settling the condition of ... the former State peasants, were by far the most extensive experiments in the way of agrarian legislation the world has ever seen. ...

That these experiments have not proved a success no competent person can now deny. Emancipation has utterly failed to realize the ardent expectations of its advocates and promoters. The great benefit of the measure was purely moral. It has failed to improve the material condition of the former serfs, who on the whole are worse off than they were before the Emancipation. The bulk of our peasantry is in a condition not far removed from actual starvation – a fact which can neither be denied nor concealed even by the official press.

Stepniak (1888) *The Russian Peasantry: Their Agrarian Condition, Social Life, and Religion.*
New York, Harper and Brothers, p. 2.

DOCUMENT 28   NICHOLAS II'S PROCLAMATION 'ON IMPROVING THE WELFARE AND ALLEVIATING THE POSITION OF THE PEASANT POPULATION', 3 NOVEMBER 1905

Nicholas II issued this proclamation during the revolution of 1905–7, during which there were widespread peasant disorders. Two weeks earlier, in another attempt to diffuse opposition, he issued the famous 'October Proclamation', in which he conceded an elected legislative assembly: the State Duma.

By the Grace of God, We, Nicholas II, Emperor and Autocrat of All the Russias ... etc. announce to all our loyal subjects:

Our heart is filled with deep sorrow by the troubles which are taking place in settlements in some districts, where peasants are inflicting violence on the estates of private estate owners. No such wilful or arbitrary [actions] can be tolerated, and the civil and military authorities ... have been ordered to use all measures to prevent and put a stop to the disorders, [and] punish the perpetrators.

The needs of the peasants, [which are close] to our heart, cannot be left without attention.

Violence and crimes will not, however, improve the position of the peasants, and can only bring great grief and misfortune to the Motherland.

The only way a concrete improvement in the welfare of the peasants [can be achieved] is a peaceful and legal way, and we have always made the alleviation of the position of the peasant population our chief concern.

Recently, we ordered the collection and presentation of information about those measures which would bring immediate benefit to the peasants.

Following consideration of this matter, we have decided:

1. Redemption payments from former seigniorial, state and appanage peasants will be reduced by half from 1 January 1906, and from 1 January 1907 the collection of these payments will cease altogether.

2. To enable the Peasant Land Bank to help peasants with insufficient land to buy more land to increase their holdings more successfully by increasing the bank's resources and establishing more favourable terms for granting loans. ...

We are convinced that then, with our combined efforts and [those] of the *best elected people from the Russian land*, who must be freely chosen by our loyal subjects, including the peasants [i.e., the State Duma], we will succeed in satisfying further pressing needs of the peasantry, without any harm to other landowners.

We hope that the peasant population, which is dear to our heart, following the Christian teachings of goodness and love, will listen to our tsarist call to preserve peace and quiet and not violate the law and the rights of other people.

Fedorov (1994) *Konets*, pp. 463–4.

GLOSSARY

appanage peasants Peasants who lived on the estates of members of the imperial family, to whom they paid dues. (Known as court peasants before 1797.) They were the subjects of reforms in the 1820s and 1830s, and again in 1858–63.

autocracy The system of government in the Russian Empire until 1906, under which there were no theoretical restrictions on the tsars' powers.

Baltic Germans The ethnically German nobility of the *Baltic provinces*.

Baltic provinces Estonia, Livonia and Kurland. The first two were formally annexed to the Russian Empire from Sweden in 1721. Kurland was annexed during the third *Partition of Poland* in 1795.

barshchina See *labour services/obligations*.

Bell, The (Kolokol) Radical journal published by Alexander Herzen in London from 1857 to 1867. It was smuggled into Russia, where it circulated among the radical intelligentsia, and was read by members of government.

Bolshevik Party Marxist revolutionary party, led by Lenin, which seized power in October 1917. Renamed the Communist Party in 1918.

boyar Aristocratic landowner in Russia before the eighteenth century.

Charter to the Nobility Charter issued by Catherine the Great in 1785 which codified the rights and privileges of the Russian nobility.

church peasants Peasants who lived on land belonging to the Russian Orthodox Church, to which they paid dues or worked. They became part of the *state peasantry* in 1762 after Peter III secularized the church's land and peasants.

commune See *village commune*.

Communist Party See *Bolshevik Party*.

conscription See *recruitment obligation*.

Crimean War (1853–56) War between the Russian and Turkish Empires. Great Britain and France joined the Turks in 1854. The Russian Empire was defeated. The peace treaty was signed in Paris in March 1856. The defeat was the catalyst for Alexander II's 'great reforms', including the abolition of serfdom.

cut offs (otrezki) The parts of serfs' land allotments under serfdom that were taken away from them at the start of *temporary obligation*.

Decembrist movement Name subsequently given to secret societies of radical army officers and some civilian intellectuals set up after the Napoleonic Wars.

Decembrist Revolt Revolt in St Petersburg on 14 December 1825 (hence name) by radical army officers against the autocracy and serfdom. The revolt was defeated.

demesne The part of the nobles' estates they set aside for their own production (with serf labour). The rest of the land was handed over to the peasants to cultivate for themselves. On many estates, demesne and peasant land were intermingled in open fields.

Descriptions of Seigniorial Estates (Opisaniya pomeshchich'ikh imenii) Descriptions of estates, including details of the serfs' land allotments and the obligations they owed in return, compiled by noble estate owners in 1858–59.

desyatina (pl. *desyatiny*)   1 *desyatina* = 2.7 acres or 1.09 hectares (2,400 *sazheny*).

dues (obrok)   Payments in cash and kind (e.g., agricultural or craft produce) made by peasants to nobles under serfdom, and during the *transitional period* and *temporary obligation* after 1861.

Editing Commissions   Four Commissions set up by Alexander II under the chairmanship of Rostovtsev in February 1858 to draft the statutes to abolish serfdom. The members included a number of key *enlightened bureaucrats*. In practice, the four commissions are better considered as sections of one body.

enlightened bureaucrats   'Enlightened' members of the bureaucracy who worked for reform in the mid-nineteenth century, e.g., the Milyutin brothers, Dmitrii and Nicholas.

free agriculturalists (svobodnye khlebopashtsy)   Peasants freed from serfdom and sold land by nobles under the terms of the decree of 1803. Formally part of the *state peasantry*.

'Great Russia'   Term for the largely ethnic Russian part of the empire, as distinct from Belorussia, 'Little Russia' *(left-bank Ukraine)*, and New Russia (southern Ukraine).

household serfs (dvorovye lyudi)   Serfs who worked as servants in nobles' houses or in skilled occupations on their estates.

inventories   Documents recording serfs' land allotments and seigniorial obligations on nobles' estates in the formerly Polish *western provinces*. They had existed before the *Partitions of Poland*, and were given force of law by the Russian government in *right-bank Ukraine* in 1847 in order to regulate noble–serf relations. (See also *wackenbücher*.)

inventory reform   Reform of 1847 regulating noble–serf relations in *right-bank Ukraine*. (See also *inventories*.)

joint responsibility (krugovaya poruka)   The principle according to which communities of peasants in the Russian part of the empire were held jointly responsible for their taxes to the state and their obligations to nobles. If peasants defaulted, their neighbours were responsible for their share. It was retained in the *Statutes of 1861* for the dues the freed serfs paid nobles during *temporary obligation* and for their *redemption payments*. It was abolished in 1903.

kulak (lit. 'fist')   Rich peasant. A derogatory term for alleged opponents of Soviet agricultural policy among the peasantry.

labour services/obligations (barshchina)   Forced labour by peasants for nobles under serfdom. Some peasants continued to work for nobles during the *transitional period* and *temporary obligation* after 1861.

land captain (zemskii nachal'nik)   Official post, filled by nobles, created in 1889 to supervise institutions of peasant self-government.

left-bank Ukraine   The part of Ukraine on the left (eastern) bank of the River Dnieper. It was absorbed into the Russian state in 1654. It was often referred to as 'Little Russia' (*Malorossiya*).

Main Committee on the Peasant Question   See *Secret Committee on the Peasant Question*

marshals of the nobility   Men elected by the nobility at district and provincial levels to manage noble affairs.

Ministry of State Domains   Ministry set up in 1838 to administer the *state peasants*.

mir   See *village commune*.

Muscovy   Name sometimes given to Russia before the reign of Peter the Great (1682–1725).

noble estate owners (pomeshchiki)   Nobles who owned land. A minority owned vast estates. Some nobles owned no land.

obligated peasants (obyazannye krest'yane)   Peasants whose relations with noble estate owners were regulated under the terms of the decree of 1842. Formally part of the *state peasantry*.

obrok   See *dues*.

Partitions of Poland   The division of Poland between the Russian Empire, Prussia and the Austrian Empire in 1772, 1793 and 1795. (See also *western provinces*.)

peace mediators (mirovye posredniki)   Officials appointed to oversee the implementation of the abolition of serfdom. Their duties included ratifying the *regulatory charters* and setting up the new institutions of peasant self-government.

peasant movement   Term used mostly by Soviet historians for unrest and disturbances among the peasantry.

peasants   (1) An unprivileged *social estate* in imperial Russian law that included most of the rural population who were neither nobles nor clergy. Until the reforms of the 1860s, peasants were divided into *appanage peasants*, *seigniorial peasants* (*serfs*) and *state peasants*. The *church peasants* had become part of the *state peasants* after 1762. (2) A term used by historians and social scientists to designate rural people who lived mainly by subsistence agriculture and were oppressed and exploited by the social elites and states of the societies they lived in.

poll tax   A tax levied on all male members of the lower orders, mainly peasants. It was introduced by Peter the Great and first collected in 1724. It was abolished in the European part of the empire in 1883–87. Poll tax censuses (known as 'revisions') were held at regular intervals between 1719 and 1857–58 to count the numbers of tax-payers.

Proclamation on the Abolition of Serfdom (sometimes referred to as the 'Emancipation Manifesto')   This was the document in which Alexander II announced the reform to the mass of the population. It was read out by parish priests in March and April 1861.

provincial committees of nobles   Committees set up in each province after November 1857 to draw up plans for the reform of serfdom on the basis of principles laid down by the government.

Pugachev revolt Revolt in 1773–74 led by Emelyan Pugachev, who claimed to be the late Tsar Peter III. He issued a fake proclamation abolishing serfdom in the Mid-Volga region in July 1774, which provoked a large-scale revolt by serfs in the region.

Razin revolt Revolt in 1670–71 led by Stepan Razin. Serfs joined in the final stages in large numbers in the Mid-Volga region.

recruitment obligation Between 1705 and 1874 members of the lower orders, mainly peasants, were liable to be conscripted into the lower ranks of the armed forces. Until 1793 service was for life. From 1834, in practice, recruits served for 15–20 years.

redemption operation The third and final stage of the reform process set in motion by the *Statutes of 1861*, during which the freed serfs bought, or 'redeemed', land allotments from nobles through the intermediary of the government. The operation came to an end in 1907.

redemption payments The payments made by peasants to the government during the *redemption operation*.

redemption sum The total amount of compensation to be granted to nobles for the loss of part of their land at the start of the redemption operation. It was calculated by capitalizing the freed serfs' *dues* under *temporary obligation* at a rate of 6 per cent a year.

regulatory charters (ustavnye gramoty) Charters containing details of the freed serfs' land allotments and the obligations they owed in return on the eve of the abolition of serfdom and during *temporary obligation*, drawn up by noble estate owners under official supervision and subject to peasant approval during the *transitional period* immediately after the formal end of serfdom in 1861.

right-bank Ukraine The part of Ukraine on the right (western) bank of the River Dnieper which was annexed by the Russian Empire during the second and third *Partitions of Poland* in 1793 and 1795. It was often referred to as the 'southwestern provinces'. (See also *western provinces*.)

rural police (zemskaya politsiya) Police force subordinate to provincial governors and Ministry of Internal Affairs.

Russian Empire The formal name of the Russian state from 1721 until the February Revolution of 1917.

Russian Orthodox Church The established church in the Russian Empire. It was part of the wider, eastern Orthodox branch of Christianity. Before 1762, the Russian Orthodox Church owned vast amounts of land and, in practice, the *church peasants* who lived on it.

sazhen' (pl. *sazheny*) 1/2,400 of a *desyatina*.

Secret Committee on the Peasant Question Committee of key advisers set up by Alexander II in January 1857 to prepare the abolition of serfdom. Renamed the 'Main Committee' in January 1858.

seigniorial obligations General term for all obligations owed by serfs to nobles. (See also *dues* and *labour services*.)

seigniorial peasants (pomeshchich'i krest'yane) Correct term for *serfs*.

serfs   *Peasants* who were bound to the estates of nobles, to whom they paid *dues* or worked *labour services*.

Seven Years' War (1756–63)   Major war between European powers. The Russian Empire was allied with the Austrian Empire and France against Prussia. Peter III pulled the Russian Empire out of the war in February–March 1762 on the brink of victory.

slavophiles   Members of an informal conservative intellectual movement which extolled the alleged virtues of Slavonic, as opposed to Western European, culture, e.g., Alexander Koshelev and Yurii Samarin.

social estate (*soslovie*)   Legal categories of the population in the Russian Empire, e.g., peasants, townspeople, nobles, clergy.

Soviet Union (or Union of Soviet Socialist Republics)   The successor state of the Russian Empire, governed by the Communist Party.

State Council   Central government institution created in 1810. It was formally responsible for approving laws before they were sent to the tsar for ratification.

state peasants   Peasants who lived on land belonging to the Russian state, to which they paid dues.

Statutes of [19 February] 1861   The Statutes ratified by Alexander II, which abolished serfdom.

temporary obligation   The second stage of the reform process set in motion by the *Statutes of 1861*, during which the freed serfs paid *dues* to, or worked for, nobles in return for the use of land allotments. The levels of dues and work, and the sizes of the allotments, were regulated by law and recorded in *regulatory charters*.

Third Section   Secret police organization established by Nicholas I in 1826 to maintain surveillance over opposition, real and potential, to the regime.

three-field system   A crop rotation common in the central regions of the Russian Empire, under which each field was sown with the winter and spring crops in successive years and then left fallow to recover its natural fertility.

township (*volost'*)   Group of several neighbouring villages. The *Statutes of 1861* created a layer of administration at township level.

transitional period   The two-year period after the ratification of the *Statutes of 1861*, during which preparations were made for *temporary obligation*.

versta (pl. *versty*)   1 *versta* = 0.66 miles or 1.06 km.

village commune (*mir* or *obshchina*).   Institutions of peasant administration at village level. Under serfdom, they were often incorporated by nobles into their estate administrations. They were reconstituted as 'village communities' (*sel'skie obshchestva*) after 1861.

village community   See *village commune*.

wackenbücher   Registers recording serfs' land allotments and seigniorial obligations on nobles' estates in the *Baltic provinces* of Estonia and Livonia. They had been introduced by the Swedish government before 1721, and were given force of law by the Russian government in 1804 in order to regulate noble–serf relations. (See also *inventories*.)

western provinces   The territories of Lithuania, Belorussia and *right-bank Ukraine*, which were annexed by the Russian Empire during the *Partitions of Poland* of 1772, 1793 and 1795. The name is sometimes also used to include the *Baltic provinces*.

westernizers   Members of an informal, progressive intellectual movement who believed that Russia should follow the path of development of Western Europe, e.g., Boris Chicherin. (They were in opposition to the *slavophiles*.)

zemstvo (pl. *zemstva*)   Elected district and provincial councils set up after 1864.

WHO'S WHO

The brief entries refer mainly to people's activities in relation to the abolition of serfdom.

Alexander II   Tsar. Reigned 1855–81. Succeeded his father, *Nicholas I*, during the Crimean War. Responsible for the enactment of the abolition of serfdom in 1861 and other 'great reforms', including local government, the courts, education, censorship, finance and military service in the 1860s and 1870s. Assassinated by revolutionary terrorists in March 1881.

Alexander III   Tsar. Reigned 1881–94. Succeeded to the throne on his father's assassination. Has reputation as reactionary and repressive ruler.

Anton Petrov (?–1861)   Peasant of Kazan province who interpreted the Statutes of 1861 in line with peasants' hopes. Executed after troops massacred protesting peasants in Bezdna. (NB Petrov[ich] was his patronymic, not his family name.)

Belinskii, Vissarion (1811–48)   Intellectual. Leading westernizer and literary critic. Called for literature to serve society. Wrote letter attacking *Gogol* in 1847.

Bibikov, Dmitrii (1792–1870)   Army officer and statesman. Governor-general of the southwestern provinces (right-bank Ukraine), 1839–52. Introduced the 'inventory reform' to regulate serfdom. Minister of Internal Affairs, 1852–55. Tried unsuccessfully to extend reform to other western provinces.

Bludov, Dmitrii (1785–1864)   Statesman. Member of several of *Nicholas I*'s secret committees on the peasant question, and *Alexander II*'s Secret and Main Committees on the Peasant Question, 1857–61. Conservative.

Catherine (II) the Great   Empress. Reigned 1762–96. Came to power in a coup against her husband *Peter III*. Seems to have recognized the need to reform serfdom, but was reluctant to act for political reasons. Some of her actions, including the provincial reform of 1775 and the Charter to the Nobility of 1785, have been interpreted by some historians as pro-noble.

Cherkasskii, Vladimir (1824–78)   Intellectual. Leading slavophile. Member of Tula provincial committee and the Editing Commissions, 1859–60. Close to enlightened bureaucrats.

Chernyshevskii, Nicholas (1828–89)   Intellectual. Strongly criticized the Statutes of 1861.

Chicherin, Boris (1828–1904)   Intellectual. Leading westernizer. Advocated abolishing serfdom in the 1850s.

Constantine Nikolaevich (1827–92)   Grand Duke. Alexander II's younger brother. He advocated reform. Appointed to the Secret Committee on the Peasant Question in late 1857. Chaired the sessions of the Main Committee in October 1860–January 1861 which approved the draft statutes.

Dolgorukov, Vasilii (1804–68)   Statesman. Minister of War, 1852–April 1856, and chief of the Third Section (the secret police), April 1856–66. Member of the Secret and Main Committees on the Peasant Question, 1857–61. Strongly opposed the abolition of serfdom on the Main Committee, exasperating *Constantine Nikolaevich*.

Eisen, Johann Georg (1717–79)   Lutheran pastor. Born in Germany, but moved to the Baltic provinces. First systematic critic of serfdom in the Russian Empire.

Elena Pavlovna (1806–73)   Grand Duchess. Alexander II's aunt (by marriage). Supported enlightened bureaucrats and advocated the abolition of serfdom.

Engelgardt, Alexander (1832–93)   Scientist and writer. Lived in internal exile on his estate in Smolensk province after 1871. Published a series of influential 'letters from the country' describing village life in the journal *Notes of the Fatherland*.

Filaret (Drozdov) (1782–1867)   Metropolitan of Moscow, 1825–67. Conservative clergyman who wrote the Proclamation on the abolition of serfdom at the invitation of *Panin*.

Gagarin, Paul (1789–1872)   Noble and statesman. Major land and serf owner. Member of the Secret and Main Committees on the Peasant Question, 1857–61. Conservative. Made last-minute amendment to Statutes in State Council in January 1861 allowing freed serfs to take small land allotments free of charge.

Gogol, Nicholas (1809–52)   Writer. Made his name with the play *The Government Inspector* (1836) and the novel *Dead Souls* (1842), which viciously satirized provincial life. He created a stir with *Selected Passages from Correspondence with Friends* (1847), which defended serfdom and advocated conservative, religious values. Attacked by *Belinskii*.

Herzen, Alexander (1812–70)   Intellectual. Left Russia to live in western Europe in 1847, and published a series of radical periodicals in London, e.g., *The Polar Star*, *Voices from Russia* and *The Bell*, which were influential among radicals and government figures inside Russia. Developed Russian version of socialism based on his interpretation of peasant communal practices.

Kavelin, Constantine (1818–85)   Intellectual. Leading westernizer. He advocated abolishing serfdom in the 1850s. Close to *Elena Pavlovna* and the enlightened bureaucrats.

Kiselev, Paul (1788–1872)   Army officer and statesman. *Nicholas I's* 'chief of staff for peasant affairs'. First Minister for State Domains, 1838–56. Responsible for reforms of the state peasants 1838–1840s. Patron of *Dmitrii* and *Nicholas Milyutin* and other enlightened bureaucrats.

Koshelev, Alexander (1806–83)   Intellectual. Leading slavophile. Advocated abolishing serfdom in the 1840s and 1850s, and called for an elected assembly in 1862. Served as a government representative on the Ryazan provincial committee, 1859–60. Close to the enlightened bureaucrats.

Lanskoi, Sergei (1787–1862)   Statesman. Minister for Internal Affairs, 1855–April 1861. Member of the Secret and Main Committees on the Peasant Question, 1857–61. Supported the abolition of serfdom. Dismissed by *Alexander II* shortly after the Statutes of 1861 were published as a concession to the nobility.

Lenin, Vladimir Ilich (1870–1924) Revolutionary and political leader. Chief theoretician and leader of the Marxist Bolshevik Party which seized power in Russia in October 1917.

Marx, Karl (1818–83) Communist economic and political theorist. Born in western Germany and lived in England after 1849, but works were very influential among Russian radicals, e.g., *Lenin*.

Milyutin, Dmitrii (1816–1912) Army officer and statesman. Prominent enlightened bureaucrat, protégé of *Kiselev* and brother of *Nicholas Milyutin*. Advocated abolishing serfdom as a necessary precursor to reforming the system of recruitment in March 1856. Minister of War, November 1861–81. Carried out major reforms of the armed forces, culminating in military service reform of 1874.

Milyutin, Nicholas (1818–72) Statesman. Prominent enlightened bureaucrat, protégé of *Elena Pavlovna* and *Kiselev*, and the brother of *Dmitrii Milyutin*. Acting deputy minister of internal affairs to *Lanskoi*, 1856–April 1861. Key member of the Editing Commissions, 1859–60, and one of main authors of the draft statutes. Dismissed, together with Lanskoi, in April 1861 as a concession to the nobility. Implemented revised terms of the abolition of serfdom in the western provinces after Polish revolt of 1863.

Muraviev, Michael (1796–1866) Army officer and statesman. Involved in the Decembrist movement, but repented and became a conservative. Minister of State Domains, 1857–61. Member of the Secret and Main Committees on the Peasant Question, April 1857–1861. Strongly opposed abolition of serfdom on the Main Committee, exasperating *Constantine Nikolaevich*.

Muraviev, Nikita (1795–1843) Army officer and revolutionary. Leader of Decembrist Northern Society and author of a constitution for Russia. Exiled to hard labour in aftermath of Decembrist revolt.

Nicholas I Tsar. Reigned 1825–55. Put down Decembrist revolt on first day of reign and acquired reputation as repressive and reactionary ruler. In reality, responsible for conservative reforms, including reforms of the state and appanage peasantry, that paved the way for the abolition of serfdom by his son *Alexander II*.

Nicholas II Tsar. Reigned 1894–1917. Survived revolution of 1905, but abdicated after outbreak of revolution in February 1917.

Ogarev, Nicholas (1813–77) Intellectual. Close associate of *Herzen*. Author of a very critical article on the Statutes of 1861 which appeared in *The Bell* in summer 1861.

Orlov, Alexis (1786–1861) Statesman. Chief of Third Section (secret police), 1844–April 1856. Chairman of the Secret and Main Committees on the Peasant Question. Conservative.

Panin, Victor (1801–74) Statesman. Minister of Justice, 1839–62. Member of the Main Committee on the Peasant Question, 1858–60. Replaced *Rostovtsev* as chairman of the Editing Commissions in February 1860. Held conservative views, but was unable significantly to alter terms of abolition of serfdom.

Paul Tsar. Reigned 1796–1801. Banned labour services on Sundays, and advocated serfs' work be divided equally between noble and serf land. Overthrown and murdered in a coup in 1801.

Perovskii, Leo (1792–1856)   Statesman. Responsible for the reforms of the appanage peasants in the late 1820s and 1830s. Minister of Internal Affairs, 1841–52. Patron of the enlightened bureaucrats.

Pestel, Paul (1793–1826)   Army officer and revolutionary. Leader of Decembrist Southern Society and author of 'The Russian Law'. Executed in the aftermath of the Decembrist revolt.

Peter (I) the Great   Tsar. Reigned 1682–1725. Responsible for Russian victory over Sweden in the Great Northern War and the annexation of the Baltic provinces. Implemented major reforms in a wide range of areas, including enforcement of noble state service, recruitment for the armed forces, and the poll tax.

Peter III   Tsar. Reigned December 1761–June 1762. Pulled Russia out of the Seven Years' War, abolished compulsory noble state service, secularized the land and peasants of the Russian Orthodox Church. Overthrown in favour of his wife, Catherine the Great.

Radishchev, Alexander (1749–1802)   Writer. Author of *A Journey from St Petersburg and Moscow* (1790) in which he attacked serfdom. Exiled to Siberia by *Catherine the Great*, but allowed to return by *Paul*.

Reutern [Reiturn], *Michael* (1820–90)   Statesman. Enlightened bureaucrat. Member of the Editing Commissions, 1859–60, and Minister of Finance, 1862–78.

Rostovtsev, Yakov (1803–60)   Army officer and statesman. First came to prominence for informing *Nicholas I* about plans for Decembrist revolt in 1825. Member of the Secret and the Main Committees on the Peasant Question, 1857–60, and first chairman of the Editing Commissions. Played a crucial role in the preparation of abolition of serfdom by convincing *Alexander II* of the need to ensure freed serfs had land and by appointing enlightened bureaucrats to the Editing Commissions. Died in February 1860.

Samarin, Yurii (1819–76)   Intellectual. Leading slavophile. Advocated abolishing serfdom in the 1850s. Member of the Editing Commissions, 1859–60.

Semenov (later –Tyan-Shanskii), Peter (1827–1914)   Geographer. Leading member of the Imperial Russian Geographical Society and a close associate of enlightened bureaucrats. Advised *Rostovtsev* on appointments to the Editing Commissions in 1859, and was himself a member.

Shuvalov, Peter (1827–89)   Noble. Chairman of St Petersburg provincial committee and member of the Editing Commissions (on the suggestion of *Alexander II*), 1859–60. Tried unsuccessfully to mobilize conservative opposition to the abolition of serfdom.

Soloviev, Yakov (1820–76)   Statesman. Senior official in the Ministry of Internal Affairs and member of the Editing Commissions, 1859–60. Enlightened bureaucrat.

Speranskii, Michael (1772–1839)   Statesman. Senior adviser to *Alexander I* and *Nicholas I*. Responsible for several reforms, including the collection and codification of law, 1826–33.

Stepniak [revolutionary name of Sergei Kravchinskii] (1851–95)   Revolutionary and writer. Active in the Populist movement in the 1870s. Escaped from Russia in 1878 after assassinating the chief of the Third Section. Publicized the cause of Russian revolutionaries and the plight of the Russian peasantry from exile.

Stolypin, Peter (1862–1911)   Statesman. Prime Minister, 1906–11. Implemented land reforms that allowed peasants to break away from village communes.

Tolstoy, Leo (1828–1910)   Writer. Portrayed peasants sympathetically in his major novels *War and Peace* and *Anna Karenina*. Owned the estate of Yasnaya Polyana in Tula province, where he tried to implement paternalistic reforms. Served as peace mediator in Tula province in 1861.

Turgenev, Ivan (1818–83)   Writer. Author of 'A Sportsman's Sketches', published 1847–51, which indirectly criticized serfdom.

Turgenev, Nicholas (1789–1871)   Intellectual and revolutionary. Member of Decembrist Northern Society. Lived in exile in western Europe from 1825. Author of *Russia and the Russians* (published in Paris in 1847), in which he criticized the existing order, including serfdom.

Unkovskii, Alexis (1828–93)   Noble politician. Chairman of Tver provincial committee which proposed radical plan to abolish serfdom in 1859. Went on to demand political reform.

Valuev, Peter (1815–90)   Statesman. Minister of Internal Affairs, April 1861–68. (Replaced *Lanskoi*.)

Zablotskii-Desyatovskii, Andrei (1807–81)   Statesman. Enlightened bureaucrat. Senior official in the Ministry of State Domains, worked closely with *Kiselev*. Member of the Editing Commissions, 1859–60.

Zaionchkovsky, Peter (1904–83)   Historian who worked in the Soviet Union. He was the author of several important works on aspects of nineteenth–century Russian political history, including the abolition of serfdom.

GUIDE TO FURTHER READING

References are given in full in this Guide only to works that are not cited in the Bibliography that follows.

Documents in English translation can be found in Vernadsky (ed.), *A Source Book for Russian History*; Dmytryshyn (ed.), *Imperial Russia: A Source Book* and Freeze (ed.), *From Supplication to Revolution*. Field, *Rebels in the Name of the Tsar* contains lengthy extracts from documents concerning the peasant protest against the terms of the abolition of serfdom in Bezdna in April 1861.

Perrie, *Alexander II: Emancipation and Reform in Russia, 1855–81* is a very good, concise, introduction. For the broader context, see the relevant volumes of the Longman History of Russia: Dukes, P. (1990) *The Making of Russian Absolutism, 1613–1801*, 2nd edn; Saunders, *Russia in the Age of Reaction and Reform, 1801–1881*; Rogger, H. (1983) *Russia in the Age of Modernisation and Revolution, 1881–1917*. Longley, D. (2000) *The Longman Companion to Imperial Russia, 1689–1917* (Harlow, Essex: Pearson Education) is a very useful work of reference.

The best single study of the whole process of abolition is still Zaionchkovsky, *The Abolition of Serfdom in Russia*. Western historians have produced a number of important monographs on aspects of the reform, in particular: Emmons, *The Russian Landed Gentry and the Peasant Emancipation of 1861*; Field, *The End of Serfdom: Nobility and Bureaucracy in Russia 1855–1861*; and Lincoln, *In the Vanguard of Reform: Russia's Enlightened Bureaucrats, 1825–1861* (which summarizes much of the author's extensive research on the bureaucracy on the eve of the reform). An abridged translation of Larisa Zakharova's important book is available as 'Autocracy and the Abolition of Serfdom in Russia, 1856–1861', *SSH* (1987), 26, no. 2.

Blum, *Lord and Peasant in Russia from the Ninth to the Nineteenth Century* surveys the history of serfdom prior to its abolition. Research published after Blum's work is discussed in Moon, 'Reassessing Russian Serfdom', *European History Quarterly* (1996), 26, pp. 483–526. For comparative perspectives, see Blum, *The End of the Old Order in Rural Europe*; Kolchin, P. (1987) *Unfree Labor: American Slavery and Russian Serfdom* (Cambridge, MA: Belknap Press); and Bush, M.L. (ed.) (1996) *Serfdom and Slavery: Studies in Legal Bondage* (London and New York: Longman). The most recent general history of the Russian peasantry is Moon, *The Russian Peasantry 1600–1930: The World the Peasants Made*.

BIBLIOGRAPHY

Acton, E. (1990) *Rethinking the Russian Revolution*. London: Edward Arnold.

Adams, B. F. (1985) 'The Reforms of P. D. Kiselev and the History of N. M. Druzhinin', *Canadian-American Slavic Studies*, 19, pp. 28–43.

Aleksandrov, V. A. (1976) *Sel'skaya obshchina v Rossii (XVII–nachalo XIX v.)*. Moscow: Nauka.

Aleksandrov, V. A. (1990) 'Land Reallotment in the Peasant Communes', in Bartlett, R. P. (ed.) *Land Commune and Peasant Community in Russia: Communal Forms in Imperial and Early Soviet Society*. Basingstoke and London: Macmillan, pp. 36–44.

Anderson, B. A. (1980) *Internal Migration during Modernization in Late Nineteenth-century Russia*. Princeton, NJ: Princeton University Press.

Anfimov, A. M. (1961) *Zemel'naya arenda v Rossii v nachale XX veka*. Moscow: Nauka.

Anfimov, A. M. (1980) *Krest'yanskoe khozyaistvo Evropeiskoi Rossii 1881–1904*. Moscow: Nauka.

Anfimov, A. M. (1984) *Ekonomicheskoe polozhenie i klassovaya bor'ba krest'yan Evropeiskoi Rossii, 1881–1904 gg*. Moscow: Nauka.

Anisimov, E. V. (1993) *The Reforms of Peter the Great*. Trans. J. T. Alexander. Armonk, NY: M. E. Sharpe.

Anisimov, V. I. (1911) 'Nadely', in Dzhivelegov et al. (eds) (1911), vol. 6, pp. 76–103.

Avrich, P. (1972) *Russian Rebels 1600–1800*. New York: Norton.

Baron, S. (1972) 'The Transition from Feudalism to Capitalism in Russia: A Major Soviet Historical Controversy', *AHR*, 77, pp. 715–29.

Bartlett, R. P. (1996) 'Defences of Serfdom in Eighteenth-century Russia', in Di Salvo, M. and Hughes, L. (eds) *A Window on Russia*. Rome, pp. 67–74.

Bartlett, R. P. (1998) 'The Free Economic Society: The Foundation Years and the Prize Essay Competition of 1766 on Peasant Property', in Hüber, E. et al. (eds) *Russland zur Zeit Katherinas II: Absolutismus, Aufklärung, Pragmatismus*. Cologne: Böhlau Verlag, pp. 181–214.

Bartlett, R. P. and Donnert, E. (eds) (1998) *Johann Georg Eisen (1717–1779) Ausgewählte Schriften: Deutsche Volksaufklärung und Leibeigenschaften im Russischen Reiche*. Marburg: Verlag Herder Institut.

Becker, S. (1985) *Nobility and Privilege in Late Imperial Russia*. DeKalb, IL: Northern Illinois University Press.

Bircher, R. (1996) 'Peasant Resistance and the Defence of Servitude Rights in Russia's South West, 1890–1914', unpublished D.Phil. thesis, Christ Church, Oxford.

Blum, J. (1957) 'The Rise of Serfdom in Eastern Europe', *AHR*, 62, pp. 807–36.

Blum, J. (1961) *Lord and Peasant in Russia from the Ninth to the Nineteenth Century*. Princeton, NJ: Princeton University Press.

Blum, J. (1977) 'Russia', in Spring, D. (ed.) *European Landed Elites in the Nineteenth Century*. Baltimore, MD and London: Johns Hopkins University Press, pp. 68–97.

Blum, J. (1978) *The End of the Old Order in Rural Europe*. Princeton, NJ: Princeton University Press.

Bohac, R. (1991) 'Everyday Forms of Resistance: Serf Opposition to Gentry Exactions, 1800–1861', in Kingston-Mann and Mixter (eds) (1991), pp. 236–60.

Bradley, J. (1985) *Muzhik and Muscovite: Urbanization in Late Imperial Russia*. Berkeley, CA: University of California Press.

Brooks, E. W. (1984) 'Reform in the Russian Army, 1856–1861', *SR*, 43, pp. 63–82.

Burds, J. (1998) *Peasant Dreams and Market Politics: Labor Migration and the Russian Village, 1861–1905*. Pittsburgh, PA: University of Pittsburgh Press.

Bushnell, J. (1994) 'Miliutin and the Balkan War: Military Reform vs. Military Performance', in Eklof et al. (eds) (1994), pp. 139–58.

Channon, J. (1992) 'The Peasantry in the Revolutions of 1917', in Frankel, E. R. et al. (eds) *Revolution in Russia: Reassessments of 1917*. Cambridge: Cambridge University Press, pp. 105–30.

Chistyakov, O. I. (ed.) (1989) *Rossiiskoe zakonodatel'stvo X–XX vekov*, vol. 7, *Dokumenty krest'yanskoi reformy*. Moscow: Yuridicheskaya literatura.

Christian, D. (1990) *'Living Water': Vodka and Russian Society on the Eve of Emancipation*. Oxford: Clarendon Press.

Confino, M. (1963) *Domaines et seigneurs en Russie vers la fin du XVIIIe siècle*. Paris: Institut d'Études slaves de l'Université de Paris.

Crisp, O. (1976) *Studies in the Russian Economy before 1914*. London: Macmillan.

Crisp, O. (1989) 'Peasant Land Tenure and Civil Rights Implications before 1906', in Crisp, O. and Edmondson, L. (eds) *Civil Rights in Imperial Russia*. Oxford: Oxford University Press, pp. 33–64.

Crummey, R. O. (1983) *Aristocrats and Servitors: The Boyar Elite in Russia 1613–1689*. Princeton, NJ: Princeton University Press.

Curtiss, J. S. (1965) *The Russian Army under Nicholas I*. Durham, NC: Duke University Press.

Curtiss, J. S. (1979) *Russia's Crimean War*. Durham, NC: Duke University Press.

Davidson, R. M. (1973) 'Koshelyov and the Emancipation of the Serfs', *European Studies Review*, 3, pp. 13–39.

Davies, R. W. et al. (eds) (1994) *The Economic Transformation of the Soviet Union, 1913–1945*. Cambridge: Cambridge University Press.

Degtiarev, A. Ia., Kashchenko, S. G. and Raskin, D. I. (1992) 'The Novgorod Countryside in the Reform of 1861', *SSH*, 30, no.4.

Dmytryshyn, B. (ed.) (1967) *Imperial Russia: A Source Book, 1700–1917*. New York: Holt Reinhart Winston.

Domar, E. D. (1989) 'Were Russian Serfs Overcharged for their Land by the 1861 Emancipation?', in Grantham G. and Leonard, C. (eds) *Agrarian Organization in the Century of Industrialization: Europe, Russia, and North America, Research in Economic History*, supp. 5, pt. B, pp. 429–39.

Domar, E. D. and Machina, M. J. (1984) 'On the Profitability of Russian Serfdom', *Journal of Economic History*, 44, pp. 919–56.

Druzhinin, N. M. (1946–58) *Gosudarstvennye krest'yane i reforma P. D. Kiseleva* (2 vols). Moscow and Leningrad: Izdatel'stvo Akademii Nauk SSSR.

Druzhinin, N. M. (1978) *Russkaya derevnya na perelome 1861–1880 gg.* Moscow: Nauka.

Dukes, P. (1967) *Catherine the Great and the Russian Nobility.* Cambridge: Cambridge University Press.

Dzhivelegov, A. K. et al. (eds) (1911) *Velikaya Reforma: Russkoe Obshchestvo i Krest'yanskii Vopros v Proshlom i Nastoyashchem. Yubileinoe izdanie* (6 vols). Moscow: I. D. Sytin.

Economakis, E. G. (1998) *From Peasant to Petersburger.* Basingstoke and London: Macmillan.

Eklof, B. et al. (eds) (1994) *Russia's Great Reforms, 1855–1881.* Bloomington, IN: Indiana University Press.

Emmons, T. (1968a) *The Russian Landed Gentry and the Peasant Emancipation of 1861.* Cambridge: Cambridge University Press.

Emmons, T. (1968b) 'The Peasant and the Emancipation', in Vucinich (ed.) (1968), pp. 41–71.

Emmons, T. (ed.) (1970) *Emancipation of the Russian Serfs.* New York: Holt, Reinhart and Winston,

Fedorov, V. A. (1974) *Pomeshchich'i krest'yane tsentral'no- promyshlennogo raiona Rossii: kontsa XVIII-pervoi poloviny XIX v.* Moscow: Izdatel'stvo Moskovskogo Universiteta.

Fedorov, V. A. (ed.) (1994) *Konets krepostnichestva v Rossii: Dokumenty, pis'ma, memuary, stat'i.* Moscow: Izdatel'stvo Moskovskogo Universiteta.

Field, D. (1976a) *The End of Serfdom: Nobility and Bureaucracy in Russia, 1855–1861.* Cambridge, MA: Harvard University Press.

Field, D. (1976b) *Rebels in the Name of the Tsar* (1st edn). Boston, MA: Houghton Mifflin.

Field, D. (1994) 'The Year of the Jubilee', in Eklof et al. (eds) (1994), pp. 40–57.

Freeze, G. (ed.) (1988) *From Supplication to Revolution: A Documentary History of Imperial Russia.* New York and Oxford: Oxford University Press.

Freeze, G. L. (1989) 'The Orthodox Church and Serfdom in Prereform Russia', *SR*, 48, pp. 361–87.

Frierson, C. A. (ed. and trans.) (1993) *Aleksandr Nikolaevich Engelgardt's Letters from the Countryside, 1872–1887.* New York and Oxford: Oxford University Press.

Fuller, W. C. (1992) *Strategy and Power in Russia 1600–1914.* New York: Free Press.

Gatrell, P. (1986) *The Tsarist Economy 1850–1917.* London: Batsford.

Gatrell, P. (1994) 'The Meaning of the Great Reforms in Russian Economic History', in Eklof et al. (eds) (1994), pp. 84–101.

Gerschenkron, A. (1965) 'Agrarian Policies and Industrialization: Russia, 1861–1917', in *Cambridge Economic History of Europe*, 6, pt.2. Cambridge: Cambridge University Press, pp. 706–800.

Gleason, A. (1994) 'The Great Reforms and the Historians since Stalin' in Eklof et al. (eds) (1994), pp. 1–16.

Gogol, N. (1847/1969) *Selected Passages from Correspondence with Friends.* Trans. J. Zeldin. Nashville, TN: Vanderbilt University Press.

Gorlanov, L. R. (1986) *Udel'nye krest'yane Rossii 1797–1865 gg.* Smolensk: Izdatel'stvo Smolenskogo Gos. Pedagagicheskogo Instituta.

Gregory, P. R. (1994) *Before Command: An Economic History of Russia from Emancipation to the First Five-Year Plan*. Princeton, NJ: Princeton University Press.

Hampson, N. (1968) *The Enlightenment*. Harmondsworth: Penguin.

Hanne, M. (1994) *The Power of the Story: Fiction and Political Change*. Oxford: Berghahn Books.

Hart, J. G. (1988) 'Razin's Second Coming: Pugachev's Rebellion in the Middle Volga Region, July–August 1774', in Bartlett, R. P. et al. (eds) *Russia and the World in the Eighteenth Century*. Columbus, OH: Slavica Publishers, pp. 506–20.

Hartley, J. M. (1994) *Alexander I*. London and New York: Longman.

Hellie, R. (1971) *Enserfment and Military Change in Muscovy*. Chicago, IL: Chicago University Press.

Hilton, R. (1973) *Bond Men Made Free: Medieval Peasant Movements and the English Rising of 1381*. London and New York: Routledge.

Hoch, S. L. (1986) *Serfdom and Social Control: Petrovskoe, a Village in Tambov*. Chicago, IL: Chicago University Press.

Hoch, S. L. (1991) 'The Banking Crisis, Peasant Reform, and Economic Development in Russia, 1857–1861', *AHR*, 96, pp. 795–820.

Hoch, S. L. (1994) 'On Good Numbers and Bad: Malthus, Population Trends and Peasant Standard of Living in Late Imperial Russia', *SR*, 53, pp. 41–75.

Hoch, S. L. and Augustine, W. R. (1979) 'The Tax Censuses and the Decline of the Serf Population in Imperial Russia, 1833–1858', *SR*, 38, pp. 403–25.

Ignatovich, I. I. (1911a) 'Krest'yanskie volneniya', in Dzhivelegov et al. (eds) (1911), vol.3, pp. 41–65.

Ignatovich, I. I. (1911b) 'Vstrecha na mestakh', in Dzhivelegov et al. (eds) (1911), vol.5, pp. 172–9.

Ignatovich, I. I. (1925) *Pomeshchich'i krest'yane nakanune osvobozhdeniya* (3rd edn). Leningrad: Mysl'.

Jones, R. E. (1973) *The Emancipation of the Russian Nobility 1762–1785*. Princeton, NJ: Princeton University Press.

Jones, R. E. (1984) *Provincial Development in Russia: Catherine II and Jacob Sievers*. New Brunswick, NJ: Rutgers University Press.

Kagan, F. W. (1999) *The Military Reforms of Nicholas I: The Origins of the Modern Russian Army*. Basingstoke and London: Macmillan.

Kahan, A. (1966) 'The Costs of "Westernization" in Russia: The Gentry and the Economy in the Eighteenth Century', *SR*, 25, pp. 40–66.

Kahan, A. (1989) *Russian Economic History: The Nineteenth Century*. Chicago, IL: Chicago University Press.

Kakhk, Yu. Yu. [Kahk, J.] (1988) *'Ostzeiskii put'' perekhoda ot feodalizma k kapitalizmu: Krest'yane i pomeshchiki Estlyandii i Liflyandii v XVIII–pervoi polovine XIX veka*. Tallinn: Eesti raamat.

Kashchenko, S. G. (1995) *Reforma 19 fevralya 1861 g. na severo-zapade Rossii*. Moscow: Mosgosarkhiv.

Keep, J. L. H. (1985) *Soldiers of the Tsar: Army and Society in Russia, 1462–1874*. Oxford: Oxford University Press.

Khodarkovsky, M. (1994) 'The Stepan Razin Uprising: Was it a "Peasant War"?', *JGO*, 42, pp. 1–19.

Kieniewicz, S. (1969) *The Emancipation of the Polish Peasantry*. Chicago, IL: Chicago University Press.

Kingston-Mann, E. (1991) 'In the Light and Shadow of the West: The Impact of Western Economics in Pre-Emancipation Russia', *Comparative Studies in Society and History*, 33, pp. 86–105

Kingston-Mann, E. and Mixter, T. (eds) (1991) *Peasant Economy, Culture, and Politics of European Russia, 1800–1921*. Princeton, NJ: Princeton University Press.

Kipp, J. W. (1975) 'M. Kh. Reutern on the Russian State and Economy: A Liberal Bureaucrat during the Crimean Era', *JMH*, 47, pp. 437–59.

Kohut, Z. E. (1988) *Russian Centralism and Ukrainian Autonomy: Imperial Absorption of the Hetmanate 1760s–1830s*. Cambridge, MA: Harvard Ukrainian Research Institute.

Kolchin, P. (1996) 'Some Controversial Questions concerning Nineteenth-century Emancipation from Slavery and Serfdom', in Bush, M. L. (ed.) *Serfdom and Slavery: Studies in Legal Bondage*. London and New York: Longman, pp. 42–67.

Kolchin, P. (1999) 'After Serfdom: Russian Emancipation in Comparative Perspective', in Engerman, S. L. (ed.) *Terms of Labor: Slavery, Serfdom, and Free Labor*. Stanford, CA: Stanford University Press, pp. 87–115, 293–309.

Kotsonis, Y. (1999) *Making Peasants Backward: Agricultural Cooperatives and the Agrarian Question in Russia, 1861–1914*. Basingstoke and London: Macmillan.

Koval'chenko, I. D. (1967) *Russkoe krepostnoe krest'yanstvo v pervoi polovine XIX v.* Moscow: Izdatel'stvo Moskovskogo Universiteta.

Koval'chenko, I. D. (1970) 'Peasant Capitalism', in Emmons (ed.) (1970), pp. 50–6.

Kropotkin, P. (1930) *Memoirs of a Revolutionist*. Boston, MA: Houghton Mifflin.

Krutikov, V. I. (1978) 'Zakonodatel'stvo o pomeshchich'ikh krest'yanakh perioda krizisa krepostnichestva (1826–1860 gg.)', in Pashuto, V. T. (ed.) (1978) *Mesto i rol' krest'yanstva v sotsial'no-ekonomicheskom razvitii obshchestva*. Moscow: Institut istorii SSSR AN SSSR.

Kukushkin, Yu. S. et al. (eds) (1998) *P. A. Zaionchkovskii (1904–1983 gg.): Stat'i, publikatsii i vospominaniya o nem*. Moscow: ROSSPEN.

Lappo-Danilevskii, A. S. (1911/1972) 'The Serf Question in an Age of Enlightenment', in Raeff, M. (ed.) *Catherine the Great: A Profile*. New York: Hill and Wang, pp. 267–89 (originally published in Dzhivelegov et al. (eds) (1911), vol.1, pp. 163–90).

Leonard, C. S. (1993) *Reform and Regicide: The Reign of Peter III of Russia*. Bloomington, IN: Indiana University Press.

Lieven, D. (1992) *The Aristocracy in Europe 1815–1914*. Basingstoke and London: Macmillan.

Lincoln, W. B. (1969) 'The Karlovka Reform', *SR*, 23, pp. 463–71.

Lincoln, W. B. (1970) 'The Circle of the Grand Duchess Yelena Pavlovna, 1847–1861', *SEER*, 48, pp. 373–87.

Lincoln, W. B. (1977) *Nikolai Miliutin: An Enlightened Russian Bureaucrat*. Newtonville, MA: Oriental Research Partners.

Lincoln, W. B. (1978) *Nicholas I*. DeKalb, IL: Northern Illinois University Press.

Lincoln, W. B. (1982) *In the Vanguard of Reform: Russia's Enlightened Bureaucrats, 1825–1861*. DeKalb, IL: Northern Illinois University Press.

Lincoln, W. B. (1990) *The Great Reforms: Autocracy, Bureaucracy, and the Politics of Change in Imperial Russia*. DeKalb, IL: Northern Illinois University Press.

Litvak, B. G. (1972) *Russkaya derevnya v reforme 1861 goda: Chernozemnyi tsentr 1861–1895 gg.* Moscow: Nauka.

Litvak, B. G. (1991) *Perevorot 1861 goda v Rossii: pochemu ne realizovalas' reformatorskaya al'ternativa*. Moscow: Politizdat.

Lyashchenko, P. I. (1949) *History of the National Economy of Russia to the 1917 Revolution*. Trans L. H. Herman. New York: Macmillan.

Macey, D. A. J. (1987) *Government and Peasant in Russia, 1861–1906: The Prehistory of the Stolypin Reforms*. Dekalb, IL: Northern Illinois University Press.

McCauley, M. and Waldron, P. (1988) *The Emergence of the Modern Russian State, 1855–81*. Basingstoke and London: Macmillan.

Madariaga, I. de (1974) 'Catherine II and the Serfs: A reconsideration of some problems', *SEER*, 52, pp. 34–62.

Madariaga, I. de (1981) *Russia in the Age of Catherine the Great*. London and New Haven, CT: Yale University Press.

Manning, R. (1982) *The Crisis of the Old Order in Russia: Gentry and Government*. Princeton, NJ: Princeton University Press.

Marks, S. G. (1991) *Road to Power: The Trans-Siberian Railroad and the Colonization of Asian Russia, 1850–1917*. Ithaca, NY: Cornell University Press.

Meehan-Waters, B. (1982) *Autocracy and Aristocracy: The Russian Service Elite of 1730*. New Brunswick, NJ: Rutgers University Press.

Mel'gunov, S. P. (1911) 'Mitropolit Filaret – deyatel' krest'yanskoi reformy', in Dzhivelegov et al. (eds) (1911), vol.5, pp. 156–63.

Melton, E. (1990) 'Enlightened Seigniorialism and its Dilemmas in Serf Russia, 1750–1830', *JMH*, 62, pp. 675–708.

Melton, E. (1993) 'Household Economies and Communal Conflicts on a Russian Serf Estate, 1800–1817', *Journal of Social History*, 26, pp. 559–85.

Miller, F. A. (1968) *Dmitrii Miliutin and the Reform Era in Russia*. Nashville, TN: Vanderbilt University Press.

Mironenko, S. V. (1989) *Samoderzhavie i reformy: Politicheskaya bor'ba v Rossii v nachale XIX v.* Moscow: Nauka.

Mironov, B. N. (1992) 'Consequences of the Price Revolution in Eighteenth-century Russia', *Economic History Review*, 45, pp. 457–78.

Mironov, B. N. (1994) 'Local Government in Russia in the First Half of the 19th Century', *JGO*, 42, pp. 161–201.

Mironov, B. N. (1996) 'When and Why was the Russian Peasantry Emancipated', in Bush, M. L. (ed.) *Serfdom and Slavery: Studies in Legal Bondage*. London and New York: Longman, pp. 323–47.

Mironov, B. N. (1999) *Sotsial'naya istoriya Rossii perioda imperii* (2 vols). St Petersburg: Dmitrii Bulanin.

Mixter, T. (1991) 'The Hiring Market as Workers' Turf: Migrant Agricultural Laborers and the Mobilization of Collective Action in the Steppe Grainbelt of European Russia, 1853–1913', in Kingston-Mann and Mixter (eds), (1991), pp. 294–340.

Moon, D. (1992) *Russian Peasants and Tsarist Legislation on the Eve of Reform, 1825–1855*. Basingstoke and London: Macmillan.

Moon, D. (1996a) 'Reassessing Russian Serfdom', *European History Quarterly*, 26, pp. 483–526.

Moon, D. (1996b) 'Decembrist Rebels, Tsars, and Peasants in Early 19th–century Russia', *New Perspective*, 2, 2, pp. 8–12.

Moon, D. (1996c) 'Estimating the Peasant Population of Late Imperial Russia from the 1897 Census', *Europe-Asia Studies*, 48, pp. 141–53.

Moon, D. (1999) *The Russian Peasantry 1600–1930: The World the Peasants Made*. London and New York: Addison Wesley Longman.

Moon, D. (2001) 'The Inventory Reform and Peasant Unrest in Right-Bank Ukraine in 1847–8', *SEER*, 79, pp. 633–82.

Morokhovets, E. A. (ed.) (1931), *Krest'yanskoe dvizhenie 1827–1869* (2 vols). Moscow and Leningrad: Gos. Sotsial'no-ekonomicheskoe izdatel'stvo.

Mosse, W. E. (1958) *Alexander II and the Modernization of Russia*. London: English Universities' Press.

Munting, R. (1979) 'Mechanization and Dualism in Russian Agriculture', *Journal of European Economic History*, 8, pp. 743–60.

Munting, R. (1992) 'Economic Change and the Russian Gentry, 1861–1914', in Edmondson, L. and Waldron, P. (eds) *Economy and Society in Russia and the Soviet Union, 1860–1930*. Basingstoke and London: Macmillan, pp. 24–43.

Nechkina, M. V. (1970) 'The Reform as a by-product of the Revolutionary Struggle', in Emmons (ed.) (1970), pp. 66–71.

Nifontov, A. S. (1961) 'Statistika krest'yanskogo dvizheniya v Rossii 50–kh gg. XIX v.' in *Voprosy istorii sel'skogo khozyaistva, krest'yanstva i revolyutsionnogo dvizheniya v Rossii*. Moscow: Izdatel'stvo Akademii nauk SSSR.

Okun', S. B. (ed.) (1962) *Krest'yanskoe dvizhenie v Rossii v 1850–1856 gg.: Sbornik Dokumentov*. Moscow: Izdatel'stvo sotsial'no-ekonomicheskoi literatury.

Okun', S. B. and Paina, E. S. (1964) 'Ukaz ot 5 aprelya 1797 goda i ego evolyutsiya', in Nosov, N. E. (ed.) *Issledovaniya po otechestvennomu istochnikovedeniyu*. Moscow: Nauka, pp. 283–99.

Okun', S. B. and Sivkov, K. V. (eds) (1963) *Krest'yanskoe dvizhenie v Rossii v 1857–mae 1861 gg: Sbornik dokumentov*. Moscow: Izdatel'stvo sotsial'no-ekonomicheskoi literatury.

Opis' del arkhiva Gosudarstvennogo soveta (21 vols) (1908–14), Spb, vol.15.

Pallot, J. (1999) *Land Reform in Russia 1906–1917: Peasant Responses to Stolypin's Project of Rural Transformation*. Oxford: Clarendon Press.

Pereira, N. G. O. (1980) 'Alexander II and the Decision to Emancipate the Russian Serfs, 1855–61', *Canadian Slavonic Papers*, 22, pp. 99–115.

Perrie, M. (1976) *The Agrarian Policy of the Russian Socialist-Revolutionary Party from its origins through the revolution of 1905–1907*. Cambridge: Cambridge University Press.

Perrie, M. (1990) 'The Russian Peasant Movement of 1905–1907: Its Social Composition and Revolutionary Significance', in Eklof, B. and Frank, S. (eds) *The World of the Russian Peasant: Post-Emancipation Culture and Society*. Boston, MA and London: Unwin Hyman, pp. 193–218.

Perrie, M. (1992) 'The Peasants', in Service, R. (ed.) *Society and Politics in the Russian Revolution*. Basingstoke and London: Macmillan, pp. 12–34.

Perrie, M. (1993) *Alexander II: Emancipation and Reform in Russia, 1855–1881* (revised edn). London: The Historical Association.

Perrie, M. (1999) 'Popular Monarchism: The Myth of the Ruler from Ivan the Terrible to Stalin', in Hosking, G. and Service, R. (eds) *Reinterpreting Russia*: London and New York: Arnold, pp. 156–69.

Pintner, W. M. (1967) *Russian Economic Policy under Nicholas I*. Ithaca, NY: Cornell University Press.

Pintner, W. M. (1980) 'The Evolution of Civil Officialdom, 1755–1855', in Pintner, W. M. and Rowney, D. K. (eds) *Russian Officialdom: The Bureaucratization of*

Russian Society from the Seventeenth to the Twentieth Century. London: Macmillan, pp. 190–226.

Pintner, W. M. (1984) 'The Burden of Defense in Imperial Russia, 1725–1914', *Russian Review*, 43, pp. 231–59.

Polnoe sobranie zakonov Rossiiskoi imperii (PSZ) (3 series, 133 vols), Spb: Gosudarstvennaya tipografiya, 1830–1913.

Predtechenskii, A. V. (ed.) (1961) *Krest'yanskoe dvizhenie v Rossii v 1826–1849 gg. Sbornik dokumentov*. Moscow: Izdatel'stvo sotsial'no-ekonomicheskoi literatury.

Pushkarev, S. G. (1968) 'The Russian Peasants' Reaction to the Emancipation of 1861', *Russian Review*, 27, pp. 199–214.

Radishchev, A. N. (1790/1966) *A Journey from St. Petersburg to Moscow*. Ed. R. P. Thaler, trans. L. Wiener. Cambridge, MA: Harvard University Press.

Raeff, M. (1966) *The Origins of the Russian Intelligentsia: The Eighteenth-century Nobility*. New York: Harcourt Brace Jovanovich.

Raeff, M. (1970) 'The Domestic Policies of Peter III and His Overthrow', *AHR*, 75, pp. 1289–310.

Riasanovsky, N. (1968) 'Afterword', in Vucinich (ed.) (1968), pp. 263–84.

Rieber, A. J. (ed.) (1966) *The Politics of Autocracy: Letters of Alexander II to Prince A. I. Bariatinskii*. Paris and The Hague: Mouton and Co.

Rieber, A. J. (1971) 'Alexander II: A Revisionist View', *JMH*, 43, pp. 42–58.

Riber, A. [Rieber, A.] (1998) 'Sotsial'naya identifikatsiya i politicheskaya volya: russkoe dvoryanstvo ot Petra I do 1861 g.', in Kukushkin et al. (eds) (1998), pp. 273–314.

Robinson, G. T. (1932) *Rural Russia under the Old Regime*. Berkeley and Los Angeles, CA: University of California Press.

Roosevelt, P. (1995) *Life on the Russian Country Estate*. New Haven, CT: Yale University Press.

Rosenberg, H. (1958) *Bureaucracy, Aristocracy, and Autocracy: The Prussian Experience, 1660–1815*. Boston, MA: Harvard University Press.

Rossiiskii gosudarstvennyi istoricheskii arkhiv (RGIA), fond 1180, *Sekretnyi i glavnyi komitety po krest'yanskomu delu*.

Saunders, D. (1992) *Russia in the Age of Reaction and Reform, 1801–1881*. London and New York: Longman.

Saunders, D. (2000a) 'P. A. Zaionchkovskii: High Society Subversive', *Kritika: Explorations in Russian and Eurasian History*, 1, pp. 167–81.

Saunders, D. (2000b) 'A Pyrrhic Victory: The Russian Empire in 1848', in Evans, R. J. W. and Pogge von Strandmann, H. (eds) *The Revolutions in Europe, 1848–1849: From Reform to Reaction*. Oxford: Oxford University Press, pp. 135–55.

Semenov, N. P. (1891) *Osvobozhdenie krestyan' v tsarstvovanie Aleksandra II: Khonika deyatel'nosti komisii po krest'yanskomu delu* (3 vols), Spb: Gosudarstvennaya tipografiya.

Semevskii, V. I. (1888) *Krest'yanskii vopros v Rossii v XVIII i pervoi polovine XIX veka* (2 vols). St. Petersburg: Tipografiya Obshchestvennaya Pol'za.

Seton-Watson, H. (1967) *The Russian Empire, 1801–1917*. Oxford: Oxford University Press.

Shakhovskoi, D. I. (1911) 'Vykupnye platezhi', in Dzhivelegov et al. (eds) (1911), vol.6, pp. 104–36.

Shanin, T. (1986) *Russia as a 'Developing Society'*. Basingstoke and London: Macmillan.

Shepukova, N. M. (1964) 'Ob izmenii razmerov dushevladeniya pomeshchikov Evropeiskoi Rossii v pervoi chertverti XVIII–pervoi polovine XIX v.', *Ezhegodnik po Agrarnoi Istorii Vostochnoi Evropy za 1963 g.* Vilnius, pp. 388–419.

Skerpan, A. A. (1964) 'The Russian National Economy and Emancipation' in Ferguson, A. D. and Levin, A. (eds) *Essays in Russian History: A Collection Dedicated to George Vernadsky.* Hamden, CT: Archon Books, pp. 161–229.

Smith, R. E. F. (1968) *The Enserfment of the Russian Peasantry.* Cambridge: Cambridge University Press.

Solov'ev, Ya. A. (1881), 'Zapiski Senatora Ya. A. Solov'eva o krest'yanskom dele. Glava vtoraya', *Russkaya starina*, 30, pp. 721–56.

Suny, R. G. (1979) '"The Peasants Have Always Fed Us": The Georgian Nobility and the Peasant Emancipation, 1856–1871', *Russian Review*, 38, pp. 27–51.

Tokarev, S. V. (1960) 'O chislennosti krest'yanskikh vystuplenii v Rossii v gody pervoi revolyutsionnoi sistuatsii', in Nechkina, M. V. (ed.) *Revolyutsionnaya situatsiya v Rossii v 1859–1861 gg.*, vol.1, pp. 124–32.

Turgenev, I. (1847–51/1967) *Sketches from a Hunter's Album.* Trans. R. Freeborn. Harmondsworth: Penguin.

Ust'iantseva, N. F. (1994) 'Accountable Only to God and the Senate: Peace Mediators and the Great Reforms', in Eklof et al. (eds) (1994), pp. 161–80.

Vasilenko, N. (1911) 'Krest'yanskii vopros v yugo-zapadnom i severo-zapadnom krae pri Nikolae I i vvedenie inventarei', in Dzhivelegov et al. (eds) (1911), vol.4, pp. 94–109.

Vernadsky, G. (ed.) (1972) *A Source Book for Russian History from the earliest times to 1917* (3 vols). New Haven, CT, and London: Yale University Press.

Viola, L. (1996) *Peasant Rebels under Stalin: Collectivization and the Culture of Peasant Resistance.* New York and Oxford: Oxford University Press.

Vodarskii, Ya. E. (1973) *Naselenie Rossii za 400 let (XVI–nachalo XX v.).* Moscow: Prosveshchenie.

Vucinich, W. S. (ed.) (1968) *The Peasant in Nineteenth-Century Russia.* Stanford, CA: Stanford University Press.

Wcislo, F. W. (1990) *Reforming Rural Russia: State, Local Society, and National Politics, 1855–1914.* Princeton, NJ: Princeton University Press.

Wheatcroft, S. G. (1991) 'Crises and the Condition of the Peasantry in Late Imperial Russia', in Kingston-Mann and Mixter (eds) (1991), pp. 128–72.

Wildman, A. K. (1996) 'The Defining Moment: Land Charters and the Post-Emancipation Agrarian Settlement in Russia, 1861–1863', *The Carl Beck Papers in Russian and East European Studies*, no.1205.

Willets, H. (1971) 'The Agrarian Problem', in Katkov, G. et al. (eds) *Russia Enters the Twentieth Century.* London: Temple Smith.

Wirtschafter, E. K. (1990) *From Serf to Russian Soldier.* Princeton, NJ: Princeton University Press.

Wirtschafter, E. K. (1995) 'Social Misfits: Veterans and Soldiers' Families in Servile Russia', *Journal of Military History*, 59, pp. 215–36.

Wortman, R. S. (1990) 'Rule by Sentiment: Alexander II's Journeys through the Russian Empire', *AHR*, 95, pp. 745–71.

Wortman, R. S. (2000) *Scenarios of Power: Myth and Ceremony in Russian Monarchy*, vol.2, *From Alexander II to the Abdication of Nicholas II.* Princeton, NJ: Princeton University Press.

Zaionchkovskii, P. A. (1968) *Otmena krepostnogo prava v Rossii* (3rd edn). Moscow: Prosveshchenie.

Zaionchkovsky, P. A. (1978) *The Abolition of Serfdom in Russia*. Ed. and trans, S. Wobst. Gulf Breeze, FL: Academic International Press (translation of above).

Zakharova, L. G. (1984) *Samoderzhavie i otmena krepostnogo prava v Rossii 1856–1861*. Moscow: Izdatel'stvo Moskovskogo Gosudarstvennogo Universiteta.

Zakharova, L. G. (1987) 'Autocracy and the Abolition of Serfdom in Russia, 1856–1861', *SSH*, 26, no.2.

Zakharova, L. G. (compiler) (1994) *1857–1861. Perepiska Imperatora Aleksandra II s Velikim Knyazem Konstantinom Nikolaevichem. Dnevnik Velikogo Knyazya Konstantina Nikolaevicha*. Moscow: TERRA.

Zakharova, L. G. (1998) 'P. A. Zaionchkovskii – uchenyi i uchitel'', in Kukuskhin et al. (eds) (1998), pp. 5–20.

Zakharova, L. G. (ed.) (1999) *Vospominiya general-fel'dmarshala grafa Dmitiya Alekseevicha Milyutina, 1860–1862*. Moscow: Rossiiskii arkhiv.

'Zakrytie inventarnykh komitetov' (1858) *Zhurnal Ministerstva Vnutrennikh Del*, part 30, sect.1, pp. 286–8.

INDEX

SEMINAR STUDIES IN HISTORY

General Editors: Clive Emsley & Gordon Martel

The series was founded by Patrick Richardson in 1966. Between 1980 and 1996 Roger Lockyer edited the series before handing over to Clive Emsley (Professor of History at the Open University) and Gordon Martel (Professor of International History at the University of Northern British Columbia, Canada and Senior Research Fellow at De Montfort University).

MEDIEVAL ENGLAND

The Pre-Reformation Church in England 1400–1530 (Second edition)
Christopher Harper-Bill   0 582 28989 0

Lancastrians and Yorkists: The Wars of the Roses
David R Cook   0 582 35384 X

TUDOR ENGLAND

Henry VII (Third edition)
Roger Lockyer & Andrew Thrush   0 582 20912 9

Henry VIII (Second edition)
M D Palmer   0 582 35437 4

Tudor Rebellions (Fourth edition)
Anthony Fletcher & Diarmaid MacCulloch   0 582 28990 4

The Reign of Mary I (Second edition)
Robert Tittler   0 582 06107 5

Early Tudor Parliaments 1485–1558
Michael A R Graves   0 582 03497 3

The English Reformation 1530–1570
W J Sheils   0 582 35398 X

Elizabethan Parliaments 1559–1601 (Second edition)
Michael A R Graves   0 582 29196 8

England and Europe 1485–1603 (Second edition)
Susan Doran   0 582 28991 2

The Church of England 1570–1640
Andrew Foster   0 582 35574 5

STUART BRITAIN

Social Change and Continuity: England 1550–1750 (Second edition)
Barry Coward   0 582 29442 8

James I (Second edition)
S J Houston   0 582 20911 0

The English Civil War 1640–1649
Martyn Bennett   0 582 35392 0

Charles I, 1625–1640
Brian Quintrell   0 582 00354 7

The English Republic 1649–1660 (Second edition)
Toby Barnard   0 582 08003 7

Radical Puritans in England 1550–1660
R J Acheson   0 582 35515 X

The Restoration and the England of Charles II (Second edition)
John Miller   0 582 29223 9

The Glorious Revolution (Second edition)
John Miller   0 582 29222 0

EARLY MODERN EUROPE

The Renaissance (Second edition)
Alison Brown   0 582 30781 3

The Emperor Charles V
Martyn Rady   0 582 35475 7

French Renaissance Monarchy: Francis I and Henry II (Second edition)
Robert Knecht   0 582 28707 3

The Protestant Reformation in Europe
Andrew Johnston   0 582 07020 1

The French Wars of Religion 1559–1598 (Second edition)
Robert Knecht   0 582 28533 X

Phillip II
Geoffrey Woodward   0 582 07232 8

The Thirty Years' War
Peter Limm   0 582 35373 4

Louis XIV
Peter Campbell   0 582 01770 X

Spain in the Seventeenth Century
Graham Darby   0 582 07234 4

Peter the Great
William Marshall   0 582 00355 5

EUROPE 1789–1918

Britain and the French Revolution
Clive Emsley   0 582 36961 4

Revolution and Terror in France 1789–1795 (Second edition)
D G Wright   0 582 00379 2

Napoleon and Europe
D G Wright   0 582 35457 9

The Abolition of Serfdom in Russia, 1762–1907
David Moon   0 582 29486 X

Nineteenth-Century Russia: Opposition to Autocracy
Derek Offord   0 582 35767 5

The Constitutional Monarchy in France 1814–48
Pamela Pilbeam   0 582 31210 8

The 1848 Revolutions (Second edition)
Peter Jones   0 582 06106 7

The Italian Risorgimento
M Clark   0 582 00353 9

Bismarck & Germany 1862–1890 (Second edition)
D G Williamson   0 582 29321 9

Imperial Germany 1890–1918
Ian Porter, Ian Armour and Roger Lockyer   0 582 03496 5

The Dissolution of the Austro-Hungarian Empire 1867–1918 (Second edition)
John W Mason   0 582 29466 5

Second Empire and Commune: France 1848–1871 (Second edition)
William H C Smith   0 582 28705 7

France 1870–1914 (Second edition)
Robert Gildea   0 582 29221 2

The Scramble for Africa (Second edition)
M E Chamberlain   0 582 36881 2

Late Imperial Russia 1890–1917
John F Hutchinson   0 582 32721 0

The First World War
Stuart Robson   0 582 31556 5

EUROPE SINCE 1918

The Russian Revolution (Second edition)
Anthony Wood   0 582 35559 1

Lenin's Revolution: Russia, 1917–1921
David Marples   0 582 31917 X

Stalin and Stalinism (Second edition)
Martin McCauley   0 582 27658 6

The Weimar Republic (Second edition)
John Hiden   0 582 28706 5

The Inter-War Crisis 1919–1939
Richard Overy 0 582 35379 3

Fascism and the Right in Europe, 1919–1945
Martin Blinkhorn 0 582 07021 X

Spain's Civil War (Second edition)
Harry Browne 0 582 28988 2

The Third Reich (Second edition)
D G Williamson 0 582 20914 5

The Origins of the Second World War (Second edition)
R J Overy 0 582 29085 6

The Second World War in Europe
Paul MacKenzie 0 582 32692 3

Anti-Semitism before the Holocaust
Albert S Lindemann 0 582 36964 9

The Holocaust: The Third Reich and the Jews
David Engel 0 582 32720 2

Germany from Defeat to Partition, 1945–1963
D G Williamson 0 582 29218 2

Britain and Europe since 1945
Alex May 0 582 30778 3

Eastern Europe 1945–1969: From Stalinism to Stagnation
Ben Fowkes 0 582 32693 1

Eastern Europe since 1970
Bülent Gökay 0 582 32858 6

The Khrushchev Era, 1953–1964
Martin McCauley 0 582 27776 0

NINETEENTH-CENTURY BRITAIN

Britain before the Reform Acts: Politics and Society 1815–1832
Eric J Evans 0 582 00265 6

Parliamentary Reform in Britain c. 1770–1918
Eric J Evans 0 582 29467 3

Democracy and Reform 1815–1885
D G Wright 0 582 31400 3

Poverty and Poor Law Reform in Nineteenth-Century Britain, 1834–1914:
From Chadwick to Booth
David Englander 0 582 31554 9

The Birth of Industrial Britain: Economic Change, 1750–1850
Kenneth Morgan 0 582 29833 4

Chartism (Third edition)
Edward Royle 0 582 29080 5

Peel and the Conservative Party 1830–1850
Paul Adelman   0 582 35557 5

Gladstone, Disraeli and later Victorian Politics (Third edition)
Paul Adelman   0 582 29322 7

Britain and Ireland: From Home Rule to Independence
Jeremy Smith   0 582 30193 9

TWENTIETH-CENTURY BRITAIN

The Rise of the Labour Party 1880–1945 (Third edition)
Paul Adelman   0 582 29210 7

The Conservative Party and British Politics 1902–1951
Stuart Ball   0 582 08002 9

The Decline of the Liberal Party 1910–1931 (Second edition)
Paul Adelman   0 582 27733 7

The British Women's Suffrage Campaign 1866–1928
Harold L Smith   0 582 29811 3

War & Society in Britain 1899–1948
Rex Pope   0 582 03531 7

The British Economy since 1914: A Study in Decline?
Rex Pope   0 582 30194 7

Unemployment in Britain between the Wars
Stephen Constantine   0 582 35232 0

The Attlee Governments 1945–1951
Kevin Jefferys   0 582 06105 9

The Conservative Governments 1951–1964
Andrew Boxer   0 582 20913 7

Britain under Thatcher
Anthony Seldon and Daniel Collings   0 582 31714 2

INTERNATIONAL HISTORY

The Eastern Question 1774–1923 (Second edition)
A L Macfie   0 582 29195 X

India 1885–1947: The Unmaking of an Empire
Ian Copland   0 582 38173 8

The Origins of the First World War (Second edition)
Gordon Martel   0 582 28697 2

The United States and the First World War
Jennifer D Keene   0 582 35620 2

Anti-Semitism before the Holocaust
Albert S Lindemann   0 582 36964 9